Focus on Computer Graphics

Tutorials and Perspectives in Computer Graphics

Edited by W.T. Hewitt, R. Gnatz, and W. Hansmann

C. Laffra E. H. Blake V. de Mey
X. Pintado (Eds.)

Object-Oriented Programming for Graphics

With 102 Figures

 Springer

Focus on Computer Graphics

Edited by W. T. Hewitt, R. Gnatz, and W. Hansmann
for EUROGRAPHICS –
The European Association for Computer Graphics
P. O. Box 16, CH-1288 Aire-la-Ville, Switzerland

Volume Editors

Chris Laffra
Morgan Stanley & Co, Inc.
1251 Avenue of the Americas
New York, NY 10020, USA

Edwin H. Blake
University of Cape Town
Computer Science Department
Rondebosch 7700, South Africa

Vicki de Mey
Apple Computer, Inc.
One Infinite Loop, MS: 301-4I
Cupertino, CA 95014, USA

Xavier Pintado
University of Geneva
Centre Universitaire
d'Informatique,
24, rue du General-Dufour
CH-1211 Geneva 4, Suisse

Coverpicture: see contribution p. 155

ISBN 3-540-58314-9 Springer-Verlag Berlin Heidelberg New York
ISBN 0-387-58314-9 Springer-Verlag New York Berlin Heidelberg

CIP-data applied for

© 1995 EUROGRAPHICS The European Association for Computer Graphics
Printed in Germany

Cover: Konzept & Design Künkel, Lopka GmbH, Ilvesheim, FRG
Typesetting: Camera-ready copy by authors/editors
SPIN 10085222   45/3142 – 5 4 3 2 1 0 – Printed on acid-free paper

Preface

This book contains thoroughly revised versions of papers submitted to and presented at the second and third EUROGRAPHICS workshops on Object-Oriented Graphics.

The second workshop was held on June 4–7, 1991, on the island Texel, The Netherlands. A report by Remco Veltkamp and Edwin Blake follows. The workshop was made possible by support of the Dutch Centre for Mathematics and Computer Science (CWI), in particular Ms. Marja Hegt, who organized all local arrangements. Further support was given by the Dutch Software Engineering Research Center (SERC), and by the Dutch Organization for Scientific Research (NWO).

The third workshop was held on October 28–30, 1992, in Champéry, Switzerland. A report by Nancy Craighill, Vicki de Mey, and Xavier Pintado follows. Support was given by Centre Universitaire d'Informatique (Object Systems Group) of the University of Geneva, Switzerland, and NeXT Inc., Switzerland.

Typesetting support for this book was given by the IBM T.J. Watson Research Center and Morgan Stanley & Co.

December 1994

Chris Laffra
Edwin Blake
Vicki de Mey
Xavier Pintado

Contents

Report on The Second Eurographics Workshop on Object-Oriented Graphics

Remco Veltkamp and Edwin Blake

Object-oriented concepts are particularly applicable to Computer Graphics in its broadest sense — interaction, images synthesis, animation, and CAD. Research in Object-Oriented Graphics has lead to a critique of the object-oriented theory. The aim of the second Eurographics Workshop on Object-Oriented Graphics was to address fundamental issues arising from the use of object-oriented techniques in computer graphics, to provide a platform to state views on relevant issues, and discuss possible research programmes to address remaining unresolved problems.

The workshop was held on June 4–7 on the island Texel, The Netherlands. A total of 30 people attended the workshop, coming from The Netherlands (10 participants), Germany (7), USA (4), Switzerland (3), France (2), Australia (1), Austria (1), Portugal (1), and Turkey (1).

1 Presentations

There were 11 full papers and 13 position papers presented. The presentations were grouped into four sessions: modelling, constraints, user interfaces, and rendering.

1.1 Modelling

This session was about issues dealing with the complexity in the design and implementation of computer graphics systems. The first paper of the workshop explores new ways to model virtual reality based on distributed control by actors, communicating via tuple spaces in the coordination language Linda. Other presentations in the modelling session were about basic mechanisms for structuring graphic objects in order to build higher structures from a kernel, flexible graphics design systems, an object oriented implementation of compound graphical objects, the representation and manipulation of structure for computer animation, and problems with database graphics systems.

1.2 Constraints

The use of constraints in managing the complexity of designing interactive graphics systems and the use of object-oriented methods for describing simulations and systems of concrete objects have been two natural methods for building large complex graphics systems. This widely acknowledged way of dealing with the complexities of modelling and interface design has had disappointingly little practical impact. This session explored some of the problems involved.

The topics covered were: the design of a co-operative, or intelligent, graphical editor for constrained objects, the satisfaction of inter-object constraints only when the objects' internal constraints are satisfied, the embedding of constraints in a prototype-based system, a discussion on object-oriented vs. declarative approaches to computer graphics, and a method for satisfaction at a geometric level, which is particularly suited for underconstrained cases.

1.3 User Interfaces

The great benefits of class inheritance in user interface design is well recognized and is finding increasing commercial application. Indeed, a great deal has already been published on object-oriented design and object-oriented design of user interfaces.

The presentations in the user-interface session described the implementation of combining a logic programming system with a user interface toolkit, an architecture developed for direct manipulation of both application and the interface objects, similar objectives in the context of a run time system and a tool for implementation, a framework for object-oriented open user interfaces, and the direct interactive generation of interactive systems.

1.4 Rendering

The last session was on rendering. A class hierarchy of geometries and associated rendering algorithms naturally lend itself for an object-oriented design. The presentations in this session discussed a toolkit for visualization of finite element calculations using alpha-numeric messages, a test environment for global illumination algorithms, ideas on object-oriented computational geometry, and volume visualization.

2 Discussions

Not all of the above mentioned topics are found in the selected papers presented in this book. It was felt that the more interesting part of the workshop was about the conceptual ideas of Object-Oriented Graphics, rather than graphic implementations using object-oriented programming techniques.

In the spirit of the constant fight between land and water in The Netherlands (we also enjoyed an excursion to particular examples of related phenomena such as the "wadden" sea, a "slufter", and plenty of dykes), we not only had discussions directly related to the papers that were presented, but also an evening discussion about Object-Oriented Graphics standards, and an ongoing discussion about constraints in Object-Oriented Graphics. The discussion about standards of Object-Oriented Graphics was meant to outline what must be provided by such a standard, and in which way. No real consensus was achieved, and this topic was seen as a major theme for the next workshop. In the discussions about constraints in object-oriented environments, not everyone was convinced that there is a problem of possible infringement of information hiding. The various approaches to a solution all have their limitations, and a more satisfying solution is yet to come.

3 Conclusion

The use of object-oriented techniques in computer graphics is a widely acknowledged way of dealing with the complexities in graphics systems. However, the field of Object-Oriented Graphics is still being explored and developed, and the problems are diverse.

In the discussions during the workshop, the following topics were found interesting research directions: parallel techniques — can computer graphics do without?; global and local relations between objects — when and how do they conflict with object-oriented concepts?; extensibility of object-oriented graphics systems — how to combine new primitives and inheritance?; operating system support — e.g. how to support persistent objects?; object-oriented graphics standards — should it be conservative, must (part of) the source code be provided?

Report on The Third Eurographics Workshop on Object-Oriented Graphics

Nancy Craighill, Vicki de Mey, and Xavier Pintado

This introduction sets the stage for the selected papers and attempts to summarize the discussions and any conclusions made during the Third Eurographics Workshop on Object-Oriented Graphics. The goal of the workshop was to begin outlining a common platform, based on a set of object-oriented primitives, for the support of graphics applications. As presentations were made, four primary topics of discussion began to emerge: design of graphics objects, object model requirements, implementation techniques and other related technology. Partly because of the diverse presentations and experiences of the attendees, we made little progress on actually identifying a common set of graphics objects. The discussions were nevertheless lively and many important issues were raised.

1 Design

The design of graphics objects (the graphics kernel) can be fairly language independent and described via class hierarchy, part-whole and message flow diagrams.

1.1 Standardization

Standardization efforts are currently under way. Most felt that a common graphics kernel could be designed but were concerned that the traditional standardization process may not produce a good design if it does not take into account the iterative nature of object-oriented design. Thus, any standardization effort should produce working prototypes and establish testbeds to evaluate the reusablity, maintainability and extensibility of their design.

1.2 Modeling and Rendering Layers

It was agreed that the graphics rendering layer should be separated from the modeling layer–there should be two distinct graphics class categories. Thus different renders can be easily swapped independent of the actual graphics model.

Designers must be careful about what information is passed back and forth between modeling and rendering objects so that encapsulation is not circumvented. It is reasonable for the modeling layer to query the rendering layer for its capabilities in order to take appropriate actions; however, these capabilities must be defined in some generic fashion.

1.3 Model-View-Controller Paradigm

Several presentations revealed that the Model-View-Controller Paradigm (MVC) can be improved by new and perhaps more efficient ways of communicating update and change messages between models and views. Traditional MVC (à la Smalltalk) can over complicate model and view implementations.

2 Object Model

Class-instance versus delegation is an issue that relates to the graphics require- ments of an object model. The object model defines "a common object semantics for specifying the externally visible characteristics of objects in a standard and language-independent way" (the OMG reference model).

2.1 Class-Instance Versus Delegation

The primary issue is whether or not class-instance is appropriate for graphics. It was argued that delegation languages may be more appropriate for graphics because of the run-time freedom to compose objects and inherit methods, thus being a better match to the way end-users manipulate and think about graphics.

However, class-instance combined with constraints and perhaps dynamic binding would provide equivalent functionality. Thus the choice of object model is more or less a preference. Therefore, standardization efforts must be careful not to inhibit the choice of different object models.

3 Implementation Techniques

3.1 Multiple Inheritance Versus Composition

Is multiple inheritance really necessary? It was generally thought that relying heavily on language constructs, such as multiple inheritance, was an artifact of a particular language; for example, implementations using statically typed lan- guages, such as C++, tend to rely heavily on multiple inheritance.

3.2 Efficiency

How do we efficiently handle thousands of graphics objects on a display? Naturally the object-oriented paradigm has some overhead costs, especially if each graphic is an interactive object. Some solutions are to implement short-cuts in the graphics kernel. For example, a hash table lookup may be used to quickly identify the target object after a mouse click, as opposed to traversing a tree structure.

4 Related Technologies

The workshop also highlighted many issues that can be seen as external influences to graphics. Many of these are future technologies that designers should anticipate.

4.1 Constraints

Constraints play an important role in graphics (i.e., in a CAD application, moving one gear affects the movement of another gear). Constraints may be geometric or non-geometric (color, texture, or other) in nature, and may be internal or external (affect other objects). There are good indications that if external constraints do not violate encapsulation then the constraint resolution problem may be exponential.

This lead to a discussion of the importance of encapsulation and the difficulties in merging different paradigms with object-oriented programming. We concluded that for special cases, breaking encapsulation can be permitted if the overall system achieves the goals of object-oriented programming: modularity, reusability and extensibility.

Although constraints are very important to graphics, constraints are not particular to graphics. Therefore, the graphics kernel should not address the constraint problem.

4.2 OMG, OODBMS and Distributed Objects

The OMG reference model was presented as a basis for evaluating and comparing different object technologies. The object-oriented graphics kernel is an example of a common facility in this architecture designed to be used by many applications. The architecture also supports object persistence via object-oriented database management systems (OODBMS), and distributed objects allowing parallel and distributed computing.

Most of this technology is very new and few systems conform entirely to the OMG reference model. However, initial experiences with OODBMS and distributed objects indicate that this technology will impact object-oriented designs and therefore should be considered when designing a common graphics kernel.

5 Summary

Discussions, such as the ones at this workshop, are far from being over. There is still some skepticism as to whether or not OOP is the right way to go for graphics. We need to see the real benefits of OOP and we need to show that OOP helps by providing solutions to graphics problems. A collection of example strategies for solving certain "known" graphics problems would be beneficial. In general, we need more experience with related object technologies to evaluate their applicability to graphics. The graphics community is not an island. It needs to address its own particular problems in the light of new technical advances and thus benefit from the work of others.

Volume I

The Second Eurographics Workshop on Object-Oriented Graphics

Co-Chairs

Chris Laffra, IBM T.J. Watson Research Center
Edwin Blake, University of Cape Town, South Africa

Programme Committee

F. Arbab (Netherlands).
J. Coutaz (France).
E. Fiume (Canada).
B.N. Freeman-Benson (USA).
M.R. Kaplan (USA).
Wm Leler (USA).
B.A. Myers (USA).
X. Pintado (Switzerland).
T. Takala (Finland).
J. van den Bos (Netherlands).
I. Wilkinson (UK).
P. Wisskirchen (Germany).

Part I

Modeling I

1

Actor-Based Simulation + Linda = Virtual Environments

William Leler

While it may be called different names – virtual reality, cyberspace, or virtual environments – the expectations are similar. We desire a way to interact completely and seamlessly with other entities, whether those entities be other individuals, synthetic individuals, or just raw information and data. Unfortunately, there is a huge gap between our dreams for virtual environments and the current state-of-the-art. This chapter explores some of the reasons for this situation, and brings together ideas from diverse fields, including object-oriented programming, parallel computation, policy management, and even computer music, in an attempt to take a fresh look at how to build the reality of our dreams.

1   Do Our Tools Become Us?

The earliest computer-generated animations were not overly concerned with the representation of reality. In *Permutations* by John Whitney, Sr., the subject matter is abstract geometry in motion [Whitney]. In *Hunger* by Peter Foldes, reality serves only as a jumping off point for a world in which animate and inanimate objects transform into each other and even motion is a form of change [Foldes]. In neither of these films is there a single static object. But both of these movies remain enjoyable, despite their age and now primitive technology.

Computer graphics then entered a commercial period largely dominated by computer-aided design (CAD) applications. CAD software is used to design objects with fixed geometry, whether they be mechanical parts, buildings, or illustrations. The commercial use of this software has been the driving force behind software development for computer graphics, including hidden surface elimination, curved surfaces and CSG. While CAD tools have given us the means to create beautiful rigid objects, software for other aspects of computer graphics has not kept up. Computer animation no longer features the amazing transformations found in *Permutations* or *Hunger*, but is instead dominated by flying logos and other rigid objects; animation driven by simple motion in space or the movement of jointed objects.

2   Virtual Environments

What distinguishes virtual environments from other media is the high degree of synergy possible between the the user (the occupant of or participant in the virtual environment) and the computer. The occupant should be an integral part of the environment; in fact, it is probably misleading to think of a virtual environment separate from the occupant (without an observer, what does it mean for a tree to fall in a virtual forest?).

Unfortunately, nowhere is the legacy of CAD software more apparent than in virtual environments, since a typical virtual environment is created using a CAD program. CAD-derived software encourages us to think of the virtual environment as an entity that exists independently of the observer (for example, a virtual building to be walked through). The resulting environments are largely static with minimal user input; any interaction is typically bolted on after the environment is "created" by the designer. Even what is considered advanced interaction, such as hitting virtual drums to make sounds, is derived from collision and interference detection algorithms developed for CAD use. More typically, the user's role is limited to putting on the eyephones and exploring; after an environment has been explored a few times it often becomes boring.

Part of the problem with virtual environments may be due to the primitive state of hardware and software, but primitive hardware and software didn't stop John Whitney or Peter Foldes. One could even argue that if advanced CAD software didn't exist, virtual environments would be more interesting. Even video games, with their flat graphics but intense interaction, are more engaging.

3   Virtual Environments in Music

It is enlightening to compare virtual realities with current work going on in the electronic music world, in particular the work creating electronic accompaniment to live musical instruments by computer (for example, the work of Daniel Scheidt [Scheidt] or George Lewis [Lewis]). In some sense these are virtual environments: the computer program takes input data from the musician in the form of MIDI data (or raw musical notes), interprets this data in some way, and then generates a response, again in the form of MIDI data (or other audible output). The musical output, in turn, is heard by the musician and affects what is played. The role of the composer/programmer is to define how the musical gestures of the musician are interpreted and the nature of the (musical) response to these stimuli.

Even though such a program is semiautonomous and can be considered a virtual environment, it is never thought of as an experience on its own, separate from the musician. Every performance of the program will be different, even with the same musician (let alone a different one).

Another difference is that a virtual environment typically assumes little or no skill on the part of the occupant, while an electronic accompaniment setup assumes at least a competent musician to supply the input, or even a virtuoso. What would it mean to have a virtuoso occupant of a virtual environment? (We already have indications that this could produce enhanced results, for example, the Mandala system by Vincent John Vincent and Frank MacDougal, which can be used by anyone, but is much more interesting under the control of an experienced user). In contrast, most existing virtual environments are much the same no matter who occupies them; evidence of the limited influence the occupant has in these environments.

Another important aspect of electronic music systems is their reconfigurability. Electronic music equipment and studios take the principles of object-oriented systems and decentralized control to their logical physical end: separate boxes with their own control that communicate via MIDI data through MIDI switchers and audio links through audio mixers. Such setups are rapidly reconfigurable, often being changed (i.e., reprogrammed) in midperformance (for example, in the work of Daniel Scheidt, where the composer/programmer is an integral part of an improvisational performance). In contrast, most virtual environments are controlled by a single program, utilizing a single stream of control. This lack of modularity makes virtual environments difficult to reconfigure.

4   Filters

CAD-influenced software encourages us to think of a virtual environment as an entity that exists independently of the occupant, and the occupant as a relatively uninfluential observer. Instead, the occupant of a virtual environment should be treated as an integral part of the environment. One way to do this is to think of a virtual environment as a set of transfer functions between the user's actions and the computer's reactions. Using engineering terminology, such a function (whose output is a function of its input) is called a filter. The filters in the virtual environment take input (possibly from the occupant), transform it in some way, and then generate output (possibly back to the occupant).

The concept of a virtual environment as a set of filters is closer to the electronic music view of a musical virtual environment. In a musical virtual environment there are often no fixed notes; sounds are created only in response to user input (musical gestures), as are the characteristics of those sounds (pitch, volume, tempo, and so on.). We can do the same thing in a virtual environment. The gestures of the occupant can be used to control the appearance and even the structure of the environment. For example, different user gestures could create different kinds of objects in the environment. Another example would be a world created out of words spoken by the occupant. Such a system could be used simply as a way to organize thoughts, or the words could become huge three-dimensional objects to create a space to be explored, or even link together like a crossword puzzle.

On a more practical level, virtual environments can be used in scientific visualization to view multidimensional data. Flat, two-dimensional computer screens are commonly used to view three-dimensional data, or, with the addition of animation and movement, four- dimensional data. But much scientific data has five or more, even hundreds of dimensions - we are not only talking about spatial dimensions here - for example, we might want to view a three-dimensional gas plasma over time under varying conditions of temperature and pressure; the data for this problem has six dimensions. Most virtual environment input devices, such as the data-glove or space-ball, or even the position and orientation of the occupant's head in the eyephones, have five or six dimensions, and combinations of input devices can be used for higher dimensions. Filters can be defined to translate from one or multiple of these input device dimensions into views that allow the occupant to explore high dimensional spaces.

Filters can also incorporate a concept of time. For example, many virtual environments recognize gestural input, but in the largely static environments common today it is not surprising that typically only static gestures are recognized. However, most interesting gestures involve a time component, for example waving, "throwing your hands up in disgust" or even the difference between shaking your head "no" and nodding your head "yes". This can be done by defining a filter that takes raw input device coordinates as input and examines them over time to recognize a set of gestures, and outputs any recognized gestures, which are then used by other filters as input. One way to build such a filter, which itself utilizes filters, is to use a simple filter to recognize static gestures, and then to feed the output of this filter into a second filter that recognizes patterns of static gestures over time. Much of the power of filters comes from their ability to be reconfigured in this way.

The designer of a virtual environment defines the filters and connects them, deciding what variables are dependent on what external input, and what variables are independent. As is common in such object-oriented systems, a toolbox of predefined filters can be supplied, or new filters that are built can be reused. Furthermore, thinking of the environment as a set of filters lets us see that the designer and the occupant need not be separate. The occupant of the environment should have the ability to change the definition of and the connections between the filters. For example, a scientist trying to interpret some six-dimensional data could choose different filters depending on the particular aspect of the data that is being explored.

5   Behaviour

The filters in a virtual environment need not be simple functions between the inputs and outputs. Instead, a filter can contain state information. This state is not static (as in current virtual environments), it is affected by the filter input (from the user or the output from another filter) and in turn affects the outputs (to the user or to another filter). When individual filters in a virtual environment are dependent on their own internal state, in addition to user input, these filters can appear to possess behaviour. In this case, we usually call these filters objects, or actors.

The rules governing these behaviours need not be complex in order to be interesting. The cells in the Game of Life (originally introduced by Conway in his now famous article in Scientific American) follow very simple rules, yet produce interesting worlds with surprisingly complex behaviour.

Behavioural models have been used in virtual environments, although usually only to control a single object in the environment. When more than one independent object possesses behaviour, things get complicated quickly. New techniques and tools are needed to manage this complexity.

6   Distributed Control

Most software is written in (and most programmers are trained using) procedural languages such as Fortran and C. These languages are based on procedural abstractions with a single, central locus of control. Unfortunately, this means that it is difficult to write software where control is decentralized. This is one reason why, among other things, parallel computers and mouse-driven user interfaces are difficult to program.

Because language strongly affects how we can think about solving a problem, the single locus of control of procedural languages makes it easier to only think about controlling a single object at a time. As a result, most computer animation and virtual environments are scripted. In a scripted system control is centralized. Like a traditional musical score or a script in a play, the script controls everything that happens. As a result there is not much variation in how the virtual environment can respond to different occupants.

The work presented in this chapter is based on two assertions. First, that interesting behaviour primarily comes from the interactions between independent actors. The music world understands this, and, even more significantly, the neuro-computer world understands this (where even the low level behaviours are modeled through the connections between simulated neurons). Second, almost in order to even think about writing software like this we need languages and tools that provide facilities for creating objects with their own locus of control and ways for these objects to communicate with each other.

There has been work done using distributed control to model independent objects in computer animation, for example, programming computer-generated birds to display "flocking" behaviour. This work has typically been called actor-based animation. It is interesting to note that most of this software has been written in LISP, a language that does provide some facilities for distributed control. Unfortunately, most of this work has not transferred so readily to the commercial world of procedural languages. Luckily, there is a new development in the procedural language world that does provide the basic structures necessary to write such software.

7   Putting the Object back into Object-Oriented Graphics

The software business is going through a revolution. Object-oriented languages and environments provide significant productivity gains over conventional languages, and programs written in these languages are easier to debug and maintain. An object-oriented language, C++, is even replacing the venerable language C in many companies and institutions. One of the major reasons for this is that object-oriented languages present a higher level of abstraction: they allow computer programs to more closely model the real- world systems they are are trying to simulate.

The concepts of object-oriented programming transfer naturally to computer graphics and virtual environments. Unfortunately, the term "object-oriented" already has a meaning in computer graphics, so we will borrow the term from animation and call these systems actor based. For animation, using our earlier terminology, we will define each actor to be a filter.

Unlike a scripted animation, in an actor-based animation the actors (objects) can operate independently (execute concurrently), so control is decentralized. Individual actors receive messages, and respond by sending more messages. Many actors will receive their input from other actors, while a few actors will receive their input from external events, such as the occupant of the virtual environment, MIDI data or even random external inputs, such as the phase of the moon. The output of some actors will correspond to objects displayed to the occupant, or sounds, while other actors may control the attributes of other objects, such as color or shape, pitch or volume.

Each actor has its own behaviour, determined by the functions encapsulated by the actor (the filter function). A set of predefined behaviours can be used, or new behaviours can be programmed. The behaviour of the entire system is then determined by how the actors communicate with each other. Because of the interaction between actors, a wide range of interesting results can be obtained based on (even slightly) different inputs.

The use of distributed control makes it easier to program much more complicated and interesting behaviours. Because each actor has its own locus of control, it is more modular. The behaviour of individual actors can be changed without any need to modify a centralized script. Instead, actors act out their own behaviour, and only synchronize when necessary, using some communication mechanism.

For example, imagine trying to write a script to control a room full of bouncing balls. Now imagine the same script, if the user is allowed to enter the room and randomly bat a few balls around. Instead of using a script, each ball should be modelled as an actor whose behaviour is to travel along a path until some other object (a wall, or the user) gets in its way. Modifying this environment to introduce gravity would not be that difficult. We could even play around with the gravitational constant. Another posibility would be to make the balls massive enough to gravitationally attract each other. In this example, communications between objects is very dynamic. A ball may need to interact with an unknown number of other objects, and even objects it was not originally designed to interact with, such as the user. Such interactions are very difficult to model using the static communication mechanisms (message passing) normally used by object-oriented systems.

8   Communication

The mechanisms used for communication between actors strongly affects their possible interactions, and consequently the behaviour of the entire system. In traditional object- oriented systems the communication paths between the objects are largely static (typically determined when the computer program is compiled), and are difficult to change when the program is running.

For a virtual environment we want to be able to make or change the connections between actors dynamically. One way to do this is by using a communication mechanism like the Linda communication paradigm developed by David Gelernter at Yale. Linda was originally developed for use on parallel computers [Leler 90], but has been used successfully in other ways (for example, for communication in a mouse-driven user-interface manager).

9   Linda

In Linda, communication takes place through an intermediary called a tuple space. Each actor in a virtual environment will have a tuple space associated with it, but actors are also free to create new tuple spaces, as desired. A tuple space behaves like a mailbox: it is a place to get data from and a place to put data. There are three primary operations defined on a tuple space:

ts.out(key, value)

Place some data into tuple space ts. Each piece of data in tuple space is identified by its key, which is a string or a number. The value can be a string, a number, or some other kind of data, including another tuple space. There can be more than one piece of data in the same tuple space with the same key (tuple space acts like a bag).

ts.in(key, value)

Remove some data from a tuple space. Tuple space ts is searched for the specified key. If found, the corresponding value is returned as the second argument of this function, and both the key and value are removed from the tuple space. If the key is not found, then the actor performing this operation blocks until the key is placed in this tuple space (by some other actor).

ts.rd(key, value)

Copy some data from a tuple space. Like the in operation, except that the key and value are not removed from tuple space.

Message passing in Linda is decoupled in space and time, and so can be much more dynamic. Messages are decoupled in space because they are sent via a tuple space, and are identified using a key. This is in contrast to message passing, where the receiver of the message must be identified explicitly by the sender. Messages are decoupled in time, since the sender of the message continues executing immediately. A message can even be sent to a receiver who is not currently executing; the message will wait in the tuple space until it is needed. Since a tuple space can be stored as the value of a key, one actor can even tell another actor who to send a message to.

Linda also uses implicit synchronization, since the receiver of a message will block until the desired key is placed in tuple space. This makes communication safe compared to something like shared memory, where extra synchronization mechanisms (such as semaphores) must be provided to keep the recipient of some data from running ahead of the provider. Unlike other implicit synchronization mechanisms, namely message passing, Linda allows the sender of a message to proceed independently of the receiver of the message. This allows the communicating entities to execute independently and only synchronize when necessary. Lastly, in Linda messages are identified via pattern matching, which supports dynamic forms of communication - including name services - that are traditionally very difficult to program. These features make Linda significantly easier to use than other communication mechanisms, and make it ideally suited to the construction of virtual environments.

10   Mechanism versus Policy

It is common for programming environments (including most operating systems) to confuse mechanism and policy. For example, even something as simple as the number of buttons on a mouse is often fixed by the operating system. A program written using such an environment often reflects the preferences of the original tool builder more than the programmer. The same thing is happening to virtual environments: the facilities provided to the environment builder end up controling what the resulting environments look like. It is difficult for tool builders to antic-ipate everything that their tools will be used for, and any policies set by the tool builders will end up as often as not hindering more than helping.

For example, when providing mechanisms to represent objects it is difficult to avoid implicitly controlling how they should be represented (what they look like). Should a graphical representation of a virtual environment have a floor or walls? Should space be cubic, cylindrical, or something else? It is often felt that such policy is unavoidable, after all, any mechanism tacitly makes a certain approach easier to use, and thus sets a policy encouraging its use.

The solution is not to avoid policy, but to separate policy from mechanism. The components that supply policies should be separated into modules called policy agents, which are used by default. One such policy agent is called an oracle. You ask an oracle a question and it provides an answer, but you generally don't care where or how it got the answer. For example, you can ask an oracle for a representation (e.g., for yourself, or for an object you have created) and it will supply one.

The oracle can make its decision based on things such as the capabilities of the underlying hardware. Consequently, the oracle will typically give different answers on different systems. For example, a representation supplied on a more capable system may be more complex.

Policy agents such as oracles are stored in Linda tuple spaces (in many cases, policy agents are themselves tuple spaces). Since policy agents are identified by name in a tuple space, a programmer can replace the default policy agent with a new one. This can be done locally (for a single user or group of users) or for the system as a whole. Thus, more sophisticated users are free to override policy, while still utilizing the base mechanisms of the environment.

11   Conclusion

This chapter explores new ways to create virtual environments based on object-oriented programming, distributed control, and Linda. Most significant is the use of Linda for communication in an actor-based (object-oriented) system, instead of the conventional use of message passing. The use of Linda for inter-actor communi-cation allows a degree of autonomy and flexibility not possible in a message passing system, as well as providing the software engineering benefits that originally made Linda popular.

The resulting system, while designed for creating virtual environments, provides benefits to many other related applications. For example, this work is directly ap-plicable to the production of animations. Other applications include the production of computer music, scientific visualization, the simulation of complex systems, and the construction of user interfaces with behaviour (like the Artificial Reality Kit from Xerox PARC).

12   Art and Technology

Current tools for building virtual environments often (inadvertently) control policy, and thus strongly affect what the resulting environments (for example, the way the CAD-influenced software favors static virtual environments). Thus, policy is often set for technological reasons alone. Unfortunately, many policy issues do not have technological answers. For example, as technologists, we know little about the best way to represent objects. As a result, computer graphics usually strives to produce the most realistic images possible, without regard to what aspects of an image are important and which are not. Typically, such images are overkill for virtual reality (and take too much time to render, anyway).

Ignoring the computational cost, a less realistic image can often be more visually effective anyway. For example, what is the best way to represent a tree? Should each leaf be modelled as a set of polygons, resulting in many thousands of polygons even for a simple tree? Would the resulting bevy of polygons even look like a tree? Would a forest represented this way even give you the feeling of being in an actual forest, or are there better ways to convey that? (And how long would it take to draw a forest represented this way?) What abstractions are necessary or possible?

These are issues that artists have been dealing with for centuries [Beirne]. What is the best way to represent a tree in a limited medium such as pencil, oil paint, or even on a computer? Is there a "best" representation? Artists will even use different representations in different situations (how many ways have artists drawn or painted trees?).

As technologists, by blindly embracing reality in our virtual environment, we ignore many other posibilities. Why should a virtual environment need to obey any laws of space and time? What would a Cubist or Futurist virtual environment behave like? Such issues have practical importance as well: can I warp space so that things I am interested in are larger or closer to me? If I am attending a meeting in virtual space and become bored, can I put time on fast forward?

Once people start interacting in virtual space, there will be questions about how people should represent themselves. Will everyone be virtually beautiful? Do I need to keep the same sex or race? Do I need to appear the same to everyone, or can I choose what I appear like to different people? Can observers choose what I look like? (Can my mother choose to see me with shorter hair? Can my boss choose to see me in a suit and tie?).

Turning the tables, how will virtual environment change our perception of the "real" world? Will we be less concerned with appearances, and more with content (as can happen through the great equalizing force of a computer mail network)? Will the relaxing of normal cause and consequence help things to get quickly out of control (again, as often happens on computer mail networks)? How will virtual environments reflect society? How will virtual environments change society? Will virtuality become the site for post-modern debates on representation? Will the virtual representation of humans change the relationship between mind and body? Will the boundary between humans and machines degenerate? Stay tuned.

References

Beirne, G., personal communication, The Banff Centre, Banff, Alberta, Canada. The Banff Centre is a professional art school doing research into the artistic aspects and issues of virtual reality.

Foldes, P., "Hunger", a computer generated short film, available from the National Film Board of Canada, Ottawa, Canada.

Leler, Wm., "Linda Meets UNIX," IEEE Computer Magazine, February 1990.

Lewis, G., performer of interactive music and virtuoso musician, Chicago, Illinois, USA.

Scheidt, D., composer of interactive electronic music, Vancouver, British Columbia, Canada.

Vincent, J., and MacDougal, F., Toronto, Ontario, Canada. "Mandala", A video space where the occupant interacts with computer generated objects by "touching" their images.

Whitney, J. Sr., "Permutations", a computer generated short film, available from Pyramid Films, Los Angeles, California, USA.

2

Meta-attributes for Graphics Collection Classes

Peter Wisskirchen

Graphics systems such as GKS, PHIGS, or GEO++ differ mainly in how graphics entities can be grouped into collections and how attributes can be assigned to them. In PHIGS, sequential structures are provided to build up multi-level hierarchies; GKS offers a single-level segment concept; GEO++ supports a set-oriented approach to handle part hierarchies. Besides the concept for collecting graphics primitives, the predominant structuring concept, additional constructs are used to filter out, select, or group specific subsets of the whole set of graphics objects. In PHIGS, the concept of name-sets allows assignment of a set of names to any primitive in order definition of filters for each of the three types of attributes, visibility, highlighting and detectability. GEO++ allows to define ad-hoc sets by using object identifiers for parts. In GKS-R, the revised version of GKS, name-sets are introduced as primary construct to assign attributes to output primitives. In this paper we introduce basic mechanisms for collecting graphics entities and for assigning attributes. These mechanisms are defined on a meta-level allowing us to extend a low-level kernel and to interpret systems such as PHIGS, GKS-R, or GEO++ as special cases of one flexible system.

1 Introduction and Overview

Many graphics systems provide mechanisms for naming and selecting graphics entities. GKS provides a segment identifier to refer to a collection of graphics primitives and to assign the attributes visibility, highlighting, and detectability to a segment. Segment identifiers are also used to insert a previously defined segment into a newly created one, the open segment, and to delete a complete segment. Besides this a pick- id is provided inside a segment to support a second level of naming used only for the pick input device [ISO, 1985, Enderle et al., 1987]. In PHIGS, structure names are provided to build up hierarchies, i.e. structure networks as acyclic directed graphs. Besides this predominant naming concept, however, additional names are used as a secondary concept to select specific subsets of a given structure network. The concept of *name-sets* introduced for PHIGS allows to assign a set of names to any primitive. These names may be used to define a *filter* for each of the three types of attributes, called *visibility filter*, *highlighting filter*, and *pick filter* respectively [ISO, 1989]. In the specification of GKS-R, name-sets constitute the central naming concept. Conceptually output primitives own a set of names as attributes and names are used to filter out specific subsets of all previously defined primitives according to various selection criteria based on the Structured Query Language (SQL) and to assign attributes to output primitives [ISO, 1990]. The object-oriented system GEO++ uses object identifiers to describe part hierarchies as predominant structuring concept. Besides this, special collection classes were introduced to collect parts from different hierarchies and to apply attributes to them [Wisskirchen, 1989, Wisskirchen, 1990]. In this paper we start with examples of two different collection classes, a set-oriented and a sequential one. Both classes differ in the aspect of how attributes are transferred to elements of the collection and how editing can be performed. Then meta-attributes are introduced which can be used to change the default strategy of whole-element inheritance of attributes. The definition of the different inheritance strategies for attributes allows to define different systems such as GKS-R, PHIGS, or GEO++ as special cases of one extensible minimal kernel. Smalltalk-80 syntax is used to describe the examples [Goldberg and Robson, 1983]. The exact specification of a graphics kernel considered in the following is left open because the concept of meta-attributes is rather general. However, the graphics kernel addressed here should fulfill the following requirements for naming graphics entities [Kansy and Wisskirchen, 1989, Kansy and Wisskirchen, 1991]:

- the kernel should be designed in the fashion that all graphics entities are direct accessible by an use of an identifier.

- all entities should be owner of their attributes.

- graphics entities should provide inquiry methods to access all information (attributes, geometrical coordinates) that may be relevant for the application programmer.

- The object-oriented kernel should know as well *graphics instances* as *masters*. The term instance, already introduced in Sketchpad [Sutherland, 1963], stands for a geometrically transformed invocation of a repeatedly used graphics entity, called *master* (see also [Foley et al., 1990]. To avoid confusions with instances in the sense of object-oriented programming we speak about *graphics items*. We suppose that graphics items own their master as *content*.

- Both master objects and graphics items can be edited and the usual graphics attributes (color, linestyle, linewidth, highlighting, detectability, visibility) can be assigned to them. Editing of a master object will update all graphics instances sharing the master object. Although these requirements sound very obvious – – in particular for kernels realized in strictly object-oriented environments – neither GKS, nor PHIGS, nor GKS-R fulfill them.

2   Collecting Graphics Objects

To start the discussion two examples of how different graphics concepts can be supported are given. For this purpose, two different graphics collection classes, GraphicsPartHierarchy and GraphicsConnection are defined, the first one to support set-oriented part hierarchies, the second one to model sequential structures. Besides different editing methods, the concept behind the class Graphics-Connection allows to inherit attributes from one component to its successors which is not possible in the case of the pure set-oriented part concept supported by the class GraphicsPartHierarchy. In addition, the two classes Part and Component are introduced for the graphics items corresponding to the above classes for master objects (cf. Figure 1).

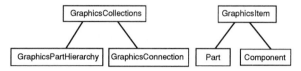

Figure 1: Set-oriented and sequential collection classes for master objects (left) and graphics items (right)

2.1   Part Hierarchies

The typical collection class for *part hierarchies* may be a non-sequential collection class. We call this class GraphicsPartHierarchy. A single primitive or an existing hierarchy, i.e., an instance of GraphicsPartHierarchy may be inserted into such a class. Primitives and instances to be inserted are considered as master objects. Usually a transformation (or any other attribute) is applied as an additional argument while inserting. The result of the insertion process (and the resulting element of the collection class) is a graphics item, in our case a part. The geometrically transformed graphics item is invoked for display only if its hierarchy is explicitly posted on a workstation. In Smalltalk-80 syntax with

        myHierarchy , GraphicsPartHierarchy new

a new empty hierarchy is created.

        aMaster , PolyLine points: nPoints

generates a master object which is inserted together with a transformation aTrans-formation into the hierarchy

        aPart , myHierarchy put: aMaster
transformedBy: aTransformation.

A part knows its master which can be inquired by:

        aPart content

and its owner which may be inquired by:

        aPart root .

A part knows also its access path, an indicator, delivered by:

```
myIndicator , aPart path.
```

The access path can be used to inquire the part from its hierarchy:

```
myPart , myHierarchy part: myIndicator.
```

As mentioned, it is allowed to insert instances of GraphicsPartHierarchy so that higher level hierarchies may be build up. The access to parts deeper in the hierarchy is possible by using a path name consisting of a sequence of indicators (ind1, ind2,..). This principle is described very detailed in [Wisskirchen, 1990].

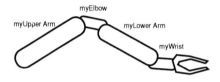

Figure 2: A robot arm as a typical example of a sequential graphics structure

2.2   Connectivity

By *connectivity*, we understand a concept to model and support the connection of components in space. Connectivity is seen as a directed (non-symmetrical) relation of type connect(a,b) between graphics items. This relation should ex-press that b is connected with a (in the sense of attached with). In connectivity, n objects are attached to each other, so that a se-quence of objects on the same hierarchical level is created. A well known example is the robot arm [ISO, 1989] with components upper arm, elbow, lower arm, wrist, hand defining a *sequence* to express the connectivity relation (cf. Figure 2). Note that PHIGS supports exclusively this type of sequential structure, although PHIGS is often used to model (set-oriented) part hierarchies which leads then to an over-specification. To supply the application programmer with a connectivity model, a sequential collection, the class GraphicsConnection, is introduced. The basic methods of GraphicsConnection are described by the following example:

```
robotArm , Connection new
myUpperArm , robotArm add: upperArm transformation: t0
myElbow , robotArm add: elbow transform: t1
myLowerArm ,  robotArm add: lowerArm transform: t2
myWrist , robotArm add: wrist transform: t3
myHand , robotArm add: hand transform: t4 .
```

The result of the sequential insertion process is a graphics item, in our case a *component*. Very similar to the non-sequential case, a component knows its master which can be inquired, for example, by

```
myWrist content
```

and its owner inquirable by

```
myWrist root .
```

A component knows its access path, in the sequential case an integer value delivered by

```
myIndicator , myWrist index
```

which evaluates in our example to 4. The access path can be used to inquire the part from its hierarchy

```
myComponent , robotArm part: myIndicator.
```

As mentioned, it is allowed to insert instances of `GraphicsConnection` so that multi- level hierarchies can be build up. The access to parts deeper in the hierarchy is possible by using a path name.

It should be noted that also mixed hierarchies can be constructed, i.e., it is allowed to insert a master object that is instance of `GraphicsConnection` into a part hierarchy and vice versa.

3   Meta-attributes

Meta-attributes are introduced to control the inheritance strategy of attributes for whole-member relations, i.e., these strategies describe how an attribute applied to a graphics collection class is transferred to its parts or components.

3.1   Default Strategy

Default strategies are not as important as in conventional graphics systems because meta-attributes allow to change the strategy very easily. Nevertheless, there should be a predefined default strategy. To define the default strategy four groups of attribute types are introduced:

- the first group contains all attribute types to describe color, linestyle, linewidth, shading.
- the second group contains detectability and highlighting.
- the third group contains visibility.
- the fourth group contains transformations which are considered to be attributes.

28   Peter Wisskirchen

Attributes of the first group, when assigned to a whole, are applied to parts or components if no attributes were assigned previously and directly to a part or component. The same default strategy is valid for inheritance from parts to subparts deeper in the hierarchy.

Consider, for example, the following assignments:

```
myElbow color: color1
robotArm color: color2
```

As a result, all components except myElbow would be receive color2 as new color. Attributes of the second group are not inherited at all. Thus, when a whole is set to detectable it becomes detectable as a whole without changing the detectability state of any sub-component. Attributes of the third group will be inherited in any case to the elements of the collection applied to, making all elements visible or invisible. Transformations are inherited from a whole to its parts or components. Thus a rotation applied to robotArm would apply the rotation to the whole arm. In the case of sequential structures, however, a transformation applied to a component would also effect the succeeding components. Thus, when we change the transformation t2 to t2new (a rotation) by

```
myElbow transform: t2new
```

then everything below the elbow rotates (see Figure 3).

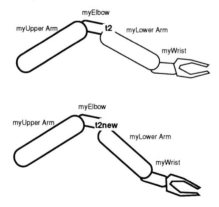

Figure 3: Rotation of the parts connected with Elbow

3.2   Controlling the Strategy

In many cases it is highly desirable do change the default strategy described above. Thus, it may be convenient, for example, to change the color of all elements of a collection regardless of color attributes assigned previously to parts or components. This leads to the requirement to control whole-member inheritance by additional capabilities. To control the strategy, special operations are provided which we call *meta-attributes*. We do without listing all different types of strategies but give some example illustrating the idea. With

```
aSet strictInheritanceFor: 'detectability'
```

all elements of the receiver are set to detectable regardless of previous assignments to single elements. The default case, mentioned above, can be achieved by

```
aSet noInheritanceFor: 'detectability' .
```

With

```
aSet weakInheritanceFor: 'detectability'
```

all elements of the set are set to detectable if no specific assignment was applied to a single element previously. An additional possibility to define the inheritance strategy is to see it as a mode. In Smalltalk-80, such a modal assignment could be modeled by a class method. Thus, with

```
Color strictInheritance
```

we can define the way of how color is inherited. This rule will take place for all subsequently assigned color attributes. To control the inheritance strategy the operations introduced above have to be supplemented by similar rules valid for sequential collections of class GraphicsConnection, for example,

```
aSequence horizontalInheritanceFor: 'color'
```

will inherit color from one component to the succeeding ones (as in PHIGS).

4   Discussion

We have introduced flexible ways to define inheritance of attributes by introducing meta-attributes. These strategies are realized as methods of graphics collection classes. In this context the question about the overall semantics of graphics collection classes will arise. In GKS collections (segments) are defined to delete and insert them and to apply three types of attributes to them. In GKS-R collections filtered out by name sets are used to apply all type of attributes and to post them to specific workstations. In PHIGS collections (structures) are essentially used as master objects to be referred by other hierarchies; collections filtered out by name-sets are used to apply the attributes detectability, highlighting, visibility. GEO++ allows to filter out collections to apply attributes to them or to edit them, collections are also used as master objects. All these operations are more or less shortcuts to apply attributes. In GEO++, however, some additional functionality of collections was defined allowing, for example, to assign specific pick sensitive areas to collections as a whole. In general, the question arises what additional semantics aspects can be assigned to a whole with a well defined meaning for any general purpose graphics system. This seems to be still an open question. Aspects valid for a graphics collection which are application specific and not general can be integrated into a general object-oriented graphics systems by defining subclasses of the collection classes shown in Figure 1. Conclusion The definition of different inheritance strategies for attributes allow to describe different systems such as GKS-R, PHIGS, or GEO++ as special cases of one extensible minimal kernel. Therefore this type of strategies should also be considered when future standards will be defined.

References

Enderle, G., Kansy, K., and Pfaff, G. (1987). *Computer Graphics Programming. GKS: The Graphics Standard*. Springer-Verlag.

Foley, J., van Dam, A., Feiner, S., and Hughes, J. (1990). *Computer Graphics – Principles and Practice*. Addison-Wesley.

Goldberg, A. and Robson, D. (1983). *Smalltalk-80: The language and its implementation*. Addison-Wesley.

ISO (1985). *Information Processing Systems: Computer Graphics – Graphical Kernel System (GKS), Functional Description*. International Standard 7942.

ISO (1989). *Programmer's Hierarchical Interactive Graphics System (PHIGS)*. International Standard ISO/IEC 9592.

ISO (1990). *New Graphical Kernel System (GKS-R)*. Working Draft. ISO/IEC JTC1 SC24 N545.

Kansy, K. and Wisskirchen, P. (1989). *An object-oriented approach towards a New API for Computer Graphics*. Document ISO/IEC JTC1 SC24 WG1 N94.

Kansy, K. and Wisskirchen, P. (1991). The new graphics standard – object-oriented. In Blake, E. and Wißkirchen, P., editors, *Advances in Object-Oriented Graphics I (Proceedings of the Eurographics Workshop on Object-Oriented Graphics, 1990)*, EurographicSeminars Series. Springer-Verlag.

Sutherland, I. (1963). A man-machine graphical communication system. In *Proceedings of the Spring Joint Computer Conference (IFIPS 1963)*, pages 329 – 345.

Wisskirchen, P. (1989). Geo++ – a system for both modelling and display. In *Proceedings Eurographics '89 (Hamburg, Sept. 1989)*, pages 403 – 414. Elsevier Publishers.

Wisskirchen, P. (1990). *Object-Oriented Graphics*. Springer-Verlag.

Part II

Constraints I

3

A Co-operative Graphical Editor Based on Dynamically Constrained Objects

Zsófia Ruttkay

A co-operative graphical editor is introduced as an efficient drawing tool for structural and functional design. The components of the artifact being designed are represented as objects. A design can be modified by direct manipulation of the 2D graphical presentation of its components. The criteria for consistency of a drawing are declared in the form of abstract rules, prescribing what relations should hold for which object instances in the drawing. In the course of the drawing process, constraints are generated from the general prescriptions and resolved dynamically, ensuring the given state of the drawing. The editing operations are defined with respect to the constraints. The graphical editor assures the consistency of a drawing on the basis of a specific constraint satisfaction mechanism. The editor is discussed with reference to the specific application domain of interactive design of planar welding fixtures. However, the basic concepts and the constraint satisfaction mechanism are general enough to be used as a framework for other domain-specific editors. The modular and open architecture of the editor assures adaptivity to other application domains.

1   Introduction

1.1   The Aim: a Co-operative Graphical Editor

There is a wide gap between the two extremities of the general drawing toolkits, such as MacDraw, and the sophisticated bulky softwares dedicated to specific needs, such as AutoCad. The former offers a set of drawing primitives too general for engineering applications, while the latter provides an environment with drawing conventions of an engineering field. However, in both cases:

- either the representation of the design is not separated from its graphical presentation at all, or it is not easily accessible by the user or an application,

- the drawing conventions and the semantics of the editing operations are wired in, cannot be defined and changed by the user.

Our concern is:

- to clearly separate the representation of a design and its *graphical presentation*, allowing the conventions for the latter to be adjusted,

- to make it possible to declare and tailor the *criteria of consistency* of a drawing,

- to support the efficient generation and exploration of *consistent drawings*.

We will not dwell on the rather technical issues of the first two points, but on the services below, closely related to editing:

- **Error-proof drawing**: In the entire course of the drawing process the consistency of the drawing is assured. The user can perform only such editing operations which do not violate the consistency of the drawing. What has been drawn so far and the general criteria of consistency determine what can be done in a given position of the drawing; the input by the user is interpreted accordingly. Only certain inevitable temporal inconsistencies are allowed exceptionally.

- **Co-operative drawing**: Each input by the user is interpreted in the context of the drawing of that very moment, and the appropriate consequences are generated and carried out automatically by the graphical editor. The user is relieved from the burden of completing and prettifying drawings.

- **Explorative drawing**: The user can explore – actually see – the consequences of a hypothetical modification, before committing himself to it. The graphical editor also provides feedback about the feasible range of a modification.

1.2   The basic technique: dynamic generation and satisfaction of constraints

Constraints [Leler, 1988] have proved to be a good basis for the purposes of interactive graphics. The prescriptions for a drawing are given as relations – *constraints* – on characteristics such as size, relative and absolute location of the graphical elements. A drawing is consistent, if all the constraints hold. The modification of a drawing may result in the violation of some constraints. A *constraint satisfaction mechanism* provides the automatic correction of the drawing, by altering certain further values in such a way that all the constraints hold again. Sketchpad [Sutherland, 1963] was the first system based on constraints to define and maintain geometric figures. When the consistency of a drawing could not be achieved by simply solving the constraints one after the other, the iterative numerical technique of relaxation was activated. ThingLab [Borning, 1979, Borning, 1985] was developed along similar lines, but with an extensible set of graphical objects and constraints. Magritte [Gosling, 1983] is an interactive graphical layout system with the power of transforming a constraint graph containing cycles into an equivalent one which does not, and hence can be solved by the method of local value propagation. IDEAL [van Wyk, 1982] is a component of a typesetting software, which can be used to secure the prescribed position and sizes of graphical objects in documents as constraints. Juno [Nelson, 1985] is a constraint language with a limited set of constraints on points, but with the means of representing constraints graphically.

In these applications the following traits are common:

- The constraints should be given in advance and can be altered one by one, only if explicitly requested by the user or an application program. As an alternative, constraints referring to different attributes of one object only are given as abstract constraints for all instances of a given object class.

- Constraint satisfaction is used in a "follow up" manner, to restore the consistency of the drawing after modification.

In order to overcome these shortcomings, we took the following novel approach:

- Constraints are prescribed in advance and in an *abstract way*, in the form of a fixed set of rules circumscribing the objects involved and giving the constraint on them. Objects belonging to different classes can be constrained.

- The consequences of a modification by the user are computed by generating the relevant constraints *dynamically*, according to the abstract rules and the instances present.

- Beside the traditional follow-up way, constraints are used also to prevent modifications which would result in unresolvable inconsistencies.

Recent research on general, incremental constraint satisfiers focuses on how to improve a given solution if the set of constraints has been altered [Freeman-Benson et al., 1990]. Our emphasis is rather on the generation of the constraints driven by the changes in the drawing, than on the power of the incremental constraint satisfaction technique. Constraints have been used with objectives similar to ours by syntax-based text and program editors [Carter and LaLonde, 1984, Logger, 1988] and user interface toolkits amalgamating object-oriented and constraint-based techniques [Hill, 1990, Maloney et al., 1989, Myers, 1989, Szekely and Myers, 1988, Vander Zanden and Myers, 1990]. While in these recent graphics systems constraints are directed and declared as characteristics of object classes, in our case non-directed constraints are used. They are prescribed separately of the declaration of object classes, in the form of rules.

1.3 The architecture: potential for a range of applications

In general, a graphical editor is an appropriate tool for design tasks with the following specifics:

- The artifact should be designed by *synthesizing* components of well-defined types.

- The feasibility of the design is expressed in terms of prescriptions for the *geometry* and *topology* of the components.

- The relevant aspects of the components can be *presented in 2D*.

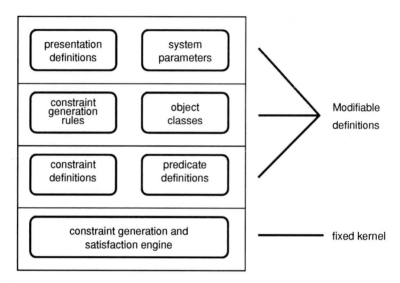

Figure 1: The layers of the modules of the graphical editor

The closed, unchangeable "engine" of our editor is based on a specific constraint satisfaction mechanism, which narrows down the possible fields of application:

- The constraints should refer to *coordinates* of specific points of graphical objects or system variables. System-variables – e.g. critical limits on distances – are set before the drawing process is started, and afterwards they are treated as constants.

- The coordinates of the graphical objects can change *continuously*.

- Each constraint is a *linear equation or inequality*.

- By an equation either *only the x or only the y coordinate* of a point is referred.

There are several application domains – mechanical engineering and architectural design, design of electrical circuits – which meet the above requirements: lines and a set of graphical symbols are used to present a design, and collinearity and ortoghonality are key composing criteria. The *modular* and *open* architecture of the editor provides basis for a range of applications. The declarations needed to define an editor for a specific design application are stored in separate modules, all of which can be modified (see Figure 1):

- By changing the *presentation definitions* and/or the *system parameters*, the graphical editor can be tuned to the needs of design environments with different drawing conventions and design parameters.

- By changing the definition of the *constraint generation rules* and/or the *object classes*, the generic design criteria and the choice of components can be altered

- By modifying the definition of constraints, the editor can be suited for domains with different design concepts.

Further on, we will discuss an editor with declarations suited to a specific application domain. However, the same concepts and mechanisms apply for other possible editor instances for different design fields.

1.4 An application: interactive design of welding fixtures

Our work was induced by the needs of the design of fixtures for welding 2D frames used for building buses. The details of the design task are discussed in [Márkus et al., 1990]. In a nutshell: a welding fixture is a lattice-like planar construct of ortoghonal bars which support clamping and positioning devices. The clamping and positioning elements are selected from a modular set. Some modules have continuously adjustable parts. The fixture body consists of a rectangular frame and 5-20 bars. On one bar there can be several clamps and positioning elements. The design task is to produce a fixture to hold the bars of a given bus-frame during the process of welding, see Figure 2.

The criteria for the fixture to be designed are of three different sources:

- *general prerequisites* for welding fixtures,

- *numerical parameters* referred by the general prerequisites,

- specification of the *given design task*, prescribing the possible location of positioning and clamping devices and a set of rectangular forbidden areas which should be avoided by the fixture body.

The design criteria refer to:

- the *structure* of the design (e.g. the fixture body should be built of ortoghonal bars, bars should support the clamping elements),

- the *topology* of the construction (e.g. no pending bars are allowed, fixture bars should avoid forbidden areas),

- the *geometry* of the components (e.g. upper and lower limit on the distance of neighbouring bars and length of bars).

1.5 An Illustrative Example

Let us assume, that in Figure 3.a. the adjustable **c** clamp should be positioned on the **b** fixture bar in order to "push" the **a** bus bar. The coordinates of the **E** and **C** points should meet the set of equations and inequalities in Figure 3.b. They should not be given explicitly, but are generated by the editor from general prescriptions such as "a clamp should always be positioned on the middle line of its supporting bar".

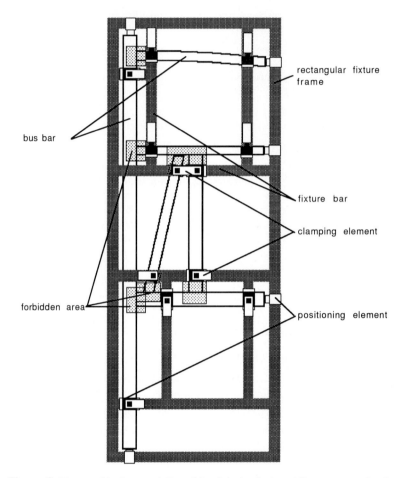

Figure 2: The graphical presentation of the fixturing task and the components of the fixture

The graphical editor assures the following:

- If the **b** bar is neither too close nor too far from the **a** bar, that is,

    6. $\mathbf{B}_x - \mathbf{A}_x - \mathbf{m} - 0.5 * \mathbf{v} \leq l_1$, and
    7. $\mathbf{B}_x - \mathbf{A}_x - \mathbf{m} - 0.5 * \mathbf{v} \geq l_2$,

    then any **E** point on of the **b** bar for which (5) holds can be selected. The x coordinate of **E** is adjusted by the graphical editor, in accordance with (1). That is, the user does not have to position the **c** clamp accurately on the middle line of the **b** bar.

- The coordinates of **C** are computed automatically, that is the adjustable part will be of the right size.

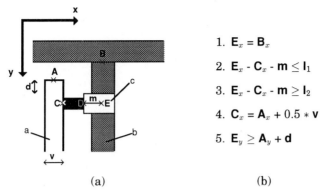

1. $E_x = B_x$

2. $E_x - C_x - m \leq l_1$

3. $E_x - C_x - m \geq l_2$

4. $C_x = A_x + 0.5 * v$

5. $E_y \geq A_y + d$

(a)   (b)

Figure 3: (a) The **c** clamping element should be positioned by giving the coordinates of its **E** and **C** points. (b) The set of equations and inequalities to be met by the drawing. **m**, **d**, **v**, l_1, and l_2 are system parameters

If the user moves the **b** bar supporting the **c** clamp along the x direction, then:

- The **c** clamp moves too, remaining on the bar. The adjustable part of **c** is readjusted continuously.

- The **b** fixture bar can be moved neither too far from nor too near to the **a** bus bar. The two extreme positions computed by (6) and (7) serve as "bumpers".

In the rest of this chapter we explain the novel functionalities of the editor and the basic concepts of its model. The chapter is structured as follows: section 2 is devoted to the modelling of design prescriptions in terms of object classes and constraints. In section 3 the editing operations are discussed. In section 4 we point out the necessity of constraint satisfaction in addition to object-orientedness, we discuss possible extensions and issues requiring further research, and finally we sum up our results. Further details, such as means provided as alternatives to direct manipulation of the drawing, the usual "householding" services of the editor as well as the technical issues of interaction, visualization and the implementation in Common Lisp are covered in [Ruttkay, 1990].

2   Constrained objects

2.1   Object classes and instances

The structural design prescriptions are captured by the definition of given graphical object classes, modelling the simple and compound components of the artifact being designed. The structure of the objects of the given class is defined by a list of typed attributes, see below. The instances of a graphical object class – graphical objects, for short Q are given by assigning values to the attributes. The value of an attribute is either an object, or a list of object instances of a class given as the type of the attribute.

class: horizontal_bar
        startpoint: point
        endpoint: point
        stating_bar: vertical_bar
        ending_bar: vertical_bar
        clamps: list
        clamp_seats: list seat
        joining_bars: list vertical_bar

For each object class a procedure to generate the graphical presentation of the instances is given, with reference to general drawing conventions (e.g. line width, filling patterns, symbols) and the specific value of some attributes of the object instances (e.g. location, size of changeable parts). The graphical object classes form a hierarchy, inheritance of attributes as well as of presentations is supported. The user can identify graphical objects only by selecting their presentation on the screen. Because of the one-to-one correspondence of the graphical objects and their presentation, further on we will use the notion "graphical object" for the objects themselves as well as for their presentation. From a given object others can be referred to in any depth, along chains of attribute names.

The two non-graphical object classes model numbers and points. The number class is defined according to the specific constraint satisfaction mechanism applied. An object instance of the number class has the following attributes:

- current_value, which can have a real number as value,

- range, which can have a closed, finite or infinite interval of the real numbers as value,

- old_value, which can have a real number as value,

- status, which can be "unknown", "changeable","changed" or "fixed".

The essential role of range in satisfying constraints will be discussed in section 2.3. The status attribute is used to guide the resolution of a conflict. For the sake of brevity we will not explain the related details neither the rather technical issues of the role of old_value in exploring a drawing.

The point objects are given by the x and y coordinates, both attributes are of number type.

2.2 Constraints

All the design prescriptions referring to the topology and geometry of the design components are given in the form of constraints: linear equations and inequalities over numerical design parameters and the coordinates of specific points of the graphical objects. The characteristics of the constraints were listed in section 1.3. A drawing presenting a design is consistent, if all the constraints prescribed for the components of the design hold.

The constraint graph consists of nodes corresponding to coordinates of points of graphical objects, to system parameters and to constraints. Each node representing

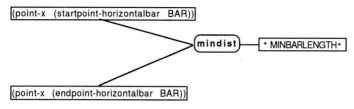

Figure 4: The constraint expressing that "the length of the horizontal bar should exceed a given limit". The limit is given as the value of the *MINBARLENGTH* design parameter

a constraint is joined to nodes representing its variables. The arcs are not directed, indicating that any of the variables of a constraint can play the role of output, while the rest of them serve as input, see Figure 4.

The consistency of the drawing is preserved by a specific constraint satisfaction mechanism, based on the following characteristics of the constrain graph, similar to but weaker than the usual *exclusion of cycles*:

- At any stage of the drawing process, the value of at most two of the numbers referred to by a constraint can be changed.

- If a number defines the value of another number via a chain of equalities, then this chain of constraints is unique.

- If a number defines the value of another number via a chain of equalities, then there cannot be given a chain of inequality constraints between the two numbers.

How and when is the constraint graph *generated*? This is a key issue, as in most cases the modification of the drawing implies modifications of the constraint graph. The following specifics of the constraint graph make possible the rule-based generation of its relevant subgraphs:

- The entire constraint graph consists of small isomorph subgraphs: the same constraints are prescribed for different tuples of object instances.

- The vast majority of the constraints are inequalities.

The first characteristic suggests that the entire constraint graph can be generated by a small set of rules prescribing what objects should be constrained in what way, referring only to names of constraints, object classes and their attributes, not to individual objects. The second characteristic assures that for the propagation of a changed value only a relatively small part of the entire graph should be known explicitly.

We took the approach of generating the relevant part of the constraint graph whenever needed, instead of storing and updating it permanently. The relevant subgraph of the constraint graph is built up on the basis of constraint generation rules. A constraint generation rule defines the objects to be constrained and the constraint itself. The left hand side of such a rule specifies the objects involved, by prescribing a conjunctions of predicates on objects. On the right hand side the name of the constraint and a list of references to point coordinates of objects and system variables are given. E.g. the design prescription "the fixture bars should avoid the forbidden areas" for `horizontal_bar` instances is formulated by the two rules below. The predicates on the left hand side of the rules identify the critical forbidden area – that is, the nearest one to the bar on each side. The constraints on the right hand side prescribe that the bar should avoid the nearest forbidden area.

```
rule forbidden_area_1
if (is_a horizontal_bar B) and (nearest_left_area A B)
then (mindist (point-x (startpoint-bar B))
              (point-x (thirdcorner-rectangle A))
              0)
rule forbidden_area_2
if (is_a horizontal_bar B) and (nearest_right_area A B)
then (mindist (point-x (firstcorner-rectangle A))
              (point-x (startpoint-bar B))
              0)
```

The *instance of a rule* is produced by binding the variables in the rule in such a way that the predicates on the left hand side hold. An *instance of a rule holds* if the appropriate constraint holds. A *rule holds* for a given drawing if all the instances of the rule hold. A drawing is *consistent* if and only if all the constraint generation rules hold.

2.3   Constraint satisfaction by interval propagation

Whenever a drawing has been modified, the constraint propagation mechanism enforces that all the prescribed constraints hold. This requires two services:

- assuring that the conflicts caused by the user's modification of the drawing can be resolved,

- updating the `current_value` of the constrained numbers in such a way that the constraints hold.

The constraints are reinforced by the widely used method of *local value propagation* [Steele, 1980], taking into account the equalities only. However, the case should be avoided when there is no solution of the set of constraints due to a modification by the user. The success of the local propagation of a changed value is provided by the use and update of the `range` of the constrained numbers. The consequences of the given set of constraints on each number instance are stored in their range attribute. The `range` of a number instance is the interval of exactly those reals, which are feasible candidates for the `current_value` of the number. Choosing any real from the range as the new `current_value`, the constraints can be resolved. The `range` of the number type objects is updated too by the so-called *local interval propagation* constraint satisfaction mechanism, which is a new generalization of the local value propagation to intervals of real numbers. In updating the `range` of objects, both the equalities and inequalities are taken into account. In [Ruttkay, 1990] a formal discussion of the method is given, with the proof of its applicability.

Constraints operate locally, relying upon the status, current_value and range of their number-type arguments. As the constraint graph is not stored, the constraint satisfaction mechanism has to generate the subgraph of those constraints which are relevant in the propagation of the consequence of a change of a given current_value on both the current_value and range of other objects. The generation of the affected constraints and the value/range propagation are performed in an interwoven way. Here we characterize the three procedures maintaining the consistency of the drawing, fully given in [Ruttkay 90].

Whenever the current_value of an object is changed – assuming that the new value is within the range of the object – the *value_propagation* procedure is activated. It identifies the objects which are constrained by equalities with the given object, and their current_value is adjusted. The adjustment of the range of objects which are constrained by an inequality and a chain of equalities with the given object is performed by the *interval_propagation* procedure.

Whenever a new object is inserted, the range of the coordinates of its points should be computed. This is done by the *interval_computation* procedure, by identifying and taking into account all the constraints prescribed for the new object and the already existing ones.

3 Editing operations

The user can edit a drawing by directly manipulating the graphical objects in the drawing. We will simply refer to selection of points and objects without going into details such as the selection of an object versus its components, or the selection of only one of the coordinates of a point, as the other one is already determined by what has been drawn before.

3.1 Drawing new objects

New simple graphical objects can be drawn one after the other. The drawing takes place as a sequence of selections of already existing graphical objects or points of the drawing. The selected objects are assigned to appropriate attributes of the object to be drawn. For each object class, one or more lists of attributes are given. The series of selected objects should confirm with the type of attributes in one of the given lists. The graphical editor can uniquely decide which attribute list is being used after at most the second selection by the user, see Figure 5. After the user has selected a point, it is decided by the editor if the selection can be accepted. Namely, the range of the attribute in question is computed, and it is tested if the selected coordinate value is in the range. If so, the selection is accepted and the new current_value is propagated. If not, the selection has to be repeated.

3.2 Moving objects

Objects can be dragged along two, ortoghonal directions by grabbing any of their points. The editor assures that an object can be moved only to such a new position that the consistency of the drawing can be restored. On the basis of the range of the appropriate coordinates of the object being moved, an interval is computed. The

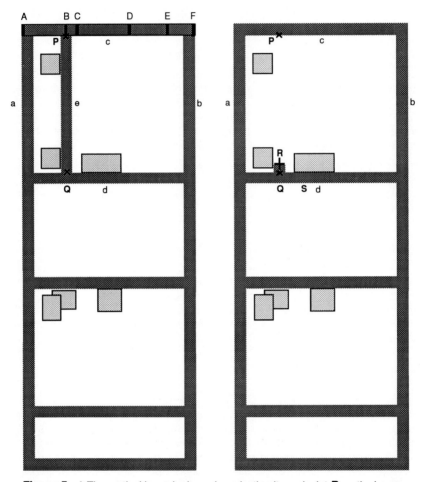

Figure 5: a) The vertical bar **e** is drawn by selecting its endpoint **P** on the bar **c**. Because of the prescriptions for bars, only points of **c** within the intervals **BC** or **DE** can be selected as **P**. As soon as **P** is selected by the user, the editor automatically computes **Q** and draws **e**. b) It is not sufficient to select the **Q** endpoint of **e** on **d**, because from the selected point a vertical bar can be drawn both upwards and downwards. As soon as the user has started to draw the line, the ambiguity is eliminated and the editor "finishes" the drawing just as in the previous case. Note that from point **S** only one joining bar on **d** can be drawn

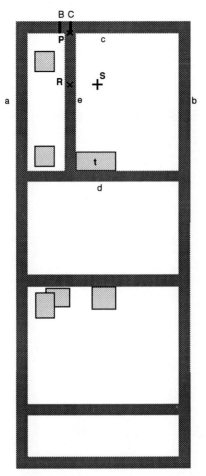

Figure 6: The **e** vertical bar can be moved horizontally within an interval: the **P** points should remain within the **BC** interval. The forbidden area **t** acts as "bumper": Point **R**, the grabbed point of **e**, cannot be moved to **S**. The forbidden area **t** cannot be jumped over by moving the **e** bar

endpoints of the interval act as "bumpers" till which the object can be moved, see Figure 6. The topology of the drawing cannot be changed by moving an object. E.g. a bar cannot "jump over" a forbidden area.

The exploration of the drawing is supported by two means:

- The extreme positions till the object can be moved is visualized (highlighted).

- The consequences of the current position of the object being moved on the current_value of the other objects are computed and visualized, see Figure 7. Hence the user can see what the entire drawing would look like if he moved the object to its current position.

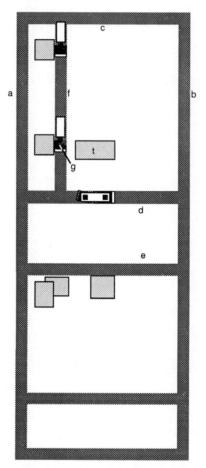

Figure 7: When the **d** bar is being moved downwards, the clamp and seats on **d** should move with the bar. The joining bar **f** is being stretched. The extreme positions for **d** are determined by the minimal distance of **d** from bar **e** and the maximal length of bar **f**

As soon as the user selects the final position, the `range` of the coordinates of the points of the objects is updated. If the user quits, the `old_values` and the corresponding drawing are restored.

3.3 Deleting objects

After deletion the remaining drawing should be structurally consistent. This is provided by defining the preconditions and consequences of deletion for each object class in the form of delete methods. E.g. a bar can be deleted only if there are no other bars joining to it. If a bar is to be deleted, then all the clamps on the bar should be deleted as well.

Note that the constraint graph of the drawing does not shrink necessarily in parallel with the deletion of objects. New rule instances may prescribe new constraints instead of the ones which have been eliminated. In most of the cases it can be proved that the new constraints hold. We will return to this question in section 4.2. In all cases after the deletion of an object the `range` of the coordinates of points of the remaining objects is recomputed.

4 Discussion

4.1 Why was object-orientedness alone not sufficient?

At the workshop a recurring question was: "Why did you take an approach other than pure object-orientedness? All you presented could have been done by using appropriate objects and message passing or delegation mechanisms." How to answer this question in my case?

Bye and large, the object-oriented paradigm lends itself naturally to model domains where objects can be classified in such a way that the behaviour of object instances can be expressed in terms of classes and instance-specific attributes. In our field the effect of an editing operation highly depends on the relative position of the element to be edited to certain other elements of the drawing. If insisting on an object-oriented approach, one should identify e.g. the forbidden area nearest to a bar by making the bar sending messages to all forbidden areas in order to find out their position. To avoid the re-execution of this kind of exhaustive search for critical constraining objects, each object could have direct pointers to the critical objects. However, in this way the objects themselves would grow large, with much redundant and only occasionally used information.

Constraints themselves could be defined and implemented as objects. We pointed out in section 2.2 that an editing operation has effect only on a small subgraph of the entire, rather bulky constraint graph. It would be inefficient to store and update all the constraints all the time. For bi-directional constraints it would require extra effort to prevent oscillations. Moreover, the instantiation of constraints – which is needed for several constraints whenever a graphical element is inserted/deleted – would require the extensive search discussed above. Defining the constraint generation rules themselves as objects would result in objects alien to real object-orientedness: the rule objects would have an overall view of and access to the real objects modelling graphical elements.

Our main claim for taking the approach of rule-based generation of constraints is the conceptual clarity, transparency and adaptivity of the declarative rule format. A new requirement can be introduced by adding a single new constraint generation rule, while in an object-oriented application all the object classes involved should be redefined. The declaration of a new constraint generation rule can be easily done by and end-user, while the redefinition of the affected object classes would require a system developer. A purely object-oriented approach would make it very difficult if not impossible to filter out a declaration of the prescribed constraints: an n-ary constraint would be mentioned in the description of all the n object classes.

Altogether: an object-oriented hacker possibly *could* implement most of the functionalities of our editor. However, that would require a solution far from the natural and easy style of object-oriented programming, and it could not be done in the orthodox way of complying to data hiding. Moreover, the rule-based approach has some advantages which could not be provided by any object-oriented implementation.

4.2   The scope of constraint generation rules

The prescription stating "the distance of two neighbouring parallel bars cannot exceed 60cm" should be met by any finished drawing. However, there are drawings – see Figure 8. – which could not be produced if this prescription were taken into account in all previous stages of the drawing process. In general, the constraint generation rules are of two kinds:

- *structure-dependent* ones,

- *structure-independent* ones.

The violation of a structure-dependent rule can be overcome by extending the drawing. In contrast, if a structure-independent rule does not hold, then it will not hold for any extension of the given drawing. In our application the quoted rule is the only structure-dependent one, which is taken into account only on the explicit request of the user.

The problem of scope of the constraint generation rules should be tackled in a more general and sophisticated way. One possibility is to chunk the constraint generation rules. As the drawing evolves, further chunks are added to the set of rules to be taken into account. The inclusion of a chunk of rules can be triggered by the user directly, or by an editing operation indirectly. Another way to handle the problem is to introduce a constraint hierarchy [Freeman-Benson et al., 1990]. The constraints with the greatest weight must hold, while the others may be relaxed. The weights change as the drawing evolves.

4.3   Non-binary constraints

The editor cannot handle constraints with more than two numbers of `changeable status`. If a constraint can be resolved by changing the `current_value` of more than one numbers involved, then a decision should be made.

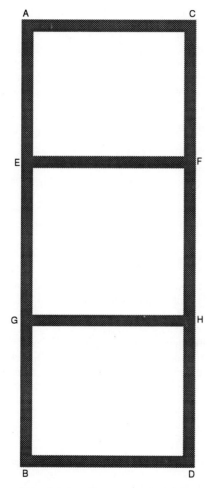

Figure 8: If no inconsistent intermediate states were allowed, this drawing could not be produced: the **AG** and **GB** distances all exceed the limit allowed. The graphical editor should only detect whether two neighbouring bars are too far from each other, and suggest the user to insert a further bar inbetween

According to the literature on constraint programming systems a conflict is resolved always by selecting one value to be changed, in one of the following three ways:

- the user is asked to decide at each occasion,

- the system decides randomly or by numerical considerations,

- the system decides but the user can override its decision. If the user is to decide, then the graphical editor should support backtracking to all previous stages where a conflict could have been resolved. A more adequate solution is if the user declares the preferences among different object classes based on application-specific knowledge. The editor chooses the value of an attribute of the least preferred object to be changed automatically.

4.4   Non-linear constraints

The linearity of the constraints provides that the set of feasible candidates for a value is an *interval* of real numbers. The interval propagation mechanism exploits only this consequence of the linearity of the constraints. Hence the linearity can be replaced by some weaker restrictions on the constraints, also assuring that the range of feasible values is an interval. One possible such a restriction is the monotonicity of the constraints in each of their variables.

4.5   Missing operations: search, cut and paste

There are no means to select other subparts of a drawing than a simple or compound object. It would be handy to have means to characterize, select , cut and paste other subparts of a drawing. The characterization of subparts of a drawing can be given in terms of object classes and attribute values, or in terms of concepts not provided by the object-oriented model, see Figure 9. In both cases, replacement of a subpart by another may produce an inconsistent drawing. The incremental and local constraint satisfaction method of the editor is not powerful enough to restore the consistency of the drawing. Only the violated constraints can be detected, and then the user has to correct the drawing.

4.6   Conclusions

A co-operative graphical editor has been presented with the following main novel services:

- preventing errors,

- support for exploration of a drawing,

- co-operative generation of consequences.

The above services are provided on the basis of dynamic generation and satisfaction of constraints on coordinates of graphical objects. Our approach has new features compared to object-oriented and constraint-based drawing systems and user interfaces:

Figure 9: The bars within the selected rectangle on the left are copied in to the selected rectangle on the right. Because the copied subpart is proportionallly distorted, the constraints prescribed for distances and length of bars do not hold necessarily in the right part

- the constraints "glueing together" object instances are declared in the form of abstract rules,

- the relevant constraints are generated when needed on the basis of the abstract rules and the current contents of the drawing,

- the generation of constraints is triggered by changes of attribute values of existing objects as well as by insertion/deletion of objects,

- the "overall effect" of the constraints on the current object instances is computed by the novel constraints propagation mechanism and stored for each object instances, making it possible to prevent unresolvable conflicts.

A prototype graphical editor for a specific application domain has been implemented in CommonLisp. The modular, open architecture, the generic concepts used to specify the application-dependent knowledge, and the not strict requirements on the individual constraints and the structure of the constraint graph guarantee that the same framework can be used for a range of potential applications.

However, as yet neither an "editor-specification" language has been worked out formally, nor tools have been forged to define and modify editor prototypes. A graphical editor shell with tools to facilitate the definition of object classes, constraints and constraint generation rules could be a further objective.

Acknowledgement

Thanks for my colleagues András Márkus, József Váncza and Gergely Krammer at the Computer and Automation Institute of the Hungarian Academy of Sciences for their comments on an earlier version of this paper.

References

Barth, P. S., "An object-oriented approach to graphical interfaces," *ACM Transactions on Graphics*, 5, 2, pages 142–172, 1986.

Borning, A. H., "ThingLab – a constraint-oriented simulation laboratory," XEROX PARC Technical Report SSL-79-3, Palo Alto, Calif., 1979.

Borning, A. H., "Defining constraints graphically," Univ. of Washington, Computer Science Dept. Technical report No. 85-09-05, Seattle, Wash., 1985.

Carter, C. A. and LaLonde, W. R., "The design of a program editor based on constraints," Tech. Report. CS TR 50, Carleton University, 1984.

Freeman-Benson, B. N., Maloney, J. and Borning, A., "An incremental constraint solver," *Communications of the ACM*, 33, 1, pages 54–63, 1990.

Gosling, J., "Algebraic constraints," CMU Computer Science Dept. Technical Report CMU-CS-83-132, Pittsburg, 1983.

Hill, R. D., "A 2-D graphics system for multi-user interactive graphics based on objects and constraints," In: Object-Oriented Graphics I (Proceedings of the Eurographics Workshop on Object-Oriented Graphics, 1990), 67 – 91. Springer-Verlag, 1990.

Leler, W., *Constraint Programming Languages*. Addison-Wesley, Reading, Massachusetts, 1988.

Logger, M. H., "An integrated text and syntax-directed editor," CWI Report CS-R8820, CWI, Amsterdam, 1988.

Maloney, J. H., Borning, A. and Freeman-Benson, B. N., "Constraint technology for user-interface construction in ThingLab II," Proceedings of the 1989 ACM Conference on Object-Oriented Programming, Systems, Languages and Applications (New Orleans, Oct. 1989), *SIGPLAN Notices*, 24, 10, pages 381–388, 1989.

Márkus, A., Ruttkay, Z. and Váncza, J., "Automating fixture design – from imitating practice to understanding principles," *Computers in Industry*, 14, 1-3, pages 99–108. 1990.

Myers, B. A.(1989) "Encapsulating interactive behaviors," Proceedings of the 1989 Conference on Computer-Human Interaction,, Austin, Texas, May 1989., pages 319–324.

Nelson, G., "Juno, a constraint-based graphics system," Proceedings of SIGGRAPH'85 (San Francisco, July 1985), pages 235–243, 1985.

Ruttkay, Z., "Intelligent graphical editor for computer-adied fixture design," Ph.D. dissertation, Computer and Automation Institute of the Hungarian Academy of Sciences, Budapest (in Hungarian), 1990.

Steele, G., "The definition and implementation of a computer programming languages based on constraints," MIT AI-TR.595, Cambridge, Mass. 1980..

Sutherland, I., "Sketchpad: A man-machine graphical communication system," Proceedings of the Spring Joint Computer Conference, (IFIPS, 1963), pages 329 – 345, 1963.

Szekely, P. and Myers, B., "A user interface toolkit based on graphical objects and constraints," Proceedings of the 1988 ACM Conference on Object-Oriented Systems, Languages and Applications (San Diego, Calif. Sept. 1988), *SIGPLAN Notices*, 23, 11, pages 36–45, 1988.

Vander Zanden, B. and Myers, B. A., "Automatic, look-and-feel independent dialog creation for graphical user interfaces," Proceedings of the 1990 Conference on Computer-Human Interaction, (Seattle, Washington, April 1990), pages 27–34, 1990.

van Wyk, C. J., "A high-level language for specifying pictures," *ACM Transactions on Graphics*, 1, 2, pages 163–182, 1982.

4

A Quantum Approach to Geometric Constraint Satisfaction

Remco C. Veltkamp

This paper presents an incremental approach to geometric constraint satisfaction that is suitable for interactive design by categorizing solutions into so called quanta. A quantum is a range of solutions with uniform geometric characteristics. In this way, the constraint management system keeps the intermediate solutions in the geometric domain, so that new geometric constraints can be interpreted on the same high level of abstraction. This approach leads to a number of advantages: the system

- can handle (perhaps temporarily) under-constrained specifications,
- represents both alternative discrete solutions and continuous ranges of solutions,
- performs satisfaction locally and incrementally,
- supports constraint inference and geometric reasoning,
- preserves the declarative semantics of constraints.

The relationships between constraints and both the imperative nature and the information hiding principle of object-oriented programming are discussed.

1 Introduction

Constraints specify dependency relations between objects which must be satisfied and maintained by the system. Constraint systems are used in applications such as geometric modeling, user interfaces [Szekely and Myers, 1988], simulation [Steele Jr. and Sussman, 1979], and animation [Badler and Kamran, 1987]. Geometric constraints can fix one or more degrees of freedom for positioning, orientation and dimensioning. For example, when a circle of fixed radius is constrained to be tangent to a fixed line segment, the position of the circle centre is restricted to two line segments parallel to the given one, at a distance equal to the radius.

A constraint satisfaction system relieves the task of the user: problems can be solved by specifying constraints, the user need not specify how to solve the constraints. It is easier to state constraints than to satisfy them. However, even if the system cannot satisfy all constraints that can occur in a given domain, it frees the user from the error-prone process of solving the many little but time-consuming problems.

The way that constraints are solved largely depends on the techniques used for representation and manipulation, see [Leler, 1988] for several approaches. Our approach categorizes alternatives and ranges of solutions into classes featuring the same characteristics, called quanta, see Section 4. We use geometric manipulation as opposed to algebraic manipulation and numerical computation to find solutions to geometric constraints. General geometric knowledge is combined with properties of (classes of) geometric objects to infer relations between geometric objects in order to satisfy constraints. This high level geometric reasoning provides geometrically meaningful solutions and tries to avoid computationally expensive algebraic and numerical methods [Arbab and Wing, 1985].

Geometric reasoning and constraint satisfaction are facilities that can be part of a basic layer of a design system, but this layer in itself is not an application system. It provides a good basis for CSG modeling and modeling with Euler operators [Mäntylä, 1988], feature-based modeling [Pratt, 1987], and intelligent human-computer interaction interfaces [Helander, 1988].

The rest of this paper is organized as follows. The next section gives an introductory classification of some constraint satisfaction techniques and an overview of systems that have been developed. Section 3 explains some shortcomings with respect to geometric modeling that motivates the present research, and Section 4 introduces the quantum approach. This is formalized in Section 5, where our system architecture is discussed, and further illustrated in Section 6, which gives some examples. Section 7 discusses additional aspects of the quantum approach; Section 8 discusses how constraints and the object-oriented paradigm relate to each other, and mentions some implementational aspects. Finally, Section 9 gives some conclusions and suggests future research directions.

2   Overview

We can classify satisfaction techniques into *structured* and *unstructured* methods. An orthogonal classification can be made into *numerical computational* and *deductive* techniques. Structured deductive techniques can exploit several methods for the *propagation of results*.

In the following subsection, I describe these techniques in more detail, in the subsequent subsection, I will mention some constraint systems that use these techniques.

2.1   Satisfaction Techniques

Unstructured Methods

Unstructured methods do not group dependent constraints into sets, and do not solve the independent sets separately. Solving the *overall set of equations* comprising all constraints is perhaps the simplest way of constraint satisfaction. Obvious drawbacks are the computational complexity and its inefficiency for interactive applications: each single change leads to solving the whole set of all equations. One way to solve the overall set of equations is by relaxation, see the following subsection.

Among the unstructured deductive systems are algebraic manipulation, logic programming, and term rewriting systems. *Algebraic manipulation*, or symbolic algebra systems are able to solve complex sets of algebraic constraints at a symbolic level [Davenport et al., 1988]. They are usually slow.

Logic programming can be classified into functional programming, based on equational logic (e.g. LISP), and relational programming, based on Horn clause logic (for example Prolog).

Augmented term rewriting as developed by [Leler, 1988] supports three features in addition to term rewriting: abstract data types, typing of variables, and binding of values to variables. The abstract data types are defined by rules. The strong ties with equational logic gives augmented term rewriting a solid theoretical foundation. As a consequence, the control mechanism is neatly separated from the problem solving rules.

Structured methods

Structured methods impose a structure on the set of constraints by grouping them into sets of dependent constraints. These local sets are satisfied independently.

Numerical computation of a local set of constraints is often done by relaxation. *Numerical relaxation* makes an initial guess at the values of the variables in an equation, and estimates the error by some heuristic. The guesses are adjusted accordingly and the new errors are estimated. This repeats until the error is minimized. A disadvantage of this method is that it will converge to only one of the roots of an equation. Moreover, *which* root is found depends on the initial value of the variable. This makes the solution unpredictable in under-constrained situations. Numerical relaxation is also computationally expensive, and can be used only in continuous numeric domains. One form of relaxation is the Newton-Raphson iteration technique for finding the root of a function. It is faster than general numerical relaxation.

A set of dependent constraints can be represented as a *network* of constraints. Structured deductive systems use some method to assimilate results of the inference process throughout the network. We mention two such methods.

Propagation of known states, or just local propagation, can be performed when there are parts in the network whose states are completely known (have no degrees of freedom). The satisfaction system looks for one-step deductions that will allow the states of other parts to be known. This is repeated until all constraints are satisfied, or no more known states can be propagated. If not all constraints can be satisfied, the remaining constraints must be resolved by some other method, for example numerical relaxation.

Propagating degrees of freedom amounts to discarding all parts of the network that can be satisfied easily, and solving the rest by some other method. This method identifies a part in the constraint network with enough degrees of freedom so that it can be changed to satisfy all its constraints. That part and all the constraints that apply to it are then removed from the network. Deletion of these constraints may give another part enough degrees of freedom so as to satisfy all its constraints. This continues until no more degrees of freedom can be propagated. The part of the network that is left is then satisfied by some other method if necessary, and the result is propagated towards the discarded parts, which are successively satisfied (propagation of known states).

Those are two methods of propagation, independent of *what* is actually propagated. We distinguish the following types of information inference and propagation.

Solution set inference makes deductions on the set of possible solutions, which are restricted by the constraints. Most frequently used are discrete value sets, or intervals of numerical values, see [Davis, 1987].

In *single solution* inference, constraint variables get assigned a single value, often numeric. Single geometric solution inference is performed by the *operational approach* [Rossignac, 1986, Arbab and Wang, 1989]. It satisfies constraints sequentially by performing operations (translation, rotation, etc.) on the geometric objects involved. An already satisfied constraint either tolerates an operation on one of its operands, or must propose a transformation to satisfy the constraint again. In this way, operations can be propagated through a constraint network until all operations are tolerated.

Local algebraic expression inference is a means to deal with loops in propagating numeric values. [Steele Jr. and Sussman, 1979] used powerful algebraic manipulation, but found that these techniques are not powerful enough to solve many interesting problems that people can solve. The way people usually solve these problems is by organizing the solution so that simple canned algebraic solutions suffice.

In *constraint* inference, implied constraints are derived and explicitly added to the network. Implied constraints can be recognized by a unification mechanism or by the use of multiple redundant views [Steele Jr. and Sussman, 1979]. They can be used to avoid extensive manipulations in cases where local propagation does not suffice. Stating constraints in a different way with the same meaning can help the constraint management system to solve the constraints locally. Otherwise the system may have to resort to techniques such as relaxation.

2.2 Constraint systems

Some systems that deal with geometry and some general purpose constraint languages are mentioned below in chronological order.

Sketchpad [Sutherland, 1963] was the first constraint-based drawing system. It satisfies constraints using propagation of degrees of freedom. When this fails, it resorts to relaxation.

Variational geometry [Lin et al., 1981] translates dimensional constraints into a single overall system of equations, which is solved numerically by the Newton-Raphson method. The dimensional constraints are defined by equations on coordinates of characteristic points. Each time a dimensional value is changed, the whole system of equations must be solved.

ThingLab [Borning, 1981] enlarges the possibilities of Sketchpad with extensibility and object-oriented techniques, so that new classes of objects and constraints can be defined. It uses both propagation of degrees of freedom and propagation of known states.

Juno [Nelson, 1985] is a simple system based on one geometric primitive: the point. It uses a Newton-Raphson iteration technique to solve constraints. The user has to supply an initial value to start the iteration.

[Rossignac, 1986] presents an operational interpretation of constraints in CSG modeling. Constraints are specified by the user in terms of relations between boundary features, and are transformed by the system into rigid motions of parts of the CSG tree. An under-constraint situation can simply not occur. The user must specify the order of evaluation and is responsible for solving conflicts.

Real general purpose languages for constraint logic programming (CLP) can be used in a wide range of applications, but are usually limited in their satisfaction power in each specific domain. Most constraint languages are biased to a more specific domain: CLP(ID) [Cohen, 1990]. For numeric constraints this yields CLP(IR) over the domain of real numbers [Heintze et al., 1987]. This is not a symbolic algebra system: it uses numerical deductions rather than unification.

Bertrand [Leler, 1988] is a rule-based system that uses augmented term rewriting. It has a form of abstract data types, which allows to define new types and constraints. Bertrand is a general purpose constraint language, but deals primarily with numeric constraints.

OTP (Operational Transformation Planning) [Arbab and Wang, 1989] provides an operational interpretation of constraints. It exploits solution reduction, i.e. only one solution is presented in an under-constrained specification (single solution inference). The satisfaction process is planned by means of symbolic reasoning on the geometric level, that is, by geometric reasoning [Arbab and Wing, 1985]. This can also involve the inference of implied constraints.

In [Emmerik, 1990] constraints relate coordinate systems. Constraints between degrees of freedom (for example between the x- and y-coordinate because of a distance constraint) are evaluated after lower-order constraints (for example one that uniquely determines the x-coordinate). This is a form of delayed satisfaction. Selection among alternative solutions to constraints is based on the minimal resulting disturbance. So, a single solution is derived for each constrained variable (single solution inference).

3   Motivation

In this section we mention some problems that motivate our current research.

Objects can be related to each other by constraints, without logically being involved in a part-whole relation. We do not want to be forced to create an artificial whole consisting of parts, in order to be able to express a constraint, as in ThingLab. Specifying constraints has a declarative flavor, and somewhat conflicts with part-whole hierarchies and information hiding, which are the hallmarks of object-oriented systems. The relation between constraints and objects is discussed in Section 8.

Many systems detect over-constrained situations, but cannot handle under-constrained cases. Indeed, numerical methods cannot solve a set of under-constrained equations. On the other hand, a CLP system for solving numeric constraints returns a set of deduced equations that constitutes the solution. In a geometric context, however, we prefer a geometrical form of the solution. The operational approach

Figure 1: Simultaneous evaluation of mutually constrained circles

and selection of alternatives based on minimal disturbance yield only one of the solutions. This may give rise to two problems:

- The proposed solution is as it was intended, but the user is not aware of the ambiguity of the specification. This may cause problems for post-processing.

- The solution is not as intended, and the user must interfere because the system cannot propose alternative solutions.

Both problems relate to the existence of alternative solutions. We distinguish several types of alternative solutions:

1. Several objects meet a specification of a variable involved in a constraint, and one or more of them must be addressed. For example, *any* circle or *all isosceles* triangles have to be addressed.

2. A constraint can have several discrete solutions. For example a circle through two points and with a fixed diameter unequal to the distance between the points, can have two positions.

3. A constraint can have a continuous range of solutions. For example, the locus of a point having a fixed distance to a fixed point is a circle.

Whether the first type of alternative solutions can be handled depends on the programming environment, for example the message passing mechanism, and is not within the scope of this paper.

Some systems mentioned above only deal with numeric constraints. Most graphics-oriented constraint systems directly translate the (geometric) constraints into a set of numeric constraints or equations. Often only linear equations can be solved. Instead, we want to solve constraints at a high level of geometric abstraction. This allows powerful reasoning, which can avoid some of the problems that occur with numeric constraints: recall that even a simple distance constraint results in a quadratic equation.

Simultaneous evaluation of mutually constrained objects is a difficult problem. Look at Figure 1 for an example. In this example, each of the two circle centres must lie on a line segment; then, the circles are constrained to be tangent to each other on the outside. It is too complex for an operational technique to translate both circles along the line segment simultaneously so as to let them touch. Delayed evaluation is then preferred to relaxation in order to deal with a geometrically meaningful representation as long as possible.

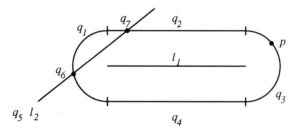

Figure 2: Quanta involved with the constraints distance(p, l_1, d) and on(p, l_2)

In this paper we focus on providing ranges of solutions and discrete alternative solutions in under-constrained situations by means of a quantum approach. In combination with geometric reasoning and delayed satisfaction this gives a more powerful problem solving capability than usually provided by constraint systems.

4   Quantum approach

Our approach to geometric constraint satisfaction is based on the reduction of both problem complexity and solution domain complexity by geometric simplification. Problem complexity reduction is achieved by expressing geometric primitives in terms of characteristic parts. For example, the position of a circle is reduced to the position of a point: the circle centre. Constraint solving then amounts to recording the solution of the constrained geometric primitives in terms of their characteristic parts.

The unit of the solution domain is a 'quantum', which is itself a geometric primitive:

> A quantum is a geometric primitive describing a part of the solution set with uniform geometrical characteristics.

We use the term quantum because it captures both 'interval' and 'region', and is more descriptive than 'solution set'. The nature of a quantum is that it describes a sharply bounded quantity of some phenomenon, in our case the geometric properties of a solution set. Note that quanta are not indivisible, nor need they be disconnected.

By means of quanta, solutions are categorized into ranges or classes featuring the same geometric characteristics. In this way, subsequent processing of the solutions can exploit the geometric properties of the quanta.

For example, the locus of a point p having a fixed distance to a line segment l_1 consists of the union of two line segments, and two half circles, see Figure 2. The solution is split into the quanta $q_1, \ldots, q_4$, representing the two line segments and two half circles. These quanta represent infinitely many alternative solutions. Incremental specification of a geometric object with constraints will successively restrict its solution domain. If p is further constrained to lie on a line l_2 (giving another quantum: q_5), the solution is restricted to the intersection of q_5 with all the alternative solutions so far. Since calculating the intersection of a line and a circle differs from intersecting two lines, we take advantage of the subdivision into quanta $q_1, \ldots, q_4$.

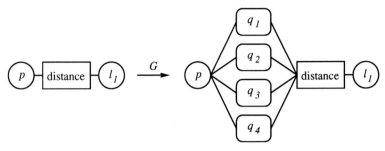

Figure 3: Network result of the quantum generating function applied to the constraint distance(p, l_1, d), corresponding to Figure 2

Some simple constraints (with a fixed second operand) and their associated quanta are listed below:

primitive	constraint	primitive	quanta
point	distance	point	circle
point	distance	line segment	2 line segments 2 half circles
point	left/right of	line	half-plane
circle	tangent	line	2 lines
circle	tangent	circle	2 circles

The same principle can be used in three-dimensional space. In general, a solution set may not be representable with a fixed set of geometric primitives, especially in three-dimensional space. In that sense the set of constraints and geometric primitives should agree with each other. In the examples in the rest of this paper, we use the primitives point, line, and circle, and the constraints on(), centre_on(), distance(), and tangent().

5   System design

The constraint system introduced here consists of a set of constraints C, a set of variables V, a set of quanta Q, a quantum generating function G, and a tolerate function T. Variables and quanta are both geometric primitives.

A constraint is a relation between a number of variables from V. The number of variables depends on the type of constraint. Depending on the constraint and the variables, quanta from Q will be associated with the variables. Constraints are multi-directional, that is, each of the variables involved constrains the others. Each constraint has a set of methods that initiate the satisfaction process, starting with the generation of the appropriate quanta. In contrast to many other systems, a method may be executed even if there is more than one undetermined variable. To make the following presentation clearer, we will only consider binary constraints.

A set of constraints, variables, and quanta can be represented as a network. We represent variables in circular nodes, constraints in rectangular nodes, and quanta in rounded rectangular nodes.

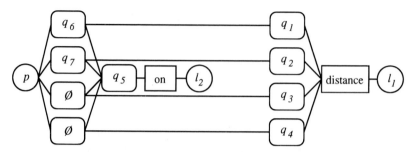

Figure 4: Network corresponding to Figure 2 after adding constraint on(p, l_2) and applying the generate and tolerate function

When a new constraint is specified, a corresponding constraint node is added to the network, connected to the variables nodes. The quantum generating function $G : (c, v_1, v_2, \{q_{1i}\}, \{q_{2i}\}) \mapsto (\{q_{1j}\}, \{q_{2j}\})$ is a mapping from a constraint, the relevant variables, and their current quanta (or none, for a new constraint), to new quanta. In the network, the quanta are positioned between the constraint and the variables, see Figure 3. The current quanta associated to a variable are those which are incident in the network.

Note that not all tuples from $C \times V \times V$ are geometrically meaningful. G is only defined for a number of relevant combinations of constraints and variables. Note further that in general several quanta for each variable can be generated, as in Figure 3.

All new quanta $\{qnew_i\}$ of each single variable, resulting from a new constraint, are intersected with all current quanta $\{qcur_i\}$ of that variable, by the tolerate function $T : (\{qnew_i\}, \{qcur_i\}) \mapsto \{qtol_i\}$. An empty quantum results when the intersection is empty. An over-constrained situation is detected when a variable has only empty quanta. Otherwise the variable tolerates the new constraint. Figure 4 shows the result of applying the generate and tolerate function after adding the constraint on(p, l_2). Between a constraint and an associated variable is a number of sequences of zero or more quanta. In the direction from the constraint to the variable, each quantum includes the next one. Where two sequences come together, the intersection determines the next quantum.

The non-empty quanta among the resulting $qtol_i$ of variable v are propagated. To each constraint c_i that has v as a parameter, the generation function is applied with quanta $qtol_i$ of v, giving new quanta for the other variable. If they differ from its current quanta, these new quanta must be tested for toleration. This propagation is repeated. In principle, the propagation need not terminate, since an infinite loop can occur. A loop can be easily detected, but in general it is not easy to determine whether a loop is finite or infinite. The constraints in a loop can be satisfied by some other method; the resulting quanta must again be propagated.

6   Examples

Consider again Figure 2. Because l_1, related to p by a constraint, is not further constrained and has no associated quantum that could be affected, there is no propagation, and p is constrained to q_6 and q_7. In general, however, a new quantum may affect the quanta of another primitive that is related to it by a constraint. A new quantum must therefore be propagated past its related constraints.

See Figure 5, where we have a point p, a line segment l, and two circles c_1 and c_2. Suppose that a point p must lie on line segment l, and circle c_1 must be centred at p. Geometric reasoning leads to the construction of the quanta q_1 and q_2, representing the loci of p and (the center of) c_1, both coincident with l. Let the next constraint be that c_1 and c_2 are tangent on the outside, giving a new quantum q_3. Circle c_1 tolerates this new constraint, resulting in q_4, which must be propagated. This means that given the constraint that c_1 is centred at p and has a quantum q_4, a new quantum q_5 for p is generated and tested for toleration. In this case, it is tolerated by p because it is fully contained in q_1. The final result is that c_1 is constrained to position q_4, and p to position q_5 (which incidentally coincides with q_4).

All this manipulating may seem superfluous, but in general the new quantum q_5 for point p can be totally different from q_4, just as the starting quanta q_1 and q_2 can be totally different. For instance when p is constrained to have a fixed distance to l.

So far, the toleration test could succeed because the intersection of two quanta was successful. It can happen, however, that the situation is too complex, or the system is not intelligent enough, to tell whether the quanta intersect. Look, for example, at the situation in Figure 6 with three fixed lines l_1, l_2, l_3, and two circles c_1 and c_2. The constraint centre_on(c_1, l_1) produces quantum q_{11}, centre_on(c_2, l_2) gives q_{21}, and tangent(c_1, c_2) gives q_{12} and q_{22}. Note that q_{12} and q_{22} are not fixed, but can move along l_2 and l_1 respectively.

Suppose now that the system is not intelligent enough to intersect a 'floating', or generic circle, with a line segment. Effectively, tangent(c_1, c_2) will be delayed until subsequent constraints allow the system to handle it. When centre_on(c_1, l_3) is specified, the system creates quantum q_{13}, a line segment coincident with l_3, see the lower part of Figure 6. Checking whether c_1 tolerates this new constraint results in the intersection of q_{11} and q_{13}, giving q_{14}. This can be more easily intersected with the generic quantum q_{12}. The result is q_{14}, because it is fully contained in q_{12}.

The resulting q_{14} is propagated. This means that, given the constraint that c_1 and c_2 are tangent and c_1 has quantum q_{14}, a new quantum q_{23} is generated, which is a

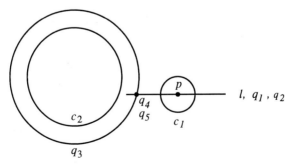

Figure 5: Quanta involved with the constraints on(p,l), centre_on(c_1,p), and tangent(c_1,c_2)

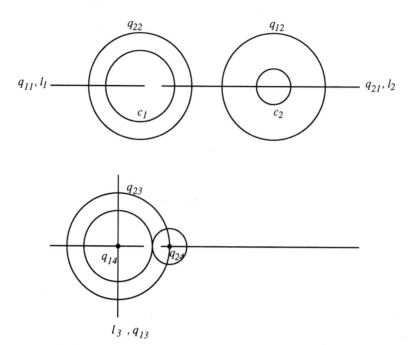

Figure 6: The quanta involved with the three constraints centre_on(c_1, l_1), centre_on(c_2, l_2), and tangent(c_1, c_2) (top), and the additional constraint centre_on(c_1, l_3) (bottom)

circle that has a fixed position. This circle can be intersected with q_{21}, giving q_{24} for c_2. The end result is that c_1 has quantum q_{14}, and c_2 has quantum q_{24}. Both quanta specify fully determined positions. Figure 7 shows the corresponding changes in the network.

7   Discussion

In the last example all variables are fully determined by constraints, after delayed satisfaction. In general, however, the solution of the given set of constraints is formed by the current quanta, and these need not specify a single position. This happens in a under-constrained specification. On the other hand, a conflict of constraints is detected when a variable has only empty quanta.

A quantum need not even be fully determined, as in our last example. Indeed, it is common to specify an assembly of geometric primitives by constraints, relative to an object that is transformed afterwards. It is therefore necessary to be able to process incomplete information. In order to keep intermediate solutions simple, we want to evaluate them as far as possible, and also use latent geometric information. Dealing with incomplete information and deriving latent information is typical in geometric reasoning.

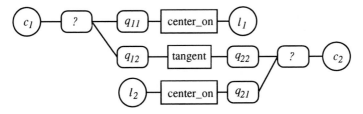

adding center_on (c_1, l_3) and applying G and T:

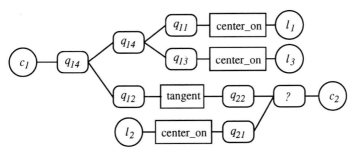

propagation:

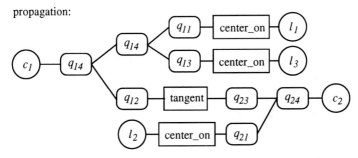

Figure 7: Some successive networks corresponding to Figure 6

Operations on a variable, such as translate, scale, mirror, and project, can be handled by performing proper corresponding operations on its quanta. These new quanta must then be propagated through the network.

For interactive CAD purposes, a constraint must also be removable. In our system, deletion from the network involves removal of the constraint as well as the sequences of quanta between the constraint and its variables. Sequences from other constraints to the same variables must be 'repaired' by intersecting the proper quanta. The resulting new quanta must be propagated through the new network. A more detailed presentation of the properties of the propagation algorithm is given in [Veltkamp and Arbab, 1992].

Our system already used geometric simplification by shrinking a circle to a point, and regarding the radius as a distance. In this way the constraint that a circle c_1 is tangent to another circle c_2 is regarded as the constraint that the shrunk c_1 has a distance to the shrunk c_2 that is equal to the sum of their radii. Geometric reasoning can be used to make the system more intelligent. In the example of Figure 6, the system is not intelligent enough to intersect a line q_{11} with a floating circle q_{12} restricted to line l_1. In this case, the same type of geometric simplification as above can be used. It can be reasoned that the intersection is necessarily a part of q_{11}, or empty. If it is non-empty, it must be that part of q_{11} that has a distance to any point on l_1, that equals the radius of q_{12}.

In order to perform such geometric reasoning more easily, we must consider implied constraints (constraint inference), not only between given constraint variables, but also between two quanta or between a quantum and a variable. The user should have no direct access to these implied constraints. For example in Figure 7, quantum q_{23} is concentric with variable c_1. For the system the addition of implied constraints is transparent, since quanta are also geometric primitives, which can be involved in constraints.

The quantum approach can also be applied to constraints in three-dimensional space, although we can run into problems when a solution set is not representable by quanta. However, a useful set of constraints and quanta can be chosen, as demonstrated in [Veltkamp, 1991]. The quantum approach can even be applied to pure numeric constraint problems. The solution is then derived with interval quanta as parameter values, instead of geometric quanta. Algebraic reasoning then takes the place of geometric reasoning.

8   Constraints and objects

Object-oriented graphics is a means to deal with the complexity of computer graphics. The geometric representation of the constraint variables and the quanta naturally corresponds to object-oriented graphics concepts. On the other hand, relationships between objects other than 'is-a' and 'part-of' hierarchies, such as constraints, cannot be suitably represented by message passing.

We distinguish two possible incompatibilities between constraints and object-oriented concepts:

- a constraint solver looks at, and sets, the constraint variables' internal data, which conflicts with the information-hiding concept in the object-oriented paradigm;

- object-oriented programming is imperative, while constraint programming is declarative in nature.

If one wants to use object-oriented methods to manage complexity in implementing a graphics system, and wants to provide constraints to the user of the system as a tool to manage the complexity of problem solving, then constraints and objects must be friends. However, message passing for constraint handling, as in [Laffra and van den Bos, 1991], is either limited to constraint maintenance, or against the object-oriented philosophy: providing all objects subject to constraints with interface methods to get and set internal data grants every other object to get and set values.

One way to restrict this, is that an object only allows value setting when its internal constraints remain satisfied, as in [Rankin, 1992]. By contrast, access to private data can be limited to constraint objects (or the constraint solver-object) only. For example C++ provides the 'friend' declaration to grant functions access to the private part of geometric objects, see next subsection. This is also comparable to the solution of [Cournarie and Beaudouin-Lafon, 1992], where special variables (slots) are accessible by constraints only.

One can argue that the encapsulation is still violated (and specifically that a C++ friend is not intended to change the internal state of an object). Alternatively one can see constraints more as a means to access information in an orderly and restricted way, than that they violate the information hiding principle. At least the responsibility for integrity is shifted from the constraint user to the constraint implementer. A problem that remains is the difficulty of debugging a constraint system, due to the global effects of constraints.

Object-oriented languages are imperative, and thus use a notion of state, particularly represented by objects. Pure constraint languages are declarative, and thus specify one single timeless state: the solution to the specified problem. However, both paradigms can be combined as is shown in [Freeman-Benson, 1990], where an imperative assignment to a variable sets a value at one moment in ime, and a declarative constraint dictates a value from that moment on. However, if the solution depends on the order in which constraints are solved, the declarative semantics is destroyed. The quantum approach uses solution set inference, which (in principle) does not depend on the order of constraint satisfaction. Delayed satisfaction can thus be used without side effects, preserving the declarative semantics of constraints.

8.1 Implementation

We distinguish the following relevant objects classes: GeometricPrimitive, Quantum, and Constraint. Instances of objects are created upon user demand, typically via a graphics interface.

A quantum can be designed as a polymorphic object which refers to a line, circle, polygon, etc. An alternative in environments supporting multiple inheritance is to let a quantum object inherit properties from geometric primitives, as well as additional properties that are specific for quanta.

The exact geometric primitive type of each individual quantum object must be known to enable correct use of the primitive. The primitives provide this type-information by means of the method whatami(). When using an object-oriented curve intersection method such as [Rankin and Burns, 1991], primitives also provide a method nearestpoint() which returns the point on the curve that is nearest to a given point. A draw() method typically calls the drawing method of the geometric primitive after a drawing style is specified, to distinguish a quantum from a design primitive.

All constraints are subclasses of the base class Constraint, and have methods draw() and satisfy(). The draw() method visualizes the constraint by connecting the operands with an arc that is labeled with a corresponding constraint icon.

The system is currently being implemented in C++ [Stroustrup, 1986] and Quintus Prolog [Quintus, 1990], which provides an interface with C. Class methods, in particular the constraint method satisfy(), may contain assertions and goals in Horn clause logic. This provides a way to exploit the geometric context of the constraint and variables, and to make the system more intelligent by geometric reasoning.

In a typical C++ implementation the above mentioned functions are virtual, to indicate that the base (super) class has a general version, and the derived classes can have different own versions:

```
class GeometricPrimitive
{
    friend class Constraint;              // grant access to private data
    private:
        Frame frame;                      // modeling coordinate system
        Color color;
        // ...
    public:
        virtual GPType whatami();         // geometric primitive type
        virtual Point nearestpoint();
        virtual void draw();
        // ...
}
```

This is only one of the many possible ways to implement the quantum approach, exploiting both object-oriented concepts and relational logic. The alternatives include an extension of (Concurrent) Prolog with object -oriented features, see for example [Shapiro and A.Takeuchi, 1983], [Zaniolo, 1984], and the language Oar [Arbab and Wang, 1989]. Object-oriented concepts can also be combined with a functional language, see for example Common Lisp Object System (CLOS) [Moon, 1989]. All these languages specify objects, hierarchies, and methods in a declarative way.

9 Conclusion

I have presented a constraint satisfaction system based on the quantum approach. This approach is suitable for interactive design because it can handle (perhaps temporarily) under-constrained specifications and alternative solutions, and performs satisfaction locally and incrementally by local propagation. The system keeps the intermediate solutions in the geometric domain, so that new geometric constraints can be interpreted on the same high level of abstraction, allowing powerful reasoning. Both alternative discrete solutions and continuous ranges of solutions are determined and propagated (solution set inference). The system can therefore easily detect ambiguity and present alternative solutions.

More research is needed to further exploit the capabilities of geometric reasoning and constraint inference. In particular implied constraints between quanta or between quanta and variables can be used by the satisfaction system to solve complex constraints more directly.

Acknowledgements

Thanks to Farhad Arbab for comments on earlier versions of this paper, and to Edwin Blake and the other participants of this workshop for all discussions. This research is part of the IIICAD project, supported by NWO (Dutch Organization for Scientific Research) under Grant NF-51/62-514.

References

Arbab, F. and Wang, B. (1989). A geometric constraint management system in Oar. In ten Hagen, P. J. W. and Veerkamp, P., editors, *Intelligent CAD Systems III – Practical Experience and Evaluation (Proceedings 3rd Eurographics Workshop on Intelligent CAD Systems, 1989)*, pages 231 – 252. Springer-Verlag.

Arbab, F. and Wing, J. M. (1985). Geometric reasoning: A new paradigm for processing geometric information. In Yoshikawa, H. and Warman, E. A., editors, *Design Theory for CAD (Proceedings of the IFIP W.G. 5.2 Working Conference, 1985)*, pages 145 – 165. Elsevier Science Publishers.

Badler, N. I. and Kamran, H. (1987). Articulated figure positioning by multiple constraints. *IEEE Computer Graphics & Applications (special issue on articulated figure animation,* 7(6):28 – 38.

Borning, A. (1981). The programming language aspects of ThingLab, a constraint-oriented simulation laboratory. *ACM Transactions on Programming Languages and Systems,* 3(4):353 – 387.

Cohen, J. (1990). Constraint logic programming languages. *Communications of the ACM,* 33(7):52 – 68.

Cournarie, E. and Beaudouin-Lafon, M. (1992). Alien: a prototype-based constraint system. In this volume.

Davenport, J. H., Siret, Y., and Tournier, E. (1988). *Computer Algebra — systems and algorithms for algebraic computation.* Academic Press.

Davis, E. (1987). Constraint propagation with interval labels. *Artificial Intelligence,* 32:281 – 331.

Emmerik, M. J. G. M. v. (1990). A system for interactive graphical modeling with 3D constraints. In *Proceedings Computer Graphics International '90*, pages 361 – 376. Sringer-Verlag.

Freeman-Benson, B. N. (1990). Kaleidoscope: Mixing objects, constraints, and imperative programming. *(ECOOP/OOPSLA '90 Proceedings) SIGPLAN Notices,* 25(10):77 – 88.

Heintze, N. C., Michaylov, S., and Stuckey, P. J. (1987). CLP(IR) and some problems in electrical engineering. In Lassez, J.-L., editor, *Proceedings of the 4th International Conference on Logic Programming.* MIT Press.

Helander, M., editor (1988). *Handbook of Human–Computer Interaction.* North-Holland.

Laffra, C. and van den Bos, J. (1991). Propagators and concurrent constraints. OOPS Messenger 2(2):68 – 72.

Leler, W. (1988). *Constraint Programming Languages, Their Specification and Generation.* Addison-Wesley.

Lin, V. C., Gossard, D. C., and Light, R. A. (1981). Variational geometry in computer-aided design. *(Proceedings SIGGRAPH '81) Computer Graphics*, 15(3):171 – 177.

Mäntylä, M. (1988). *An Introduction to Solid Modeling.* Computer Science Press.

Moon, D. A. (1989). The common lisp object-oriented programming language. In Kim, W. and Lochovsky, F., editors, *Object-Oriented Concepts, Databases, and Applications.* ACM Press/Addison Wesley.

Nelson, G. (1985). Juno, a constraint-based graphics system. *Proceedings SIGGRAPH '85, Computer Graphics*, 19(3):235 – 243.

Pratt, M. J. (1987). *Form Features and their Applications in Solid Modeling, Tutorial SIGGRAPH '87.*

Quintus (1990). *Quintus Prolog User Manual.* Quintus Computer Systems, Inc.

Rankin, J. R. (1992). A graphical object oriented constraint solver. In this volume.

Rankin, J. R. and Burns, J. (1991). Coordinate frames and geometric approximation in graphics object oriented programming. In E. Blake, and P. Wißkirchen, editors, *Advances in Object-Oriented Graphics I*, pages 131 – 148. Springer-Verlag.

Rossignac, J. R. (1986). Constraints in constructive solid geometry. In Crow, F. and Pizer, S. M., editors, *Proceedings of the 1986 ACM Workshop on Interactive 3D Graphics*, pages 93 – 110. ACM Press.

Shapiro, E. and A.Takeuchi (1983). Object-oriented programming in concurrent Prolog. *New Generation Computing*, 1(1):25 – 48.

Steele Jr., G. L. and Sussman, G. J. (1979). CONSTRAINTS. *APL Quote Quad*, 9(4–Part 1):208 – 225.

Stroustrup, B. (1986). *The C++ Programming Language.* Addison Wesley.

Sutherland, I. (1963). Sketchpad: A man-machine graphical communication system. In *Proceedings of the Spring Joint Computer Conference (IFIPS)*, pages 329 – 345.

Szekely, P. and Myers, B. (1988). A user-interface toolkit based on graphical objects and constraints. In *Proceedings of the 1988 ACM Conference on Object-Oriented Programming Systems, Languages, and Applications*, pages 36 – 45. ACM.

Veltkamp, R. C. (1991). Geometric constraint management with quanta. In Brown, D. C., Waldron, M., and Yoshikawa, H., editors, *Proceedings of the IFIP TC5 / WG5.2 Working Conference on Intelligent Computer Aided Design, Columbus, Ohio, September 1991).* To be published by North-Holland.

Veltkamp, R. C. and Arbab, F. (1992). Geometric constraint propagation with quantum labels. In B. Falcidieno, I. Herman, and C. Pienovi, editors, *Computer Graphics and Mathematics*, pages 211 – 228. Springer-Verlag.

Zaniolo, C. (1984). Object-oriented programming in Prolog. In *Proceedings of the IEEE International Symposium on Logic Programming*, pages 265 – 270. IEEE.

5

A Graphics Object-Oriented Constraint Solver

John R. Rankin

The development of computer graphics constraint systems has been of considerable interest in recent years. It is desirable that constraints may be dynamically incorporated into selected graphics output primitives, and also into graphics segments as a whole at the time of their interactive construction. The constraints usually take the form of coupled equations or inequations limiting the rendition of graphics primitives or segments. After a few constraints have been defined in the graphics constraint system, the interaction of these rules becomes quite complicated, and it has been necessary to provide a constraint equation solver to resolve these interactions and take control over the decisions for the rendition of all graphics primitives and segments.

From another direction, the object-oriented programming paradigm has been found to be very effective in producing large pieces of maintainable and extendable standard graphics software. When graphics object-oriented programming is applied to graphics constraint systems the constraint solver is found to violate a basic principle of object-oriented programming, as in particular, the constraint solver needs to look at the internal data of every graphics object and will also adjust the internal parameters of graphics objects in order to fit the solution which it finds of the complex constraint equations. Consequently, the question of the compatibility of graphics constraint programming and object-oriented programming is currently a topical issue.

This paper discusses an alternative approach to the constraint solver code. This new approach forms a harmonious and natural integration with the object-oriented programming paradigm and does not require complex equation entry by the user. We investigate the application of geometric iteration processes which are shown to be very naturally expressed in the object-oriented paradigm, and a number of conjectures concerning the behaviour of these processes are formulated. Furthermore, constrained geometric objects are built from previously constructed geometric objects, or from a set of ready-made geometric elements with inbuilt constraints. Our results show that this approach satisfactorily maintains constraint integrity. Some examples using this new approach to constraint solving are also described. A technique for dynamically constructing constrained graphics segments (objects) is described using a new algorithm the "Democracy Algorithm" which generalizes this approach. An implementation of the ideas has shown that the method is practical and that only a small amount of number crunching is required before the constraints are satisfied.

1 Introduction

Computer graphics programming has reached a stage where application programmers are required to produce software where the graphics objects visible on the
screen have their own built in intelligence with respect to maintaining their own
integrity and individuality, and also with respect to the distinctiveness of their
interaction with other screen objects. It is thus becoming necessary to find ways
of building this level of intelligence into the graphics and making it easier for the
application programmer to achieve his objectives. This is the area of constraint
programming [Leler, 1988], where things are not just drawn or even animated,
but move and change according to strictly enforced rules, the constraint equations.
A number of experimental constraint projects have already been built and there
are some emerging on the commercial scene [Rankin, 1990a, Fertey et al., 1990,
Nelson, 1985, Rankin, 1990b, Leler, 1988]. Simulation of physical systems such as
the cold water dispenser + beaker with thermometer + oven with adjustable flame
+ controls selectable and operable on the screen by means of the mouse pointer as
described in [Coutaz and Bass, 1988] are systems where the constraints are already
hard-coded into the program and cannot be varied. The CAD package [Khoubyari,
1990] and Borning's ThingLab [Borning, 1986] (discussed also in [Rankin, 1990a])
are systems where the user can dynamically create screen objects and interactively
define their constraint equations to the system. In these general constrain systems,
the aim is to allow the desired constraints to be interactively entered by the system
user at the same time that the object to be constrained is being constructed on the
screen. The constraints typically take the form of equations or inequations relating
the geometric parameters that lie behind the graphics images being displayed. In
many of these systems it is required that the user enter the constraint equations
as algebraic expressions. There are however many difficulties with this traditional
technique. One is that the user needs to know or remember what range of functions
the system recognizes (such as which trigonometric functions, square roots and
other powers, logarithm and exponential functions) so that acceptable algebraic
expressions can be entered. The functions provided may not enable the user to encapsulate the geometric constraint desired, or conversely, the functions may be too
general and allow constraints which are not natural to the geometry but which the
user could easily enter by slight mistakes in the algebra. This approach requires
the user to be proficient with complex algebra when his competence may in fact
lie in geometric construction and visualization. A further difficulty is that the user
has to be able to relate each algebraic variable he enters to the visual geometry
in some way. This is a design and implementation problem. A related implementation problem is that of designing a suitable format for the user to be representing
and entering algebraic relations. Another difficulty is that of making the code to
interpret the input algebraic expressions and then to be able to use the entered
equations for determining a solution of the constraints. The more constraint equations that are entered into the system, the more complex their interaction becomes,
and the more difficult it becomes to solve them.

object-oriented programming is now finding extensive application in graphics programming. The OOP paradigm enables programmers to produce more bug-free,
maintainable and extendible graphics code. Each graphics entity or graphics output primitive typically becomes an object class with its own methods for creation,
display, animation, attribute setting and destruction. OOP systems allow libraries

of such objects to be extended as and when new objects are needed without having to recompile the old code. In this way distributed binary codes can be extended locally or by supplier updates without the need to refer to the proprietry source codes. When the advantages of OOP are brought to bear on the new problems of constraint programming we find that incompatibilities occur in the areas of encapsulation and extensibility. With encapsulation, an objects private data is supposed to be inaccessible to all code except the objects own methods. The traditional constraint equation solver however is a piece of code that needs to know every bit of internal information of every graphics entity involved in the constrained object and its environment. This code must not only read the private data of OOP objects but must also rewrite that data in setting up the solution to the constraints that it arrives at. With extensibility, new graphics entities should be able to be added to the system without recompilation. However the traditional constraint solver is hard coded to recognize only a given set of graphics entities, and would need recoding and recompilation if new entities were to be added to the system.

The work described in this paper addresses this compatibility problem, and attempts to provide an harmonious integration of OOP and constraint programming. To do so the traditional approach to entering constraints as equations is rejected in favour of a new approach presented in [Rankin, 1990a, Rankin and Burns, 1990a, Rankin and Burns, 1990b] making use of *schematic diagrams* to represent what linkages between entities are set up in the constrained geometry. As described in [Rankin, 1990a], because geometry is based on points, and the mouse pointing system is a useful way of entering or selecting point data for geometric operations, we have chosen to *encode all geometric message passing as point sets* [Rankin, 1990b]. The schematic diagrams indicate the traffic of this point data between geometric components and are reminiscient of digital electronic circuit diagrams. The schematics very easily map to OOPs code. Loops in the schematic circuits result in iteration in the OOP code. Just as electronic circuits designed for particular functions, can have undesirable transient signals due to feedback, and yet establish output voltage levels from the inputs very rapidly, so we also expect that OOPs code derived from the schematic diagrams would likewise resolve constraint problems rather rapidly. Our experiments have indicated that this is indeed often the case. Geometric functional iteration does seem to provide a new and simple way of solving complex geometric constraint equations. A similar iterative technique implemented in hardware, has been previously applied to algebraic problems. This technique is called the CORDIC technique, and a survey of its capabilities in given in reference [Fulcher, 1990].

In this paper we shall illustrate simple applications of the schematic diagram approach to some constraint problems. Then we will look at a generalized approach that depends heavily on the new features that the OOP paradigm provides for the systems programmer. The generalized approach makes use of the new algorithm perhaps appropriately called the Democracy Algorithm which is described in this paper. It allows the user of the constraint system to interactively construct constrained screen objects. The algorithm has been tested in a program called GICS with pleasing results. The GICS program avoids the need for the user to generate schematic diagrams on the screen (by making some limiting assumptions about what the user will want to do), and this has the advantage that it ensures that every constructed constrained screen object starts in a feasible configuration.

According to certain observations described in section 4, this provides confidence that the Democracy Algorithm will operate successfully.

2   Hierarchies of Graphics Object Classes

By a graphics entity (or GE) we mean a simple graphics output primitive such as a line segment, a circle, an elliptic arc, a polyline and so forth. The underlying graphics library provides us with the GEs and from these we go on to produce combinations of GEs into useful visual screen objects or graphics objects (GOs) also known as graphics segments. A layer of software is provided to bundle code for each GE into an OOP object with a standard set of methods. (We called this software layer the constrained GE or CGE library.) This is illustrated in Figure 1 and the standard methods required for each GE in the CGE library are listed in Table 1. The GEs themselves can and mostly do have internal constraints. The maintenance of an internal GE constraint is the responsibility of the GEs own methods, and the implementation of this poses no difficulty. The complexity comes when various constrained GEs are built together into a compound GO for which explicit constraints about the way the GE components link together must be specified by the user. We refer to the latter kind of constraint as an external constraint. We will first consider some of the internal constraints.

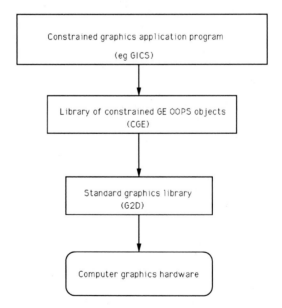

Figure 1: Software layers in the construction of a constraint system. The standard graphics library is not necessarily written in OOP code.

In order to describe the way schematic diagrams help solve constraints we will start by listing some very simple types of constraints. While the geometric iteration algorithm has wide generality, it has proven sufficient, given our limited time and

Notes:

FDPS = finite defining point set = the input point set.

TPS = the tag point set = the output point set.

GE = graphics element (basic graphics output primitive).

GO = graphics object (a composition of GEs).

entity = the generic term for a GE or GO.

The methods:

entity.create
> dynamically creates an instance of the entity class.

entity.init(FDPS)
> sets the internal parameters for the entity, such as the length of fixed length line segments, using an initial user-entered FDPS.

entity.display
> draws the entity on the graphics screen in its current configuration, erasing it first if it is already visible.

entity.erase
> smart erasure of the entity from the screen restores any previous background graphics properly.

entity.assign(FDPS)
> assigns new input point values to the entity.

entity.enquire(TPS)
> returns the current point values defining the entity.

entity.nearest_point(P: point_type; vas S: point_type)
> returns the nearest point S on the entity to the given point P.

entity.destroy
> terminates the existence of a dynamically created instance of the entity class.

Table 1: Standard GOOP entity methods.

resources, to consider only a small subset of the possible graphics output primitives and consider only two dimensional cases. In particular, most of our tests concern the connecting together in various ways, of varieties of constrained line segments and occasionally circles and polylines.

With regard to line segments the following strains were considered:

- unconstrained line segment

- fixed length line segment

- fixed length hanging line segment

- fixed angle line segment

- fixed angle and length line segment

- fixed end point line segment

For each of these constrained graphics entities (GEs) there is an object class and corresponding schematic box. The point data inputs to any of these boxes are P and Q, the *desired* end points of the particular variety of line segment. The point data outputs of the boxes are labelled P' and Q'. (See Figure 2.) The points P' and Q' are the *actual* end points that the constrained GE was able to adopt given its inputs after working out its own internal constraints. We will now describe each of the GE classes listed above.

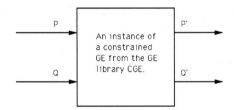

Figure 2: The schematic box for a GE instance from the GE OOP library has a set of input points, output points and the box is labelled with the name and type of the GE concerned. For the case of line segments suitable inputs and outputs are the end points of the line segment.

For an unconstrained line segment, the end points P and Q can be any non-coincident positions in space, and the outputs will be the same as the inputs i.e. P' = P and Q' = Q. For a fixed length line segment, say of length a, input P determines the starting position for the GE, and the end position is on the line PQ and such that the line segment has the length a.

The geometric transfer equations are therefore:

$$P' = P \tag{1a}$$

$$Q' = P' + a_*(Q - P)/|PQ| \tag{1b}$$

For the fixed length hanging line segment, the conditions are the same as for the fixed length line segment except that Q' is required to be lower than P', i.e.:

$$Q'.y < P'.y \tag{2}$$

If the result of the computation in equation [1b] violates inequation [2] then Q.y is reset to P'.y and Q' is recomputed by equation [1b] until the inequation [2] is satisfied. For the fixed angle line, P determines the first end point through which the line must pass, i.e. P' = P, and then Q' is the nearest point [the nearest point method was shown to crop up in a wide variety of geometric problems in references 1 and 4] to Q on the line through P' at the original angle a to the horizontal that the line segment was created with. For the fixed angle and length line segment Q' is independent of Q, and is determined by P', the length of the line a, and its angle a. For the fixed point line segment, the first end point cannot be changed (P' = constant), but the second end point can be anywhere in space (i.e. Q' = Q). Other constraints we have used include the wall object and the railing line segment described later. It may be noted that the algebraic expression of these natural geometric internal constraints, in terms of x and y components, is often mathematically messy to deal with, and not the simple mathematical functions one might wish for. The geometric approach is therefore more preferable than the algebraic approach for this practical reason also.

It is clear that as object classes, many of these classes are subclasses of others, and that they form a hierarchy of descendents from the line segment class. Indeed many of the constraints mentioned so far could be combined with others to form new constrained line segments within this hierarchy. As descendents of the line segment class, the constrained classes inherit data and methods from their ancestors. So also, if we extended the library of GE objects (CGE) to include strains of (constrained) circles, strains of area filled polygons and so on then we would be introducing several new hierarchy trees each with their separate direct inheritances.

We now come to considering the composition of the constrained GEs described above into new GOs. Since in general there would be several class hierarchies emanating from the basic set of unconstrained GEs, and since GOs can be composed from any selection of GEs coming from any of these classes, we can expect to need the OOP notion of multiple inheritance. However, only one GO class is necessary. We require that this new GO class provide the same list of useful methods that every GE class has as given in Table 1 and this is not difficult to implement in terms of the GE class methods. The FDPS for the GO is the long list of points consisting of all the FDPSs for each constituent GE in the order in which the GE was added in to the GO. Similarly the output tag point set is the concatenation of all output points from the constituent GEs in the same order. The methods for the GO (see Table 1) are constructed as sequences of calls to the corresponding method in each constituent GE with the appropriate parameters taken from the point lists where necessary. However the implementation for the nearest point method for the GO takes a different structure: the seed point is fed into the nearest point methods of each GE in the GO and the closest output point to the seed point is returned. The grouping of GEs into GOs using external (user defined) constraints is described in the next section by means of the schematic diagrams.

3   Schematic Diagrams

The schematic diagrams link the input point sets and output point sets of any selection of constrained GEs to define the composite GO geometrically. There is a straight forward transformation from schematic diagram to OOPs code. Consider a linkage from output (point) A_i from the schematic box of graphics element GE1 say, connecting to input (point) B_j of schematic GE2. In this circumstance we say that input j of entity GE2 is *controlled* by output i of entity GE1. The corresponding OOPs code then consists of a sequence of method calls: first a call to the GE1.enquire method to read the A_i point value, then (sometimes) a call to the GE2.enquire method to find the current values of the other inputs to GE2 that are not linked to (ie controlled by) another GE output, and then finally a call to the GE2.assign method to assert the desired inputs for GE2. A sequence of schematic boxes connected previous to next becomes a sequence of such calls down the sequence of boxes. If the tail of the sequence of schematic boxes rejoins the start of the sequence then a loop in OOPs code is required. Some simple examples will illustrate this idea. For more complex schematic diagrams and for interactively created schematic diagrams we resort to the Democracy Algorithm which is described in section 5.

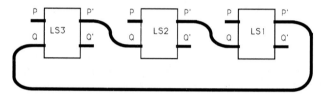

Figure 3: The schematic diagram for three line segment GEs constrained to form a triangle. The constraint equations are effectively:(LS1.Q = LS2.P', LS2.Q = LS3.P' and LS3.Q = LS1.P'.

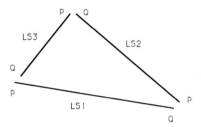

Figure 4: The triangle Graphics Object (GO) represented in Figure 3 as three component Graphics Elements (GEs), unconstrained line segments knit together end point to end point.

Figure 3 shows a schematic diagram that defines the external constraints for the construction of a triangle out of unconstrained line segments, LS1, LS2 and LS3, and the corresponding geometry is depicted in Figure 4. If the user selects point LS1.P with a pointing device and moves it to a new point X, then when the LS1 object receives the message LS1.P = X, then its outputs are adjusted according to its own internal constraints giving new output points LS1.P' = X, and LS1.Q' = LS1.Q for this strain of GE. Then the schematic diagram implies that LS3 must adjust so that its input LS3.Q = LS1.P'. Likewise LS2 adjusts so that LS2.Q = LS3.P'. Note that in the combined GO only the P inputs of each line segment are useful for being selected and moved. The external constraints embodied in the schematic diagram then ensure that the three line segments reform as the closed triangle. Only one iteration of the schematic loop is necessary in this case to restore the integrity of the GO. Once this is achieved, then the GO is (intelligently erased and then) redisplayed.

This example behaves in a more interesting manner when we replace some or all of the unconstrained line segments with various other constrained line segment strains. The OOPs code representing the schematic diagram will then iterate more than once in its quest for a solution. The looping continues until the point value fed back to the start of the loop is roughly equal (to the screen precision) to the current point value at the start of the loop and then the GO is redisplayed. (A boolean function called "roughly_equal(A,B : point_type)" is provided in the CGE library for this purpose.) It is then also interesting to observe the effects of different sized disturbances on different connections in the schematic circuit. For instance in the case where we make a triangle from fixed equal-length line segments, small displacements in P inputs end up only slightly rotating and shifting the triangle. Large displacements however cause it to translate a large distance and rotate always such that the edge opposite the end point moved is perpendicular to the direction of motion and nearer to the point moved to. And in this case, the manipulation of the Q inputs does have an interesting effect: the triangle is rotated with only a very small translation no matter how far away Q is taken. Figures 4a to 4d illustrate the phenomena. It becomes an interesting exercise learning how to manipulate these controls (selecting P or Q inputs for a given side of the triangle and then moving them) to position and orient the triangle in any desired configuration.

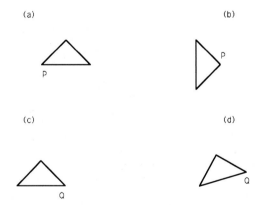

Figure 5: Pulling point P on fixed length line segment 1 away to the left causes the triangle to move left and rotate as shown. Pulling Q on line segment 1 to point X causes the triangle to rotate as in (d).

Similar test cases involving polygons of any number of sides and any combination of constrained GEs were investigated as well. Another example was the multiple pendulum constructed from fixed length hanging line segments. Figures 5a and 5b show the schematic diagram used for a triple pendulum. It was observed that by applying a shift to any join in the pendulum caused the pendulum to change configuration to accept the new position if it was a valid one. A time motion applied

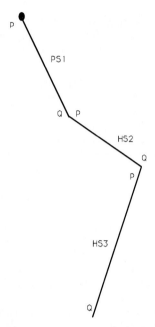

Figure 6: The screen appearance of a triple pendulum built from three hanging fixed length line segments PS1, HS2 and HS3. PS1 also has its initial end point P immovable.

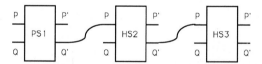

Figure 7: A schematic diagram depicting the external constraints applying in the triple pendulum of Figure 6. PS1 is a fixed position fixed length line segment - changes on its inputs P and Q only effect the output point Q' and P' remains the same point. HS2 is a hanging fixed length line segment which is constrained to join on to the end of PS1, ie HS2.P = PS1.Q'. Similarly HS3 is a hanging fixed length line segment constrained to join on to the end of HS2 via HS3.P = HS2.Q'. If the Q end point of PS1 is displaced to point X then a call to the GO display method will show that HS2 has moved to keep contact with that end point of PS1. If however end point P of HS2 is moved to some point X then a call to the triple pendulum display method will show that in this case the new constraint solution is the same as the original constraint solution (and the pendulum has not moved).

to any joint would then make the pendulum swing somewhat realistically even if the equations for the disturbance of the joint were not actually solutions for the motion of a physical triple pendulum. As the schematic diagram for this GO does not include any loops, there is no iteration in this case and the constraints are quickly satisfied in one pass.

A further constraint object called the wall-type was implemented. This has a method called "test(R : point_type; var S : point_type)" which receives a point R and tests to see if it is inside the wall or not. If it is not inside then the method returns S = R. If however the point R is inside the wall then the method sends back point S which is the nearest point on the wall surface to R. The wall type GE is initialized by two points P and Q. The x component of P is used for the position of the (vertical) wall, and the x component of Q is used to say if the wall is on the left or the right of P.x. The wall-type GE was used in conjunction with the multiple pendulum, and it was required that no output point of a hanging fixed length line segment could be inside the wall. Every time a disturbance caused an end point to enter a wall, left or right, the code iterates until the endpoint is at the wall surface. An example of this is shown in Figures 6a and 6b. It was found that the schematic diagram generated new feasible solutions very rapidly to the precision of the graphics screen.

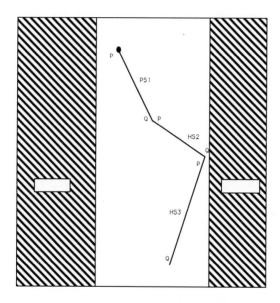

Figure 8: The screen appearance of a triple pendulum when the user has selected left and right walls. If any of the end points of any of the line sements go left of xleft or right of xright then an iteration process rearranges the pendulum to a feasible solution with the point concerned just touching the wall face.

Another kind of external constraint GE created was the railing line segment. This is just a line segment to which other line segments can be attached. Suppose that line segment LS is attached at point LS.P to the railing RL. If a disturbance is applied to end point P of LS, say moving it to point X, then the external constraint embodied in the schematic diagram brings LS.P' back to a point on RL which is the nearest point on RL to X. In this way constructions can appear to consistently slide up and down the railing as the user twiddles point positions. We also looked at implementing the obstruction constraint whereby two line segments cannot cross

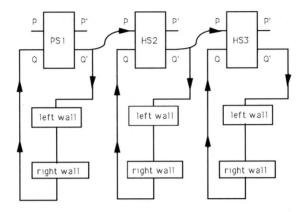

Figure 9: A schematic diagram to represent the triple pendulum which is constrained to lie between a left and a right wall as shown in Figure 8. An input point to a wall object is passed to the test method which outputs the correct point not in the wall.

over each other. This constraint involved using the intersection schematic described in [Rankin, 1990a].

As another example we used the nearest point method to cause an arbitrary shape to move in such a way that it maintained contact with an arbitrary surface entered by the user. A truck profile moves along the mountainous horizon with both wheels correctly placed on the ground. (See Figure 10.) Figure 11 shows the geometric constructions used in implementing this. The user points to a screen position, X say, and the front wheels of the truck are then drawn such that they touch the horizon polyline (a GE object provided in the CGE library) at the nearest point on the polyline to X. Essentially a circle (another GE provided in the CGE library) is constructed for every new placement of the front wheels. The circle is intersected with the polyline via the geometric iteration algorithm described in reference [Rankin, 1990a]. Once the intersection point Y is known, the truck object is appropriately rotated and drawn on the screen.

A point join of say point A on GE1 to point B of GE2 is termed fully constrained (or doubly linked) if GE1.A controls GE2.B and GE2.B controls GE1.A, otherwise it is termed underconstrained. For example, the singly linked triangle of Figure 3 is underconstrained. It is easily shown that underconstrained polylines consisting of at least one single link may not retain integrity (i.e. may fall apart) when the geometric iterations start depending on the firing order. Tests also showed that the firing order for the component GEs in a constrained GO made a difference to the final equilibrium solution that the iterations settle on. If the three line segments of a triangle were pulled widely apart and then geometric iterations brought them together again, the six possible firing sequences produced six different resolutions with different convergence times. (See Table 2.) In general the number of iterations, the time taken and the time per iteration for the doubly linked triangle (Figure 13) were all less than or equal to the corresponding values for the singly linked triangle

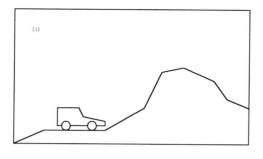

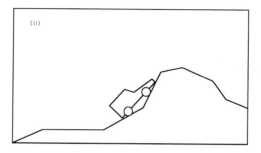

Figure 10: The van is constrained to move along a constant surface only. Initially a random polyline is entered as the constraint surface, then the user digitizes a point X. The program then puts the front wheel of the car at the nearest point on the polyline to X and then rotates it so that the back wheel also just touches the polyline. Nearest point and circle polyline intersections are used extensively.

(Figure 12). A conclusion from these tests is that we should always try to ensure that joins of points are doubly linked.

4   Observed Behaviour

The author has posited and tested a number of conjectures regarding this method of geometric iteration derived from a schematic diagram for the resolution of constraint problems. In general these conjectures are difficult to prove mathematically, mainly due to the complexity of the algebraic equations which correspond to the natural geometric constraints, and also due to the mathematical complexity in repeatedly applying these functions to themselves.

Observation 1:
A geometric iteration process either converges strictly monotonically to a limit point, or diverges strictly monotonically, or converges monotonically to a metastable condition.

A metastable condition is where the iterations oscillate between two or more limit points. Arriving at the metastable condition does not mean that a feasible solution of

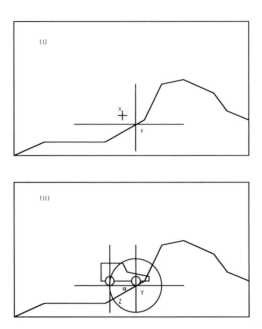

Figure 11: In (i) the user digitizes a point X on the screen and the horizon polyline returns its nearest point Y. In (ii) the front wheel of the van is located at Y and a circle with radius equal to the wheel base is constructed about Y. The intersection algorithm intersects the circle with the polyline to give point Z. The van is then rotated by the indicated angle.

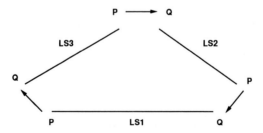

Figure 12: A singly linked triangle: the position of end point LS1.P controls the position of end point LS3.Q, and so on around the triangle, as in Figure 3.

the constraints does not exist as was seen in [Rankin and Burns, 1990a] - it simply means that the algorithm was unable to reach any feasible solution. Monotonic divergence implies that the GO will rapidly disappear altogether off the graphics screen. A proof of this behaviour pattern for the case of intersection problems was outlined in [Rankin, 1990a]. For constrained GO cases, convergence means that all defining points converge, and divergence and metastability of the iterations means that any of the defining points in the graphics object exhibit divergence or metastability as the number of iterations increases.

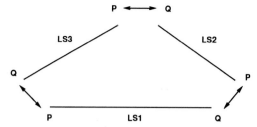

Figure 13: A doubly linked triangle: end point LS1.P controls the position of end point LS3.Q and vice versa, and similarly at the two other joints around the triangle.

Notes:

NI = number of iterations taken.
MS = time taken in milliseconds.
T/I = time per iteration in milliseconds.

Timings:

	singly linked triangle			doubly linked triangle		
Sequence	NI	MS	T/I	NI	MS	T/I
1 2 3	7	220	31.4	6	160	26.7
1 3 2	13	380	29.2	9	270	30.0
2 3 1	6	170	28.3	6	170	28.3
2 1 3	13	380	29.2	13	380	29.2
3 1 2	7	220	31.4	6	160	26.7
3 2 1	12	330	27.5	13	330	25.4

Table 2: Timings for various sequences.

Observation 2:
If the set of constraints has no feasible solution then the geometric iteration will diverge.

We can easily find examples where the algorithm diverges. Consider for instance a fixed length line segment with non-zero length where the output point Q' is fed in as the new input end point P. The line segment will very quickly go to infinity. Another example is to get the algorithm to find the triangle satisfying the requirement that the sum of the lengths of two sides of the triangle is less than the length of the third side. Both of these examples apply geometric constraints that cannot be satisfied and for which the algorithm rapidly diverges.

Observation 3:
If there are feasible solutions to the set of constraints, then there is a basin of attraction such that if the seed point is selected in this basin then convergence on a solution is assured.

Again as this observation applies to any of the defining points in the iterations implied by the schematic diagram. In contrast to the geometric intersection prob-

lems considered in [Rankin, 1990a], there are many Voronoi diagrams and basins
of attraction for the constrined geometric objects because there is generally more
than one defining point in the schematic diagram.

Observation 4:
*If there are feasible solutions to the set of constraints, then the iteration process will
either converge to a single limit point inside the feasible solution subspace, or else it
will oscillate between two limit points both of which are outside the feasible solution
subspace.*

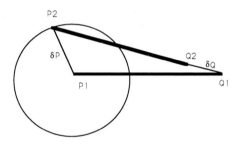

Figure 14: The fixed length line segment P1Q1 has end point P1 moved to the
position P2. The internal constraint for this GE then sets the other end point to Q2
a point on the line P2Q1 at distance a from P2 towards Q1. The consequence of
moving P1 by $\delta P = P2-P1$ is that Q1 moves by $\delta Q = Q2-Q1$. The length of vector
δQ is always less than or equal to the length of vector δP.

The following points are significant in proving these theorems. Firstly, if the set of
linkages in the schematic diagram forms a directed graph (i.e. has no loops) then no
iteration is involved and the constraints will always be solved in one pass through
all links and so the above observations become trivially true. When we have loops
in the schematic diagram we must consider the size of the feedback disturbance
compared with the size of the input disturbance. Suppose that a vectorial point
displacement of $\delta \mathbf{P}$ is forced in at the start of the loop. This travels down the links
of the loop and finally comes back to the start of the loop as a vectorial displacement
$\delta \mathbf{Q}$. If we always have $|\delta \mathbf{Q}| < |\delta \mathbf{P}|$ then it can be expected that the iterations will
converge rapidly. For example, this condition can be easily shown to be virtually
always true in the case of disturbing fixed length line segments. Figure 14 shows a
displacement $\delta \mathbf{P}$ of end point P resulting in a displacement $\delta \mathbf{Q}$ in Q' which is always
such that $|\delta \mathbf{Q}| <= |\delta \mathbf{P}|$, equality holding only when $\delta \mathbf{P}$ is parallel to $\mathbf{PQ}$. Disturbing
one end of a string of non-collinear fixed length line segments linked end to end
will therefore result in a much smaller disturbance on the last end point along
the string. This proves convergence for the case of geometric iterations to restore
a disturbed single polygon loop from an initial (feasible) configuration. Programs
visualizing examples of these cases gave rise to some exotic curves depicted in
Fugure 10. The envelopes in Figure 15 and Figure 16 arise from considering all
possible first displacements of the vertices of the polygon (whose edges are of fixed
length) arising from the disturbance of the first vertex of the polygon where $|\delta \mathbf{P}|$ is
a fixed parameter of the curves.

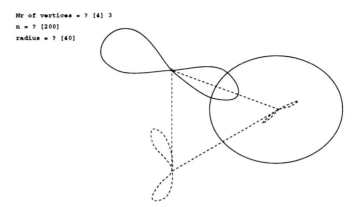

```
Nr of vertices = ? [4] 3
n = ? [200]
radius = ? [40]
```

Figure 15: The envelopes of first moves for the vertices of a triangle composed of (equal length) fixed length edges. The displacement of the first vertex is to any point on a circle of radius 40 units centered on that vertex. Note that the resulting displacements of the third end point form a small curve entirely within the circle of radius 40.

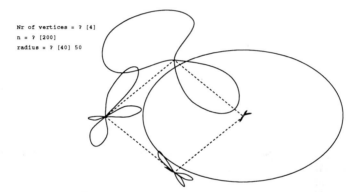

```
Nr of vertices = ? [4]
n = ? [200]
radius = ? [40] 50
```

Figure 16: The envelopes of first moves for the vertices of a square composed of fixed length edges. The displacement of the first vertex is to any point on a circle of radius 40 units centered on that vertex. Note that the resulting displacements of the fourth end point form a small curve entirely within the circle of radius 40 (smaller than the resulting curve of Figure 15). The envelopes for the square are also more complex than the envelopes for the triangle.

5   Interactive Construction and the General Democracy Algorithm

For interactive construction of a constrained GO, we need to be able to represent the network of connections in the corresponding schematic diagram as a dynamic data structure that grows as the user adds more constrained GEs and external constraints between the constrained GEs. The first step in doing this is to construct a linked list of all the constrained GEs that the user calls upon in chronological order as he uses them. He may for instance be selecting instances of GE strains from a menu. Upon selecting a GE for use, the software must dynamically allocate the object on the heap, and create a list node containing a pointer to that object. The user determines the parameter values for the selected GE by placing it on the screen using a pointing device such as the mouse to specify its finite defining point set (FDPS - the input parameters for the GE - see reference [Rankin, 1990a]). The nodes in the list contain other useful information such as slots for entering the input points and output points, GE graphics attributes (such as colour) and the pointers needed for maintaining the linked list. Additionally the list nodes contain the schematic diagram link pointers. For each of the input points there is a slot for a pointer to a GE object (the "from pointer") and a parameter ID integer. The pointer if not nil indicates that that particular input point comes from (i.e. is controlled by) the output point given by the parameter ID of the GE object pointed to. These slots serve to provide the source information for obtaining the input point values from. If the from pointer is nil then the input value is taken from the corresponding input point slot in the node, otherwise the contents of that input point slot are replaced with the point value of the output point pointed to by the from pointer. This processing is done only when the geometric iteration algorithm fires up. The implementation of this data structuring is somewhat involved and requires variant records of object pointers and so forth.

We have now described the data structure dynamically constructed at run time, which lists all GEs used in a schematic diagram, and embodies all connections between GEs in the schematic diagram through the from pointers. We next need to be able to fire up the activity of the schematic diagram, and get it iterating through to a constraint solution. Whereas with the hard coded geometric iteration OOPs code the order of calling the object methods is known in advance, such is not the case here. Therefore we have relied on a new general approach called the Democracy Algorithm which works as follows. There is one code loop only - a continual loop through all GEs in the GE list. Each GE node is tested in turn to see if its constraints are satisfied or not. To test a GE node, the input point values are first sought, a snap-shot is taken of these values and then they are applied via the GE.assign method for the indicated GE of that node. Next the GE.enquire method for the GE of that node is called up to fill in the output point values into the appropriate slots in the node. The snap-shot values are compared with the output values (using the "roughly_equal" procedure). Any significant differences mean that the constraints are not yet fully satisfied for that GE and the looping will need at least another iteration. Even though this algorithm works on paying attention to individuals and their needs in an order not suggested by the schematic diagram (which might be compared with an organization chart indicating the chain of commands) it has been shown to work just as well and enable constraint resolution to be achieved. Each time around the loop we recheck constraint satisfaction for each GE because satisfaction in one iteration does not necessarily mean satisfaction in the next iteration due to changes induced into the outputs of other GEs that affect the GE in question. This algorithm is highly suited to parallel processing architectures which would arrive at the constraint solution at a speed roughly proportional to the number of processors.

A general graphics interactive constraint system program called GICS was implemented to test these ideas. Figure 17 shows a typical screen that the user works with, and a GO constructed on the graphics area. The different strains of GEs are coloured differently by the program (but shown in Figure 17 with labels instead) to enable the user to visually distinguish them. Again we are working, in the current

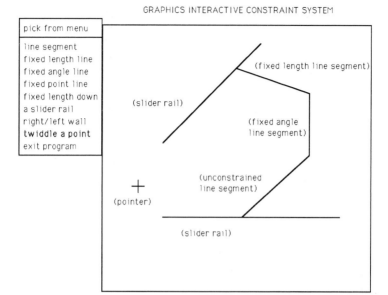

Figure 17: One of the screen views in the GICS program. After (several constrained GEs have been selected from the menu and drawn on the screen using the graphics pointer system, the user can select "twiddle" and then observe the effects of shifting some of the points around.

version, with varieties of constrained line segments only. All the tests that were done with hard coded geometric iteration algorithms derived from schematic diagrams were repeated on the GICS program and the constrained GOs were observed to maintain their integrity and respond rapidly to disturbances equally well as in the simpler hard coded cases.

The GICS program constructs constrained GOs interactively without reference to a schematic diagram by making the following reasonable assumptions. Whenever the user places a line segment LS such that LS.P is roughly equal to an end point of any other line segment previously drawn, then the user wants that second end point to control the input point LS.P. Likewise for the placement of end point LS.Q. Furthermore, if end point LS.P is roughly equal to the nearest point to LS.P on any of the railing line segments in the dynamic list then it is assumed that the user wants end point LS.P to be constrained to lie on and slide along that railing. Likewise for the placement of end point LS.Q on or near railing line segments. Because the user does not have access to the schematic diagram there are some limitations on how to make constrained GOs. For example, the controlling entities have to be drawn before the controlled entities. This means also that closed loops in control are not available. Another consequence is that constraint links also cannot be changed. Another consequence of this interface is that triple joints have to be constructed carefully - double linkage is not possible and then the order of firing can mean the difference between constraints being maintained or failing to be maintained. Also when interacting with the screen image of the GO alone, input and output points at a vertex cannot be visually distinguished, and similarly the desired end point cannot be distinguished when two line segments meet at a vertex. A more powerful constraint systems design program is clearly called for: one in which the user can interactively edit schematic diagrams. Nevertheless a significant advantage of this direct screen approach though is that the GO is always created in a feasible solution initially. The conjectures in section 4 then would indicate that we will have convergence to screen precision in finite time as is indeed observed.

6   Conclusions

We have found that geometric iterations are very efficient at finding new feasible solutions to geometric constraint systems which have been disturbed away from an initial feasible solution. Schematic diagrams which state precisely the nature of the geometric constraints in the composition of the GO from various strains of GEs are used in place of sets of equations. The geometric iteration OOPs code derives directly from the schematic diagrams. The cases where the constraints are known and fixed beforehand are easily dealt with by hard coding the OOPs geometric iteration code derived from the schematic into the application program. The more general case where constrained screen objects are constructed ad hoc by the user require a delicate data structuring and extensive use of the dynamical allocation facilities of OOPs objects and then the also the associated facilities for calling up the methods of these temporarily created objects. Nevertheless the geometric iteration method was found to generalize to an algorithm here called the Democracy Algorithm. According to the Democracy Algorithm, each object/person in the population gets an equal chance at getting his own constraints/needs satisfied and these chances cycle through every object/person until such time as all constraints/needs are acceptably met. Our initial indications on testing the Democracy Algorithm are that it works very effectively. However, different firing sequences converge to different solutions. A program that tested the algorithm enables a great variety of constrained GOs to be interactively constructed and disturbed. The program actually by-passes the need for the user to construct a schematic diagram for each GO by making some restrictive assumptions about what the user wants to be linked together. As a result of this, all constrained GOs constructed by the program are initialized in a feasible solution for the GO. This is desirable not only because the user immediately sees what he wanted to construct, but also because, by the observations given in section 4, the Democracy Algorithm has the best chance of finding a new feasible configuration for the GO after it has been disturbed. Since GOs can be built up using previously created GOs as components, we can have separate Democracy Algorithms running at all levels in hierarchically constructed GOs with each Democracy Algorithm maintaining the integrity of a GO at a given level in the hierarchy. The Democracy Algorithm is highly suited to OOP on parallel processor hardware. Both the hard coded geometric iteration technique and the Democracy Algorithm are techniques for solving constraints that are very neatly fitted into the OOP paradigm unlike the traditional approach to the constraint resolution problem.

References

Borning, A. H., "Defining Constraints Graphically", Computer Human Interaction Conference Proceedings, Boston, Apr 13 – 17, 1986, ACM, pp. 137 – 143, 1986, New York.

Coutaz, J., "Architecture Models for Interactive Software: Failures and Trends", Engineering for Human-Computer Interaction, Elsevier Science Pub., pp. 137 – 153, IFIP 1990.

Coutaz, J. and Bass, L., "Ergonomics and Software Principles for the Construction of Interactive Software", Proceedings of the Advanced User Interface Seminar, IFIP WG 2.7, University of Melbourne, Australia, pp. 8 – 121, Nov 21 – 23, 1988.

Fertey, G., Peroche, B. and Zoller, J., "Creating 3D scenes with Constraints", Proceedings of the Eurographics Workshop on Objected Oriented Graphics, pp. 65 – 87, 1990.

Fulcher, J., "CORDIC Survey", LRA, (VCH Publishers, Inc) Vol 2, pp. 93 – 100, 1990.

Khoubyari, S., "A What-if Tool For CAD", Personal Workstation Magazine, Vol 16, pp. 16 – 23, May 1990.

Leler, Wm., "Constraint Programming Languages", Addison-Wesley, 1988.

Nelson, G., "Juno, a constraint-based graphics system", SIGGRAPH '85 Proceedings, Volume 19, Nr 3, pp. 235 – 243, 1985.

Rankin, J., "Intersection Algorithm Using Graphics Object Oriented Programming Under Constraints", Technical Report 10/90, 1990.

Rankin, J., "Computer Graphics Software Construction", Prentice-Hall, pp. 115 & 155, 1990.

Rankin, J. and Burns, J., "New Geometric Intersection Algorithm Based On Object Oriented Programming", Proceedings of the Eurographics Workshop on Objected Oriented Graphics, pp. 89 – 107, 1990.

Rankin, J. and Burns, J. "Coordinate Frames And Geometric Approximation In Graphics Object Oriented Programming", In Blake, E. and Wisskirchen, P., editors, *Advances in Object-Oriented Graphics I (Proceedings of the Eurographics Workshop on Object-Oriented Graphics, 1990)*, pages 131 – 148, Springer-Verlag, 1990.

Sutherland, I. E., "Sketchpad - A Man-Machine Graphical Communication System", Proceedings of the Spring Joint Computer Conference, pp. 2 – 19, 1963.

6

ALIEN: A Prototype-Based Constraint System

Eric Cournarie and Michel Beaudouin-Lafon

The main objective of the work reported in this article is the use of constraints in graphics and user interfaces. We believe that constraints need to be integrated in a powerful programming paradigm in order to be usable in large-scale systems. The system we present embeds constraints in a prototype-based model. A prototype object (a template) contains internal constraints, and exports slots so that instances of the prototype can be further constrained. Instantiation uses delegation to share constraints between instances. As a consequence, changing a template has an immediate effect on all its instances. The model also features generic templates and skeletons to create complex constrained objects. The system is open and extensible: new constraint types can be defined and alternative solvers can be used. The basic solver uses local propagation.

The article presents the model and the constraint system. Then we discuss the performance of the current implementation. Two running applications are described: a graphical editor for constrained objects and a graphical environment for the Occam parallel programming language. The last section compares ALIEN to other existing systems.

This work is partially supported by the AVIS-UIS project, within the framework of the Eureka Software Factory, and by CNRS Greco de Programmation.

1   Introduction

The idea of using constraints for graphics is now widespread and a number of systems actually use them. The nice properties of constraints are now well-known, such as their ability to describe relationships in a declarative instead of algorithmic ways. There is also significant works on constraint solving techniques so that constraints now seem ready to be used widely in graphics as well as other domains.

The reality, however, is that few real size systems actually use constraints. It might be that constraint systems cannot handle large-scale systems (thousands of constraints) with an acceptable response time. It might also be that beyond a certain number, constraints are difficult to master by the programmer. The motivation behind the work reported in this article is this second assumption: programming with constraints is not easy, and structuring mechanisms are needed to help the programmer maintaining large systems driven by constraints.

Our first attempt has been to use an object-oriented framework and try to integrate constraints in this framework. We were not satisfied with the result because of a number of problems raised by the pure (i.e. class-based) object-oriented paradigm. Nevertheless the object-based approach was still tempting, and we actually moved to a prototype-based model. The reasons for this final choice are described in the first section of this paper. The following sections go into more details about ALIEN, our prototype-based constraint model and system. Then we describe some applications being developed with this system. In the final section ALIEN is compared with other related work.

2   ALIEN : From Objects to Prototypes

The aim of ALIEN is to provide the programmer with a simple model to create and manage constrained objects, especially in a graphics world. The kinds of activity we expect from the programmer is to create objects, use constraints to describe their internal rules, put objects together and specify constraints between them, reuse existing objects and change their behavior. A major goal is to have the system support large applications with good performance and programming ease.

The first version of ALIEN was based on a pure object-oriented model, i.e. a model based on classes, instances and inheritance. We finally rejected this model after having identified the following weaknesses with respect to our goals.

A class defines the behavior of a set of objects, and all the instances of a class have the same behavior. This means that a new behavior usually leads to the definition of a new subclass. Such subclassing is needed even if objects differ in detail. Defining many classes is not only cumbersome, it also limits reusability. For instance, if we want to create a fixed-width rectangle, we must create a specific subclass of the class rectangle, and instantiate this new subclass. Alternatively, we could instantiate a rectangle and add a fixed-width constraint to it, but this would mean that rectangles must know how to handle constraints, and that constraints have access to the internals of a rectangle. Both are difficult to accept in a pure object-oriented model.

Another drawback of classes is that they freeze the behavior of objects. There is no strong support for dynamically modifying or enhancing this behavior, especially in compiled languages. For instance it is difficult to change the fixed-width rectangle class into a fixed-height rectangle class dynamically, with an immediate effect on all the instances of that class. Class-based languages just do not expect classes to change.

Finally, class-based languages do not allow the sharing of common properties between objects of distinct classes, unless the classes are tied by an inheritance link. For instance, it is not possible for an ellipse class to use the fixed-width property defined in our fixed-width rectangle class. Even with multiple inheritance, one can hardly imagine inheriting the fixed-width rectangle class from the rectangle class and a fixed-width object class, because there is no simple means to describe an abstract fixed-width object class.

These problems suggest the use of a model that supports the dynamic aspects that we need: instance-level properties, dynamic modification of classes and free inheritance of properties. For this reason, ALIEN is now based on prototypes instead of classes and instances. It uses delegation instead of instantiation.

Prototypes and delegation support the sharing of properties [Lieberman, 1986]. Such a technique provides an important gain in flexibility, because the local modification of a shared property has a global impact on the system. In addition, delegation allows prototypes to change their behavior dynamically. Another feature of prototypes is that all objects are potential prototypes and hence can generate new objects. There is no longer a difference between the generators and the generated objects, like with classes and instances. Self [Ungar and Smith, 1987] demonstrates the flexibility of the prototype model.

The status of constraints in our model must be clearly defined. Constraints are relationships between objects. We use them to define behaviors declaratively instead of having those behaviors hard-coded by the programmer. Thus, constraints are objects that can be created at run time. The constraint solver is a part of the run-time environment that supports and manages these constraint objects.

To sum up this model, constraints define the behavior, prototypes support sharing and dynamic modification of behaviors and objects provide the general framework of the system.

3   Objects and Slots

In ALIEN, we call *slots* the instance variables that can be connected to constraints. Slots are typed: basic types include integer slots, character slots, color slots, etc. Composite slots are similar to the records found in many programming languages. A composite slot contains a number of slots and is itself a slot, i.e. it can be connected to constraints. For instance, a point slot holds two integer slots, one for the X coordinate and one for the Y coordinate. Thus, one can constrain the entire point, or only the X coordinate, or both of them.

An object in ALIEN contains one composite slot, representing the attributes of the object. For instance, the composite slot of a rectangle has two point slots for its shape, color slots for its background and border color and an integer slot for its thickness (figure 1). New slots can be added to the objects dynamically. An object can also contain the usual instance variables, which have no impact on the constraint system, and thus will be ignored from now on.

A slot behaves like a normal variable in a programming language. The only difference is that the constraint solver is run when a slot is assigned a new value. Thus, the constraint solver is invisible to the user of ALIEN.

During the resolution, a slot keeps its new intended value in a *candidate*, used as a temporary value. This has two advantages: first, it is possible to backtrack on some choices. Second, constraints are able to use the old value of the slot. For instance, a constraint between a point and a line can state that the point must stay on the same side of the line. Such a constraint needs the old and new positions of the point to check whether it is verified.

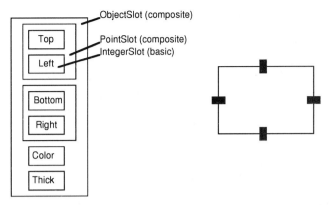

Figure 1: Slots. A rectangle contains 6 basic slots and 3 composite slots: two points and the whole object. The right part of the figure shows the graphical representation of rectangles and constraints that we use in the remaining of the article.

There is no limitation on what kind of value a candidate can hold. For instance, if a constraint defines that a point must stay on a line, then the candidate of this point can hold the equation of the line instead of one arbitrary point of the line. If the same point is under another constraint like a fixed distance from a given point, then the candidate value will become (in the best case) the set of two points satisfying both constraints.

Slots are eventually updated with their candidates when the constraint solver has finished. If a candidate holds a non unique value (like the equation of a line or a set of points), it is asked to choose one. In order to satisfy the principle of least astonishment, it should select the nearest value according to its initial value. When a slot is actually updated with its final value, its owner object is notified. In a graphics environment, this is used to redisplay the object.

Slots, Constraints, and the Object-Oriented Paradigm

One may be surprised that we use slots to define constraints on objects. A big virtue of the object-oriented paradigm is to provide for encapsulation of data. Slots may look like a way to expose the internal state of an object to the outside world. In effect, constraints in ALIEN do change the values of the slots they are connected to, thus bypassing any access protocol that the object may want to impose. A more traditional approach would be to ask the object for the value of a slot and to ask an object to change the value of a slot. This can be used in a constraint-based system, as examplified by Rankin in another chapter of this volume [R. Rankin, 1991]. Nevertheless, we feel that slots provide an interesting alternative, without breaking the object-oriented paradigm.

In order to encapsulate its state, an object can define an access protocol for a slot by adding internal constraints on that slot. These constraints will be handled by the constraint solver, like any other constraint. If this happens to be impractical or insufficient, one may use a slot like an active value: reading or writing the value of a slot triggers a method of its owner object, which can then implement any access protocol to its internal state. This feature can be related to prototype-based languages like Self which have unified state and behaviour by using messages to access the state. This makes it possible to define fake state variables which are actually computed. Our slots provide the dual view of this unification, by which the behavior is triggered by state changes.

4   Templates, Instantiation and Cloning

A *template* is a prototype that contains component objects (possibly other templates), internal constraints, and exported slots, i.e. slots that are visible from outside the template. The main property of templates is their ability to use delegation. A template has a set of *proxies*, which are themselves templates. When a slot of a template is modified, this triggers the constraints on this slot as well as the constraints defined in the proxies of this template. This is achieved by delegating the modification to the proxies, as shown in figure 2. By changing the set of its proxies, a template may borrow the behavior of other templates dynamically.

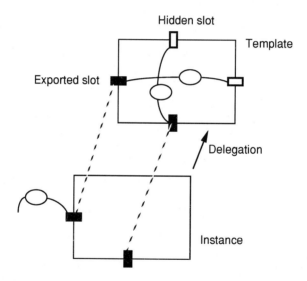

Figure 2: Proxy. An instance delegates the assignment on its slots to its proxy.

The usual way to produce a template that has a proxy is by instantiating an existing template. In figure 3, two levels of instantiation are used to define an object made of two vertically aligned rectangles. Note that there is no distinction between generator templates and final objects: the instance INST is a template, which can be instantiated again. Note also that instantiation duplicates the slots of the generator while it shares its internal constraints. Slots must be duplicated because each instance will have different values for them. Constraint sharing maintains "live links" between templates, so that adding or removing constraints in a template has the expected effect on all its instances, with no overhead.

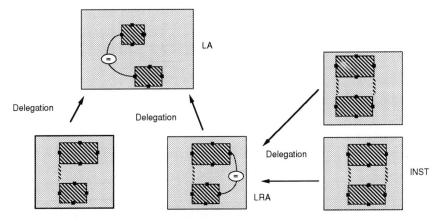

Figure 3: Templates. LA is a template containing two rectangles constrained to be left-aligned. LRA is an instance of LA, with an additional right alignment constraint. INST is an instance of LRA, and thus inherits these two behaviors. In this example, INST does not define any new constraint so that INST and LRA have the same behavior. The dashed lines indicate inherited alignment constraints.

As an example, a constraint could be added to LA to specify a fixed distance between the two rectangles. LRA, INST and the other instances would inherit this new constraint. This means that a resolution would take place to compute the values of the slots that are now under the new constraint. A similar resolution would take place if a constraint was removed, or modified.

As an alternative to instantiation, templates can also be cloned. Cloning duplicates the slots as well as the internal constraints of the template. A cloned template has no proxy, hence it looses any link with its generator.

It is worth noting that delegation does not change the semantics of the constraints. When a resolution takes place, the result is the same as if all templates had been cloned instead of instantiated. For the solver, delegation only implies some extra bookkeeping to know exactly which constraints are involved in the proxies of the objects.

Genericity

A template may contain parameters, thus defining a *generic template*. Instantiation or cloning of generic templates involves argument-passing, as shown in figure 4. The generic template becomes a proxy of its arguments. Like a normal template, the constraints of a generic template are shared through delegation. Cloning a generic template creates a new template by copying the arguments as well as the constraints and slots of the generic template.

A side effect of generic template instantiation is to provide *composition* (see figure 5). Composition is achieved by plugging one generic template into another, by cloning or instantiation. The arguments of one of the generic templates are parameters of the other one. They are still arguments in the final template.

Figure 4: Generic template. A generic template containing two horizontally aligned objects is instantiated with a rectangle and an ellipse. The dashed lines represent the constraints inherited from the generic template.

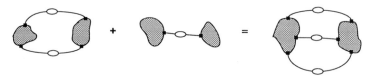

Figure 5: Composition of generic templates. A generic template containing two horizontally aligned objects is composed with a generic template containing two objects with a fixed horizontal distance. The result is a generic template containing two horizontally aligned objects separated by a fixed distance.

Iterative Constraints

Iterative constraints are an experimental feature of ALIEN. Iterative constraints provide a way to capture in a declarative way the insertion and removal of objects in a "constrained set". The objects in a constrained have similar constraints, like for instance the items in a menu. The constrained set automatically changes the constraints when an object is added to or removed from the set. A constrainted set is represented by a *skeleton* which is a specialized generic template, whose parameter objects are distinghuished elements of a list (first, previous, current, next). Constraint are defined between the different parameters. Figure 6 shows a sample skeleton for a vertically aligned list.

Skeletons are special generic templates because they are associated to a set of objects. The set is monitored by the skeleton so that each change triggers a new instantiation. To perform this instantiation, the skeleton needs to know the semantics of its parameters. For instance the list template knows which element is the first, the previous, the current, etc. Thus creating a skeleton not only requires the creation of the generic template, but also the definition of the instantiation method. This is currently hard-coded in the skeleton, but of course we would prefer a declarative specification, which we have not found yet.

5   Constraints

A constraint in ALIEN is an object. The word "object" is used here to refer to the class-instance model: constraints belong to classes in the usual sense. A sample constraint class is the class of linear constraints. Classes for equality and inequality can be subclasses of the linear constraint class. Another sample constraint class is the class of fixed distance constraints. Constraints are multiway: they are not oriented.

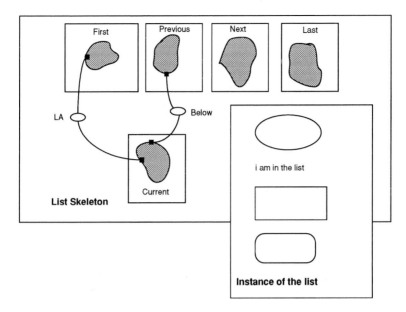

Figure 6: Iterative constraint. Each item of the list is aligned with the first element and each item is a fixed distance below the previous one. When the text was added to the list, the Below constraint between the ellipse and the rectangle was removed, an LA constraint between the text and the first element (the ellipse) was added, and two Below constraints where added (one between the text and the ellipse, the other between the rectangle and the text).

All constraints contain:

- a set of *entries*. An entry can be linked to at most one slot, while a slot can be linked to several entries. Entries, like slots, are typed.

- a *level* in the hierarchy.

- a *rule*, i.e. a predicate that tests whether the constraint is satisfied or not.

- a *satisfaction method*, which computes the new values of unknown slots.

- an *internal state* private to the constraint.

As an example, a linear constraint has a variable number of entries, one for each variable in the linear equation or inequality. The state of a linear constraint contains the coefficients of the variables and the constant value of the equation. A fixed distance constraint is simpler: is contains two entries of type point, and a state holding the distance to keep between the two points.

Control over Constraint Behavior

ALIEN offers two means for controlling constraint behavior: global control over the network of constraints and local control over a particular constraint. Global control is necessary to specify what happens when the network of constraints is over-constrained or under-constrained. This also has the advantage of preserving the principle of least astonishment. Global control of over-constrained systems is addressed by a *hierarchy*, as introduced by Borning et al. [Borning et al., 1989]. Resolution of a hierarchy of constraints proceeds by solving all higher-level constraints, and adding one level after the other until no solution can be found. Hence, with such a hierarchy, the user can assist the system in finding which constraints to leave unsatisfied. Under-constrained systems are easier to manage because one can assume that each slot has a constraint to keep its previous value. Such implicit stay constraints have the lowest level in the hierarchy.

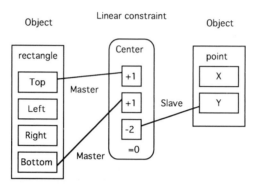

Figure 7: Master and Slave entries. The point on the right is vertically centered with respect to the rectangle. The constraint represents the equation Top + Bottom - 2Y = 0 . The constraint state contains coefficients +1, +1, −2 and the constant 0.

Local control is used to help the system in solving a particular constraint. First, a multiway constraint may be turned into a one-way constraint by using two different entry types: *master* or *slave*. When the slot of a master entry is modified, the constraint can modify any other slot. When the slot of a slave entry is modified, the constraint can only modify slave slots or its internal state. In figure 7, the point is centered vertically with respect to the rectangle; moving the rectangle results in moving the point. On the other hand, moving the point does not modify the rectangle but the alignment, represented by the constraint's state (in this case the constant and/or the coefficients). If the slave entry was a master, moving the point would reshape the rectangle.

Another means of local control addresses the problem of ambiguities. In the previous example, if all entries are masters, then moving the point must change the rectangle. However there are many ways to reshape a rectangle so that a given point is centered vertically. To give a hint to the constraint, entries can be given the *prefer_stay* property. The constraint will then try to leave such entries unchanged. In our example, if the entry corresponding to the top slot was flagged prefer_stay, the constraint would change only the bottom slot of the rectangle. If both the top and bottom entries were flagged, the constraint would be solved on both. In this case it would try to minimize the change of both slots. Moving the point would then result in moving the whole rectangle.

As shown by this simple example, achieving a good control over constraints is not easy. It must be pointed out that global control is used by the solver, while local control is used by the constraints. Each control is independent of the other. This is an important feature, to insure that different constraint classes can have different local controls available, and to insure that the strategy of the constraint solver can be changed without changing the constraints.

Granularity of Constraints

Constraints in ALIEN have different levels of abstraction. Low-level constraints like linear equations connect basic slots. High-level constraints connect composite slots. Because objects are made of one composite slot, constraints on objects can be defined. Typical constraints that can be defined only on objects (or composite slots) include topological constraints like stay-inside or do-not-intersect. These constraints can be defined only by using global information on the objects to which they apply.

A number of geometric constraints apply to points and thus have medium granularity. Such constraints include fixed-distance between two points, fixed orientation of a segment, fixed angle between three points, etc. Defining a point as a composite slot instead of a basic slot is important because constraints can be set on the individual coordinates of the point as well as on the point itself.

The solver handles constraints on composite slots as if they would apply to each component of the composite slot. Hence, the granularity of constraints has no particular semantics for the solver. In particular, granularity does not define the hierarchy of constraints, which is defined independently.

6   Constraint Solving

Constraint solving has to deal with several challenges. First of all, a constraint network can be under- or over-constrained, depending on whether the constraint has more than one solution or no solution at all. Finding all the solutions can lead to a combinatorial explosion. Thus, the constraint solver must avoid this explosion, but still deduce useful and expectable results. On the other hand, if there is no exact solution, one can expect the solver to give the "best" one, according to some error measure.

However, general constraint satisfaction is NP-complete [Mackworth, 1977]. This means that a particular constraint solver is most of the time application dependent. We think the solution is to provide an easy way of changing the solving technique, even at run-time. In ALIEN, a basic constraint solver is used, but it is able to delegate the work to a more specialized solver. Such a solver can easily added to the architecture of ALIEN. Thus, particular applications can use ALIEN and still provide their own solver.

The basic solver of ALIEN is based on local propagation. Local propagation is the fastest technique, although it fails in some cases, in particular when there are cycles. Local propagation does not make any assumption about constraint types, unlike other solving techniques. For instance a numerical technique like relaxation works only with linear constraints. With local propagation, any kind of constraint can be used.

Our approach is to have an extensible system, by separating as much as possible the constraint solver from the constraints. However, in order to be able to call a specialized solver, one must know the constraint types involved at resolution time. This is why our solver splits the work into two phases: first, it collects all constraints that are suspected to be unsatisfied, then it calls the resolution module on this set.

To insure the separation between the solver and the different constraint types, a constraint must have three properties: it has to be able to tell whether it is satisfied or not (its rule), to resolve itself (its satisfaction method) and to say whether it has enough information to be solved. This last property is used by our local propagation resolution to order the constraints to solve, taking into account their level in the hierarchy.

As already stated, the impact of delegation and constraint sharing on the solver is minimal. When collecting shared constraints, the solver keeps the reference of the instance that initiated the delegation. This reference will be used at resolution time to get the values of the instance slots on which the constraint will work. When the constraint is solved, the new values are returned to this referred instance.

History of Resolution

An interesting improvement of the constraint solver is based on the history of previous resolutions. This is motivated by the assumption that the constraint solver is often triggered in the same way (that is by modifying the same slots). For instance, in the context of graphics, when objects are dragged, the same resolution is done for each move of the mouse. Keeping a history has two major advantages: the constraints need not be collected again, because they are the same as for the previous resolution, and the previous ordering is still valid. Thus, the solver needs only call the constraint resolution methods.

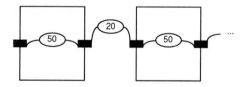

Figure 8: Example 1. n rectangles are constrained to have a constant width and to be 20 pixels apart from the previous one. Performance is measured when the left side of the first rectangle is dragged.

This improvement is invalid if anything has changed between the two resolutions, like for instance if constraints have been added or removed. We are currently studying the integration of the delta-blue algorithm [Freeman-Benson, 1988] in the solver to optimize the insertion and deletion of constraints. This integration is made difficult by our constraint sharing.

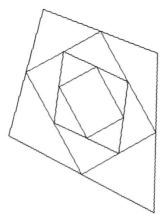

Figure 9: Example 2. Performances are measured when a corner of the outer quadrilateral is dragged

Performance

Performance has been measured in two situations, which are related to experiments with ThingLab II [Maloney et al., 1989]. The first one (figure 8) features a simple ordering of constraints while the second (figure 9) is the "famous" nested quadrilateral example [Borning et al., 1989].

Our measurements are split into two times, corresponding to the two tasks of the solver. The first time measures only resolution, while the second sums this resolution with the time spent in collecting the constraints. The time to draw is not taken into account as it depends on the graphics subsystem. The last time, playback time, indicates the successive resolution time due to the history optimization described in the previous section. These measures have been performed on a Sparc workstation.

Example 1:

Rectangles	Constraints	Resolution time	Total time	Playback time
250	499	0.1	0.4	0.1
500	999	0.4	0.7	0.2
1000	1999	0.7	1.5	0.4
2500	4999	1.9	3.9	1.2

Example 2:

Quadrilaterals	Constraints	Resolution time	Total time	Playback time
10	92	0.3	0.3	0.0
20	192	1.4	1.4	0.0
30	292	3.5	3.6	0.1
50	492	10.7	11.0	0.1

These examples show that the critical point of our basic solver is the resolution phase, i.e. the ordering of constraints. A possible optimization, which we have not tried yet, is to keep track of the last computed slot. Further constraints to solve are most of the time near this slot (this is the strong assumption of local propagation).

The last set of measures shows the impact of instantiation: the rectangles of the first example have been instantiated from a fixed-width rectangle template. The table below shows a time factor of 5 when using instantiation. The difference is due to the frequent switches between the instances, especially while collecting constraints. We have not yet optimized instantiation like we have optimized the basic solver. We expect to have a time factor of 2 with a few simple optimizations, which we think is acceptable. The gain in memory space has not been quantified yet.

Example 1 with instantiation:

Rectangles	Constraints	Resolution time	Total time	Playback time
250	499	0.5	2.2	0.3
500	999	1.8	7.4	1.2

7   ALIEN for Graphical Applications

The intended use of ALIEN is to build graphical applications. It is developed for this purpose within the project Avis-UIS, a subproject of the European Eurêka Software Factory (ESF) project. The model defined by ALIEN is being used in a semantic drawing tool now under development within Avis-UIS. The applications described in this section are currently running. The first one is a graphical editor for constrained objects, which we use to test ALIEN. The second one is a graphical programming environment for the parallel programming language Occam. Both applications use XTV [Beaudouin-Lafon et al., 1990], a graphical toolbox that we have developed also within Avis-UIS. XTV provides extensible structured graphics and input handling on top of the X Window System

ALIEN is currently implemented in C++, as a library of classes. The source code is around 16000 lines and the compiled library is 530 Kbytes on a Sparc. ALIEN is *not* a language, although the model it is based on would easily lead to a language. We found that the cost of designing and implementing a new language was not worth the trouble. A library makes it easy to integrate ALIEN into applications, while having a language would imply the development of applications with this language. Because in most applications constraints are only a tool, we believe that providing a library is better than providing a language.

A Graphical Editor for Constrained Objects

Although we do not want to define yet-another-language to validate ALIEN, building constrained graphical objects with a conventional language is sometimes tedious. Thus, the first application developed with ALIEN is a graphical editor to build and test constrained graphical objects.

The editor is dedicated to prototyping objects and their behavior. First, an objet can be designed in an editing view. Its slots are displayed and the user can bind constraints, which have a graphical appearance, to them. Then the user can test the object and its behavior in a separate view. In this view the objects can be exercised by moving and stretching them. This runs the constraint solver, and tests its ability to work in real time. Once a new object has been designed, it can be used as a component for another object. It may also be stored in a file for later use. A run-time library is available so that applications can use objects built with the editor.

The editor is merely used to test ALIEN, to demonstrate its features, and to validate new ideas. As an interactive tool, it needs many improvements, in particular to represent the constraints graphically. Juno [Nelson, 1985] or Fabrik [Ingalls et al., 1988] present significant work in this area.

A Graphical Programming Environment for Occam

To validate ALIEN from the applications point of view, we use it to develop a graphical environment for parallel programming with Occam: EPO^{++}. This environment is based on the graphical visualization and editing of parallel programs. A program is represented by a control graph (see figure 10). Nodes of the graph represent various components of the program : constructor processes like PAR, ALT, SEQ and so on, elementary processes like assignment, input, output, etc.

This graph supports user interaction, enabling static analysis of the program. Constructor nodes can be opened or closed, showing or hiding the code inside this node. A node can be displayed in another view, in order to focus on a subpart of the program. Communications are included in the graph and can be displayed by selecting either input or output processes. Finally, variables can be inspected, by opening a variable sub-window on any node that defines variables. At run time, the graph reflects the current state of the processes, showing active points (i.e. current instructions) and updating variables.

The interface is connected to an Occam interpreter and scheduler. Our first implementation of this environment [Mourlin and Cournarie, 1989] led to numerous problems: layout of the graph, consistency between active points on the graph and the current instructions, consistency between variables and their graphical representation. The use of ALIEN has solved these problems. The layout is addressed by pure graphical constraints. For instance, each node is a fixed distance below its parent, and a parent node is centered over its subgraph. Generic templates are used to instantiate the arcs. Although in this case all nodes are made of the same graphical objects, changing the presentation of a node would not affect the constraints that tie the arcs to the nodes.

Separating adjacent subgraphs by a fixed distance raises a difficulty as a node may be opened and replaced by a subgraph, thus changing the nodes that must be constrained. To solve this problem, a subgraph has a virtual extent object, containing four slots. The right slot of the extent is constrained to be equal to the right slot of the rightmost node of the subgraph. Similar constraints are set with the other slots. Fixed size constraints are set between the slots of the extents of two adjacent subgraphs. When a subgraph is opened or closed, it needs only change the internal constraints of its extent.

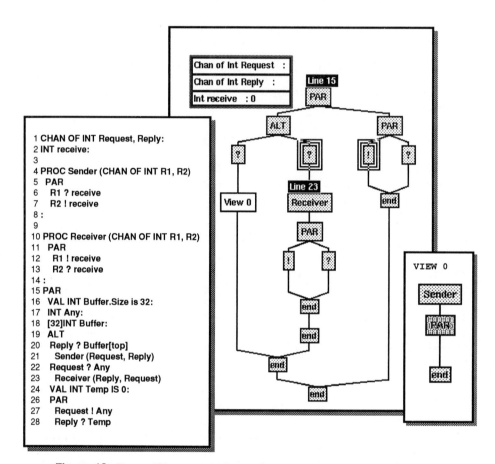

```
1 CHAN OF INT Request, Reply:
2 INT receive:
3
4 PROC Sender (CHAN OF INT R1, R2)
5  PAR
6    R1 ? receive
7    R2 ! receive
8 :
9
10 PROC Receiver (CHAN OF INT R1, R2)
11  PAR
12    R1 ! receive
13    R2 ? receive
14 :
15 PAR
16   VAL INT Buffer.Size is 32:
17   INT Any:
18   [32]INT Buffer:
19   ALT
20     Reply ? Buffer[top]
21     Sender (Request, Reply)
22     Request ? Any
23     Receiver (Reply, Request)
24     VAL INT Temp IS 0:
26     PAR
27       Request ! Any
28       Reply ? Temp
```

Figure 10: Epo++. "?" represents input, "!" represents output. The highlighted nodes (right son of ALT and left son of PAR) show an ongoing communication. Process *Sender* is closed in the main graphical view, and partially open in the subview VIEW0 (the PAR construct is closed). The variables window has been opened on the first PAR construct.

With this example, we do not want to pretend that ALIEN is able to layout any graph. Here, we are concerned with directed acyclic graphs. To handle general graphs, one must provide a better solver than ours. Indeed, a solver based on local propagation can hardly address such problems.

EPO^{++} manages the consistency between graphics and the Occam interpreter by semantic constraints. Constraints are placed between the Occam code in the interpreter and the node representing this code in the control graph. An instruction has a boolean slot, connected by a constraint to the color slot of the node representing that instruction. When this instruction is executed, the interpreter sets the boolean to true, causing the node to be hilited. Breakpoints are handled similarly. Variables are stored directly in slots by the interpreter, so that variable windows are straightforward to implement. Used that way, constraints give a behavior similar to active variables [Henry and Hudson, 1988].

8   Related Work

In this section we compare ALIEN to a number of existing constraint-based systems, especially those which are dedicated to graphics. ALIEN does not introduce any fundamental new idea in object-oriented programming or constraint systems. Rather it attempts an integration of known models, methods and techniques to make constraints really usable. The systems presented in this section have been, among others, the source of inspiration of ALIEN.

ThingLab [Borning, 1981,Borning and Duisberg, 1986] is probably one of the best known systems that uses constraints. ThingLab has a graphical editor quite similar to ALIEN's to create constrained objects. The main difference between ALIEN and ThingLab is that ThingLab uses a class-based approach, namely the classes of its implementation language Smalltalk. Thus instantiating constrained objects leads to copying the constraints, whereas ALIEN uses sharing and delegation. Moreover, there is no other way to structure constraints than instantiation. Constraints in ThingLab are very general, like in ALIEN. However, ThingLab requires that each constraint provide the set of possible resolution methods, so that the solver knows which one to apply given a set of input and output variables.

ThingLab introduced the notion of constraints hierarchy, and we have used this notion in ALIEN. Besides this, the solver of ThingLab is more powerful than ours, because it uses the sophisticated delta-blue algorithm for incremental insertion and removal of constraints. On the other hand, it is probably more difficult to change the solver in ThingLab than it is with ALIEN. The performance of ALIEN looks better than the performance of ThingLab, although this is very difficult to compare because of the difference of hardware and software environments. As an interpreted system, ThingLab actually looks very efficient. We have been concerned by the performance of ALIEN only recently, and we expect to be able to gain a lot in future versions, by tuning the implementation and by using other algorithms.

Another constraint-based system for use with graphical applications is the Garnet set of tools [Myers et al., 1990]. The constraint system of Garnet is a new version of Coral [Szekely and Myers, 1988]. Garnet uses constraints in a rather pragmatic way. Constraints are unidirectional, so that there is no ordering of constraints to be done at resolution time. This gives very good performance (3500 constraints per second) much better than other constraint systems. However, if we count only the playback time, then the performance of ALIEN does compare to the performance of Garnet.

A powerful feature of Garnet is to provide lazy evaluation. This means that constraint resolution only solves the variables that are of interest to the user. For instance, it is not necessary to compute the positions of objects that are not visible. This however seems to be applicable only to unidirectional constraints, since with multiway constraints, one cannot foresee the contribution of a given constraint to the value of a given variable. Lazy evaluation also raises the problem of which variables are "of interest". Although the constraint system itself does not use prototypes, other subsystems of Garnet do. The graphical object system defines aggregates, with propagation of changes to the instances. Unlike ALIEN, this is not based on delegation, but the comparison is difficult: constraints in Garnet are not objects but formulas, so that the notion of sharing constraints does not apply to Garnet. There is a further interesting similarity between ALIEN and Garnet: the Lapidary interface builder supports prototypes with parameters, which are instantiated by giving arguments. This is similar to ALIEN generic templates, except that it is available only at a higher level of the Garnet system, not at the very heart of the constraint system as with ALIEN.

We have described ALIEN as the integration of constraints in a prototype-based model. Other integrations have been studied, namely the integration of constraints and logic programming and the integration of constraints and imperative programming. In CLP [Jaffar and Lassez, 1987], the integration of constraints with logic programming consists in replacing the concept of unification in a logic program by the concept of constraint solving. This is expected to be more general as well as more intuitive to use. Bertrand [Leler, 1987] uses a similar approach and addresses constraint solving by augmented term rewriting. CLP has been used in building graphical user interfaces, as reported in [Ege, 1989], and Bertrand could be used for graphics as well. The integration we attempt with ALIEN is quite different to the integrations we just described. ALIEN tries to integrate *constraints* in a structured model, while CLP and Bertrand integrate *constraint solving* in a programming model. The focus is different, and the two approaches could actually be merged together.

The integration of constraints and imperative programming is done in Kaleidoscope [Freeman-Benson, 1990]. This language makes it possible to state constraints as well as to assign expressions to variables and to use control structures like in imperative programming languages. This is achieved by introducing time as an explicit notion, and by associating a stream of values to each variable. We feel that ALIEN offers an integration that can be compared to Kaleidoscope although the means are different: Kaleidoscope is a language whereas ALIEN is a library. As a language, Kaleidoscope must address all the needs of the programmer; as a library, ALIEN relies on the client application and its supporting language. The ability to describe timed constraints (constraints that hold only for a given period of time) is a powerful feature of Kaleidoscope that ALIEN misses. Conversely, genericity in ALIEN has no equivalent in Kaleidoscope, nor in any other constraint system we know of.

9   Conclusion and Future Work

We have presented in this paper a new model that integrates constraints with prototypes. We have shown applications of the model and we have compared it with existing systems. Our goal is to make constraints usable in large-scale applications. This requires abstractions for the programmer without sacrificing efficiency at run-time. We believe that the abstractions defined with ALIEN are useful to the programmer, and that performance is acceptable, although more work is needed. Our first experiments show that programming with constrained objects is much easier than programming with constraints and objects. Wiring together slots and objects and constraints by hand is much more difficult and error-prone than using predefined components and tuning them to one's specific needs. We could compare this to programming with an assembly language versus programming with a high-level language. Genericity supports the idea of constrained objects very efficiently. One can imagine libraries of generic templates to choose from when creating an application.

Work on ALIEN is continuing. The model is now stable enough to undertake the task of specifying its semantics. We feel this is a major step to the real understanding of structuring constraints. Iterative constraints need to be investigated further as they are only experimental at this moment. We also want to study the applications of constraints to the description of the *dialogue* of user interfaces: we have shown how ALIEN can describe the graphical behavior of objects, but we would also want to describe how the user can create, delete and manipulate these objects. The editor already restricts the editable parts of the objects based on the visibility of slots, but this is far from sufficient. We beleive that the general paradigm of constraints applies to such specification of interactive objects.

References

Beaudouin-Lafon, M., Berteaud, Y., and Chatty, S., Creating direct manipulation applications with Xtv. In *Proc. EX'90*, November 1990.

Borning, A., Duisberg, R., Freeman-Benson, B.N., Kramer, A., and Woolf, M., Constraint hierarchies. In *Proc. OOPSLA'87*, pages 48–60, October 1987.

Borning, A., The programming language aspects of Thinglab, a constraint-oriented simulation laboratory. *ACM Transactions on Programming Languages and Systems*, 3(4):353–387, October 1981.

Borning, A., and Duisberg, R., Constraint-based tools for building user interfaces. *ACM Transactions on Graphics*, 5(4):345–374, October 1986.

Ege, R.K., Direct manipulation user interfaces based on constraints. In *Proc. COMP-SAC'89*, pages 374–380, September 1989.

Freeman-Benson, B.N., The DeltaBlue algorithm: an incremental constraint hierarchy solver. Technical Report 88-11-09, Dept. of Computer Science, University of Washington, November 1988.

Freeman-Benson, B.N., Kaleidoscope : Mixing constraints, objects and imperative programming. In *Proc. ECOOP-OOPSLA'90*, pages 77–87, 1990.

Henry, T.R., and Hudson, S.E., Using active data in a UIMS. In *Proc. ACM Siggraph Symposium on User Interface Software*, October 1988.

Ingalls, D., Wallace, S., Chow, Y.Y., Ludolph, F., and Doyle, K., Fabrik: A visual programming environment. In *Proc. OOPSLA'88*, pages 176–190, September 1988.

Jaffar, J., and Lassez, J-L., Constraint logic programming. In *Proc. 14th Annual ACM Symposium on Principles of Programming Languages*, pages 111–119, January 1987.

Leler, Wm. *Constraint Programming Languages*. Addison-Wesley, 1987.

Lieberman, H., Using prototypical objects to implement shared behavior in object oriented systems. In *Proc. OOPSLA'86*, pages 214–223, September 1986.

Mackworth, A.K., Consistency in networks of relations. *Artificial Intelligence*, 8(1):99–118, 1977.

Maloney, J.H., Borning, A., and Freeman-Benson, B.N., Constraint technology for user-interface construction in ThingLab II. In *Proc. OOPSLA'89*, pages 381–388, October 1989.

Mourlin, F., and Cournarie, E., A graphical environment for Occam programming. In *Proc. of the First International Conference on Applications of Transputer*, August 1989.

Myers, B., Giuse, D., Dannenberg, R.B., Vander Zanden, B.T., Kosbie, D.S., Pervin, E., Mickish, A., and Marchal, P., Garnet, comprehensive support for graphical, highly interactive user interfaces. *IEEE Computer*, pages 71–85, November 1990.

Nelson, G., Juno, a constraint-based graphics system. In *Proc. SIGGRAPH'85*, pages 235–243, July 1985.

Rankin, J.R., A graphics object-oriented constraint solver. In *Second Eurographics Workshop on object-oriented Graphics*, June 1991.

Szekely, P.A, and Myers, B., A user interface toolkit based on graphical objects and constraints. In *Proc. OOPSLA'88*, pages 36–45, September 1988.

Ungar, D., and Smith, R.B., Self: The power of simplicity. In *Proc. OOPSLA'87*, pages 227–241, October 1987.

Part III

User Interfaces I

7

Extending an Advanced Logic Programming Environment by an Object-Oriented User Interface Management System

Heinrich Jasper

Visualization and manipulation of knowledge is of great importance for any knowledge based system. Window based user interface management systems (UIMS) allow building flexible and easy to use interactive graphical user interfaces. There is a need to integrate such UIMS into knowledge base programming environments. This paper addresses the integration of UIMS into the logic programming environment PROTOS-L. Our approach provides a small set of built-in predicates that defines an easy to use object-oriented interface to UIMS within the logic programming language. This interface is realized by the PROTOS-L window manager and presented by a simple text editor in this paper. Its implementation is based on a multiple process concept with asynchronous communication in order to cope with long lasting inference processes. The prototype of the PROTOS-L window manager is implemented on top of the standard user interface toolkit OSF/Motif.

The work reported here was carried out within the EUREKA project PROTOS (EU 56) when visiting the Institute for Knowledge Based Systems of IBM Germany Scientific Center.

1   Introduction

Within the international EUREKA project PROTOS [Appelrath, 1987] tools for building expert systems based on the logic programming principle are designed and implemented. One such tool is the PROTOS-L system [Beierle and Böttcher, 1989], a compiler based logic programming environment. The PROTOS-L language is designed to support software engineering principles like strong typing and modularization. Furthermore, the PROTOS-L system provides advanced tools for building expert systems like a deductive relational database and a high level interface to user interface management systems (UIMS).

Applications that provide interactive graphical user interfaces create, manipulate and destroy visual objects dynamically. This behaviour is most naturally implemented using an object-oriented programming approach. Such object-oriented interfaces to UIMS offer classes of which applications can create instances.

A class defines a set of attributes and methods. Attributes are specified by name, value class and default value. Methods have a name unique within the class and are invoked by messages. For example, messages can be used to manipulate the attribute values of instances or to send messages to other instances. Classes are organized in a hierarchy and provide an inheritance mechanism. This means that a class knows about the attributes and methods of all its ancestors in the class hierarchy.

An instance of a class, usually called object, is created by sending a method to the desired class. The object itself is manipulated by sending messages to it. Attributes and methods defined by a class or inherited from ancestor classes are known to all objects of that class. Within an application, the objects may be organized in a hierarchy, too. This allows for inheriting attribute values from ancestor objects. Thus it is easy to manipulate an attribute value of a set of objects: just redefine the value in an ancestor object and all heirs will get the new value. The instances of the classes of a user interface management system (usually called widgets, i.e. an abbreviation of window gadgets) can be visualized on displays, e.g. as windows or graphical objects, and allow for direct manipulation.

The communication between application and UIMS is done by message passing in object-oriented environments. These messages are created by events due to user interaction. Methods are either defined by the UIMS or by the application. The application provides methods to handle those user events (for example pushing a button created by the application) that are specific to the application. These methods are installed into appropriate predefined slots of an object. They are called callbacks. Within the PROTOS-L system callback procedures are implemented as deterministic relations, i.e. relations that consit of exactly one "solution".

Whenever some event occurs in the UIMS (e.g. as the result of a user action) it invokes the corresponding callback. This event handling is done by a predefined method of the UIMS, called the "event handling loop". This method receives all events and distributes them to methods either installed by applications or defined in the UIMS.

The architecture of the PROTOS-L window manager (hereafter called PWM) consists of four major parts: the class manager (PCM), the object manager (POM), the PROTOS-L windows interface (PWI) and the PROTOS-L callback manager (PCBM). The class manager provides all classes known to the UIMS and organizes them in a hierarchy. The object manager manages the set of actually known objects. These are those objects created by PROTOS-L applications and additionally some predefined objects having unique names (cf. section 4). The PWI provides a set of built-in predicates (built-in predicates define a library in logic programming languages) to the PROTOS-L programmer that allows for creating and manipulating objects. The callback manager invokes the PROTOS-L procedures that correspond to events that occured in the window system.

The global architecture regarding message passing between PROTOS-L, PWM and UIMS is visualized in figure 1. The PROTOS-L system communicates with the

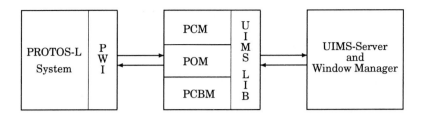

Figure 1: PROTOS-L window manager (PWM) architecture

PCM, POM or PCBM via a set of built-in predicates (cf. section 2). The PCM/POM/ PCBM in turn communicate with the UIMS via library calls (cf. section 3 and 4). Of course, both communication channels are bidirectional.

The next section explains the built-in predicates that the PWM provides to application programmers. This is followed by a section presenting an example editor implemented with these predicates. In the fourth section the concepts of the implementation of the PCM and POM on top of OSF/Motif are outlined. A summary is given in the last section.

2   PWI: The Programmer's Interface

The overall design goal of the PROTOS-L programmer's interface, the PWI, was to provide a set of built-in predicates in the PROTOS-L language that is as small as possible. Thus it is not feasible to set up a one-to-one mapping between methods of classes and built-in predicates, since this would result in a huge amount of built-in predicates (cf. the approaches described in [BIM, 1988], [Quintus, 1990] and [IF/Prolog, 1990]). Furthermore, such a one-to-one mapping is not easily manageable because it is inflexible regarding changes and enhancements to the PWM: adding a new class or changing the arguments of a method requires changes to the built-in predicates.

Therefore, the built-in predicates provided by the PWI are defined as an abstraction of methods, called generic methods. All methods of the classes are mapped to these generic methods. Four generic methods were identified in the object-oriented UIMS. These generic methods allow:

- creating a new object,
- assigning values to attributes of one object,
- asking for one object or for the values of the attributes of some object and
- calling a method of an object.

For each generic method there exists one built-in predicate in the PWI. These built-in predicates can be detailed as follows:

1. pwm_new(class_name, attribute_value_list, object)

The built-in predicate pwm_new creates a new object as an instance of an existing class. The class itself is denoted by its name which is represented as a string in the first argument of pwm_new. The second argument of pwm_new specifies a list of attribute-value-pairs. These define those attributes of the new object that will initially differ from the defaults provided in the class description. The third argument returns the object identifier.

Due to the strong typing principle of PROTOS-L, the elements of the attribute_value_list must have a value of one of four different PROTOS-L types. These are integer (i_attr), string (s_attr), pwm_object (o_attr) and pwm_goal (p_attr), the latter two being abstract types in the PWI. Each attribute-value-pair is denoted as a term with functor i_attr, s_attr, o_attr or p_attr respectively, the first argument of which is the attribute name (a string) and the second argument is the respective value.

Values of type pwm_object are object identifiers known to the POM. A pwm_goal is a callback, providing application dependent actions for events occurring in the user interface. A pwm_goal is defined as an ordinary subgoal in the body of PROTOS-L rules. As soon as a corresponding event occurs the goal is called as the actual goal in PROTOS-L. The proof of this goal can in turn cause other events and thus other goals to be called.

For example a call of

(G1) pwm_new("XmText", i_attr("width", 500) . i_attr("height", 400) . nil, Text)

creates a new object of the class XmText having values 500 for the width attribute and 400 for the height attribute. (In PROTOS-L lists are written with an infix dot operator separating head and tail. They are finished with the predefined term "nil".) An abstract handle for this object is unified with the PROTOS-L variable "Text" (which of course must be of the corresponding type pwm_object).

2. pwm_send(object, attribute_value_list)

This built-in predicate updates values of attributes of a given object. The attribute_list is defined as above.

For example a call of

(G2) pwm_send(Text, s_attr("text", "This is a text.") . nil)

assigns the string "This is a text." as actual value of the text attribute of the object unified with the "Text" variable, cf. example (G1).

3. pwm_get(object, attribute_value_list)

This predicates asks for actual values of an object and unifies them with the variables in the attribute_value_list. The retrieved values may differ from the last assignment done by a call to pwm_new or pwm_send as a result of interactive changes (mostly due to user interaction) of the state of the windows and their contents on the screen.

For example calling

(G3) pwm_get(Text, i_attr("width", W) . s_attr("text", T) . nil)

will result in retrieving the values of width and text of the object denoted by the "Text" variable and unifying them with the variables W and T respectively. Of course, the types have to be correct: in this case W must be of type integer and T of type string. The values of W and T may differ from the initial settings, e.g. W may be unequal to 500 (cf. (G1)) as a result of window resizing and T may "contain" an arbitrary string as a result of user updates on the initially assigned and displayed text (cf. (G2)).

This built-in predicate may be used to query the object identifier of some (predefined) object, too. For example a call to

(G3') pwm_get(Multi_line, s_attr("name", "MULTI_LINE_EDIT").nil)

retrieves the object named "MULTI_LINE_EDIT" and unifies its object identifier with Multi_line.

4. pwm_call(object, method, attribute_value_list)

This built-in predicate is used to call methods of objects. The first argument of pwm_call references the object and the second argument denotes the method via a string. The third argument is a list of attribute-value-pairs that is mapped to the parameters of the method. Since the parameters in this list are named no ordering of the elements of the attribute_value_list according to the ordering of the parameters of the method is necessary.

For example

(G4) pwm_call(Text, "destroy", nil)

calls the destroy-method known by all objects. This method has no arguments, thus the attribute_value_list is empty (equal to nil). In this case it will destroy the object referenced by the "Text" variable, e.g. as created in goal (G1).

The four predicates described above allow for creating and manipulating arbitrary objects as instances of the classes known to the PCM. In order to call the "event handling loop" there exists a fifth built-in predicate, namely **pwm_start(display-parameters)**. The argument of pwm_start is system dependent (e.g. for specifying the display to be used) and is normally left empty. In the following section an example shows how these predicates are used to create a simple interactive window based editor.

3   Example: an Editor

The following example is part of an application that demonstrates the development of a window based user interface in PROTOS-L. This example uses, among others, the text class of OSF/Motif in order to implement an editor that manipulates files. The application is called "xmeditor" and e.g. documented in [OSF1, 1990]. A description of the text class itself can be found in [OSF2, 1990]. The reimplementation of a smaller part of the "xmeditor" in PROTOS-L using the PWI built-in predicates is described in this section. The editor consists of the parts depicted in figure 2.

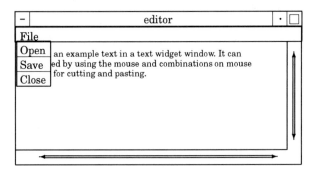

Figure 2: The example editor

The steps to develop a window based application are sequenced in the usual way: first define all the necessary objects and then implement the appropriate procedures and assign them as callbacks. After this call the "event handling loop" via pwm_start. The built-in predicate pwm_start is normally the last goal that is activated in a PROTOS-L application using windows.

In the "xmeditor" example an application shell, a text window and a menubar are created. Having finished this, the event loop of the window system is started. This is denoted by the following initial PROTOS-L rule (specified as a deterministic relation with keyword drel) that defines a predicate "editor" of arity 1. Calling this procedure starts the "xmeditor" application. The argument of the editor predicate is the name of the file to be initially edited.

```
drel editor : string.
editor(File) <- create_shell(Shell) &
                create_text(File, Shell, Text) &
                create_menubar(Shell, Text) &
                pwm_start("").
```

An application shell is the basic window for applications written on top of OSF/Motif. It is the root object in the object hierarchy of applications using windows. The application shell is created by the deterministic relation create_shell that is defined by the following PROTOS-L rule; attribute values are defined as in [OSF2, 1990]:

```
drel create_shell : ?pwm_object.
create_shell(Shell) <- pwm_new("ApplicationShell",
                            s_attr("name", "editor").
                            i_attr("shadowThickness", 0).
                            s_attr("managed", "true").nil,
                            Shell).
```

The text window is create via the next PROTOS-L rule. First the identifier of a predefined object named "MULTI_LINE_EDIT" is retrieved. After this the text window is created and the deterministic relation openfile (see below) is called, which assigns the contents of a file to the text window.

```
drel create_text : string x pwm_object x ?pwm_object.
create_text(F, S, T) <-
    pwm_get(Multi_line, s_attr("name", "MULTI_LINE_EDIT").nil) &
    pwm_new("Text",
                o_attr("parent", S).
                i_attr("rows", 60).
                i_attr("columns", 120).
                s_attr("resizeWidth", "true").
                s_attr("resizeHeight", "true").
                s_attr("scrollVertical", "true").
                s_attr("scrollHorizontal", "true").
                o_attr("editMode", Multi_line).
                s_attr("wordWrap", "true").nil,
                T) &
    openfile(F, T).
```

The menubar is created via the deterministic relation create_menubar. It consists
of one button for calling a pulldown menu. The pulldown menu itself consists of
three buttons, that allow for opening and closing a file and for saving the actual
text displayed in the text window.

```
drel create_menubar : pwm_object x pwm_object.
create_menubar(S, T) <-
    pwm_new("MenuBar", o_attr("parent", S).nil, MBar) &
    pwm_new("PulldownMenu", o_attr("parent", MBar). nil, PDMenu) &
    pwm_new("CascadeButton",
                o_attr("parent", MBar).
                o_attr("subMenuId", PDMenu).
                s_attr("labelString", "File").
                s_attr("mnemonic", "F").
                s_attr("managed", "true").nil,
                _) &
    pwm_new("FileSelectionDialog",
                o_attr("parent", PDMenu).
                p_attr("okCallback", open(_, _, T)).
                p_attr("cancelCallback", cancel(_)).nil,
                Open) &
    pwm_new("PushButton",
                o_attr("parent", PD_Menu).
                s_attr("labelString", "Open").
                s_attr("mnemonic", "O").
                s_attr("managed", "true").
                p_attr("activateCallback", open_Menu(_, _, Open)).nil,
                _) &
    pwm_new("PushButton",
                o_attr("parent", PD_Menu).
                s_attr("XmNlabelString", "Save").
                s_attr("XmNmnemonic", "S").
                s_attr("managed", "true").
                p_attr("XmNactivateCallback", save(_, _, T)).nil,
                _) &
    pwm_new("PushButton",
                o_attr("parent", PD_Menu).
```

```
          s_attr("XmNlabelString", "Close").
          s_attr("XmNmnemonic", "C").
          s_attr("managed", "true").
          p_attr("XmNactivateCallback", close(_, _, T, S)).nil,
          _).
```

Within a call of the procedure create_menubar seven objects are created. These are the menubar as a child of the application shell widget, the pulldown menu, a cascade button (called "File") as a child of the menubar that is connected to the pulldown menu, the three buttons mentioned above and a file selection dialog widget, which is visualized when the activate callback of the open button is invoked, cf. the deterministic relation "open_Menu" below.

The procedure openfile which is called as the last subgoal in create_text opens a file (stream), reads the stream as a string (cf. second argument) from that file, closes the file and assigns the string as well as the filename to the text object. It is defined as follows:

```
drel openfile : string x pwm_object.
openfile(Filename, Text) <-
        open_instream(Filename, string, Stream) &
        get_term(Stream, String) &
        close_instream(Stream) &
        pwm_send(Text, s_attr("filename", Filename).
                       s_attr("value", String).nil)
```

The deterministic relations (procedures) installed as callbacks of the buttons are defined below. They consist of

- an open procedure that assigns a new file and string to the text object and unmanages the file-selection-dialog object,

- a cancel procedure the unmanages the file-selection-dialog object,

- a open_Menu procedure that manages the file-selection-dialog object,

- a save procedure that writes the actually displayed string into the corresponding file and

- a close procedure that works in the same way as the save procedure but additionally calls the destroy method of the top object of the application and therefore destroys all objects.

Callbacks may have arbitrary arity but the first two arguments must have type pwm_object each, if they exist. The first argument will be instantiated with the object identifier of the object to which the event belongs that invoked the callback. The second argument is instantiated with an object that describes the event which caused the callback to be invoked.

```
drel open : pwm_object x pwm_object x pwm_object.
open(W, Data, Text) <-
        pwm_get(Data, s_attr("filename", Filename).nil) &
```

```
        openfile(Filename, Text) &
        pwm_get(W, o_attr("parent", Parent).nil) &
        pwm_send(Parent, s_attr("managed", "false")).

drel cancel : pwm_object.
cancel(Widget) <- pwm_get(Widget, o_attr("parent", Parent).nil) &
                  pwm_send(Parent, s_attr("managed", "false")).

drel open_Menu : pwm_object x pwm_object x pwm_object.
open_Menu(_, _, Menu) <-
        pwm_send(Menu, s_attr("managed", "true").nil).

drel save : pwm_object x pwm_object x pwm_object.
save(_, _, Text) <- pwm_get(Text, s_attr("filename", Filename).
                                   s_attr("value", String).nil) &
                    open_outstream(Filename, string, Stream) &
                    put_term(Stream, String) &
                    close_outstream(Stream).

drel close : pwm_object x pwm_object x pwm_object x pwm_object.
close(_, _, Text, Shell) <- save(_, _, Text) &
                            pwm_call(Shell, "destroy", nil).
```

The example given here is only a smaller part of the "xmeditor" application which originally provides two pulldown menus, one for file handling (open, close, save, save-as, new) and the other for editing (cut, copy, paste and clear). The code used in PROTOS-L for the complete "xmeditor" example is only about 30 percent of the original example which is written in C and covers 25 pages of source code.

To our opinion, this example demonstrates how easily complex user interfaces are implemented using the PWI (and OSF/Motif). Furthermore, it is well known that the logic programming paradigm allows for rapid prototyping and flexible application development. Therefore, PROTOS-L together with the PWM will allow for incrementally building advanced knowledge based system like those production planning systems (job shop scheduling) that are the subject of the PROTOS project.

4   Implementation on Top of OSF/Motif

A PROTOS-L application using the PWI results in the software architecture depicted in figure 3. Only those parts of an application regarding user interface management are visualized. The bottom software layer (e.g. hiding operating system peculiarities) is the X library of the X window system. Upon this the Xt intrinsics library is provided which allows for building widget class hierarchies. Using these intrinsics (and some features of the X library as well) the OSF/Motif library builds its widget and gadget classes.

The next layer is provided by the class and object manager of the PWM. These managers are based on the OSF/Motif class hierarchy. Additionally, these managers need some procedures provided by the Xt intrinsics and the X libraries. This layer provides the PWI to the PROTOS-L applications. An advantage of the approach of the PROTOS-L window manager is that it prevents the programmer from details

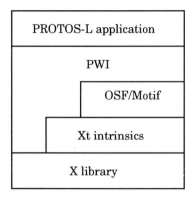

Figure 3: Software architecture of applications using PWM.

regarding different libraries, unlike the OSF/Motif library where every application additionally uses procedures from the Xt intrinsics and the X library.

The architecture of the implementation of the PROTOS-L window manager (PWM) is given in figure 4. It consists of three major layers: the PROTOS-L inference system, the PROTOS-L window manager itself and the X window system. The PROTOS-L inference system consists of the inference engine and a module for the windows interface, realizing interprocess communication (IPC) to the PWM.

The architecture of the PWM consists of six modules, one for the PWM part of the IPC to the inference engine that realizes the built-in predicates of the PWI, one for initializing the PWM, i.e. the class (PCM), object (POM) and callback (PCBM) managers, one for the isolation of the X interface and the three major parts, namely PCM, POM and PCBM. The PCM and the POM are discussed in detail below.

All classes known at the PWI are managed by the PROTOS-L class manager (PCM). Class descriptions are maintained on a secondary device which is a file in our prototype. Running a PROTOS-L application, the class descriptions are loaded from this file and an internal tree representation of the class hierarchy is constructed before the first built-in predicate of the PWI is executed. Each node in this tree structure represents one class. It holds information about all attributes of that class, their respective value class and default value (which is NULL, if unknown). Furthermore, it preserves information about all methods known to a class.

The classes known to the PCM are mapped to corresponding features of OSF/Motif. OSF/Motif is an object-oriented UIMS (at least to a certain extent) providing widget classes (e.g. objects/tools having an associated window) and gadget classes (windowless tools/objects). It is based on the X window system ([Scheifler et.al., 1988]) and implemented as a widget set on top of the Xt intrinsics ([Young, 1989]). OSF/Motif as well as the X window system are implemented in C (basically on UNIX workstations). Unfortunately, OSF/Motif is not object-oriented in every detail. For example the methods known to the objects of one class are ordinary C procedures that are not directly linked to that class as methods.

Therefore, it is not possible to maintain a one-to-one mapping between classes and their features in the PCM and the corresponding classes and features of OSF/Motif.

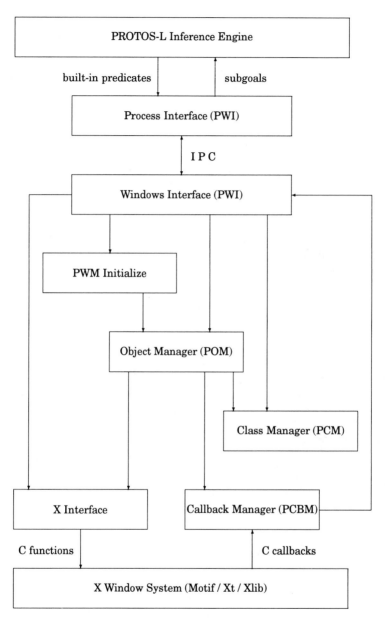

Figure 4: The PWM process and module architecture (arrows indicate the flow of messages)

Instead, the PCM provides an object-oriented abstraction of non object-oriented features of OSF/Motif. These are mappings of attributes and methods to C functions of the Xt intrinsics and X window system libraries. Additionally, in order to provide a truly object-oriented interface in the PWI it is necessary to maintain classes in the PCM that have no corresponding class in the UIMS. Especially, there exist integer and string classes in the PCM which have no counterpart in OSF/Motif.

All objects created in a PROTOS-L session via the PWI built-in predicates are managed in the PROTOS-L object manager. Whenever a new object is created, its consistency is checked against the PCM class descriptions. The objects are organized in a hierarchy. This hierarchy is maintained as a tree in the POM. Each object holds a reference to the class of which it is an instance. This reference is used when manipulating an object in order to check the changes against the class descriptions. Predefined objects must be maintained in the POM. For example in the OSF/Motif library there exist enumeration types (in the C language) that are used to describe predefined features of classes and instances, see e.g. the object named "MULTI_LINE_EDIT" in the example given in the previous section. Each predefined object has an unique name in the POM. They are maintained in an object file of the PWM and loaded into the POM immediately after the classes are loaded.

The PROTOS-L inference system, the PROTOS-L window manager and the X window system with OSF/Motif run in seperate processes. Typically, the UIMS runs a process of its own just because it has to cope with other applications. The PROTOS-L inference system and the PROTOS-L window manager run in distinct processes in order to cope with user interaction while running long lasting inference processes in PROTOS-L. Otherwise the following two problems will occur:

- User interaction is suspended as long as a callback lasts. This is not feasible in knowledge based applications, since a callback might start an inference process that lasts for several minutes or even longer.

- All intermediate results are displayed when a callback is finished. This may result in a lot of changes to the visualized objects at some moment. But, the inference process normally generates intermediate results in some sequence the user wants to watch and react on.

In order to circumvent the problems mentioned above the PROTOS-L inference system and the PROTOS-L window manager run in two asynchronous processes. They communicate via message passing. Each call of a built-in predicate of the PWI results in both, sending a corresponding message to the POM which in turn notifies the X window system. The PCBM sends messages to PROTOS-L in order to invoke callback procedures. These callback procedures are managed by PROTOS-L normally one after the other. In order to cope with long lasting processes, callbacks can be specified to interrupt the actual inference process. This results in storing the actual state of the inference process and the processing the interrupting callback. As soon as the latter has finished, the former inference process is resumed. Intermediate results of PROTOS-L inference processes are visualized as soon as they have been established.

5   Summary

The PROTOS-L window system offers a high level interface for programming window based user interfaces. Objects of an object-oriented UIMS are created and manipulated using four generic methods. An implementation on top of OSF/Motif provides all classes of OSF/Motif to the PROTOS-L programmer. In opposite to other approaches (see e.g. [IF/Prolog, 1990] and [Quintus, 1990], where one-to-one mappings between OSF/Motif procedures and built-in predicates are provided) the PWM establishes a flexible integration of UIMS. Especially, other widget sets (e.g. the Athena or HP widget sets) may be installed instead of or in addition to the OSF/Motif widget set. This will not change the interface but allows for using the same built-in predicates to access the new classes and objects.

There exist several approaches to integrate graphical and user interface capabilities into e.g. Prolog programming environments. Most of these use a set of built-in predicates that map the functions of the UIMS one-to-one to Prolog, see for example [BIM, 1988], [IF/Prolog, 1990] and [Quintus, 1990]. The approach of the ProWindows system of [Quintus, 1988] is similar to the approach adopted here since it uses generic methods, too. But the "event handling loop" must be implemented by the Prolog programmer in the ProWindows system. Thus, all approaches known to us lack the simplicity of the message passing approach adopted for the PROTOS-L window manager.

The approach described here has been implemented on RS/6000 workstations under AIX 3.0. It has been tested by two complex knowledge based applications, a system for interactively planning of train connections and an application in the area of job shop scheduling. Experiences with the latter showed the necessity of the multiple process architecture, since the planning algorithm lasted for more than fifteen minutes and the planning staff did not accept this time period where it could not interact with the planning system. Therefor, the planning stuff was allowed to interrupt the actual planning process and to ask for information about the jobs planned so far. This behaviour could easily be implemented with the asynchronous process mechanism of the PROTOS-L window manager.

Acknowledgements

I am greatly indebted to O. Herzog for enabling my visit and P. Greissl for supporting my work at the Institute for Knowledge Based Systems of IBM Germany. In particular I am grateful to C. Beierle, G. Meyer and M. Zeller for many fruitfull discussions and to M. Schenk for the implementation of the prototype.

References

Appelrath, H.-J., Das EUREKA-Projekt PROTOS, in Brauer, W., Wahlster, W., (eds.), Proceedings GI-Kongress Wissensbasierte Systeme, IFB 155, Springer Verlag, 1987.

Beierle, C., Böttcher, S., PROTOS-L: Towards a Knowledge Base Programming Language, in W. Brauer, W. Wahlster (eds.), Proceedings GI-Kongress Wissensbasierte Systeme, IFB, Springer Verlag, 1989.

BIM Prolog Graphic Package, BIM, Everberg (B), 1988.

OSF/Motif Schnittstelle für IF/Prolog, Interface GmbH, München (D), 1990.

OSF/Motif Programmer's Guide, Open Software Foundation, Prentice Hall, Englewood Cliffs (NJ), 1990.

OSF/Motif Programmer's Reference Manual, Open Software Foundation, 1990.

Quintus ProWindows User's Guide, Quintus Computer Systems Inc. Mountain View (CA), 1988.

Quintus ProXt User's Guide, Quintus Computer Systems Inc. Mountain View (CA), 1990.

Scheifler, R.W., Gettys, J., and Newman, R., X Window System, DIGITAL Press, 1988.

Young, D., The X Window System: Application and Programming with Xt (Motif Version), Prentice Hall, Englewood Cliffs (NJ), 1990.

Appendix: PWM programmer's interface: built-in predicates (PWI)

```
pwm_object := abstract.


pwm_goal :=    % call of a deterministic PROTOS-L relation (e.g. p_rel) having
               % arbitrary arity. If p_rel has arity > 0, the first argument
               % must have type pwm_object (will be instantiated with a widget
               % identifier). If p_rel has arity > 1, the second argument must
               % have type pwm_object (for callback data), too. The other
               % arguments must be ground when installing an object of type
               % pwm_goal as callback to some object. This type must not be
               % used in PROTOS-L programms, i.e. a callback must not be
               % instantiated to a variable.


pwm_attribute := {i_attr: string x int,       % named integer attribute
                  o_attr: string x pwm_object, % named pwm_object attribute
                  p_attr: string x pwm_goal,   % named callback attribute
                  s_attr: string x string}.    % named string attribute


drel pwm_new  :  string x list(pwm_attribute) x ?pwm_object.


drel pwm_send :  pwm_object x list(pwm_attribute).


drel pwm_get  :  ?pwm_object x ?list(pwm_attribute).
                 % In general undetermined deterministic behaviour, if the
                 % first argument is not instantiated. This case is useful
                 % for retrieving identifiers of predefined named objects.


drel pwm_start : string.
```

8

An Object-Oriented Architecture for Direct Manipulation Based Interactive Graphic Applications: The MAGOO Architecture

Mário Rui Gomes, Rui Pedro Casteleiro, and Fernando Vasconcelos

Magoo is a C++ implementation of OO-AGES, an object-oriented model that copes with the requirements of Direct Manipulation based Interactive Graphic Applications both at the user interface and at the semantics level. The OO-AGES is based on the Client-Server concept and the Responsibility-Driven approach.

An overview of the OO-AGES model is given and the main Magoo classes are described. The current Magoo version includes a object-oriented encapsulation of both X-Window and Motif Xtoolkit that will be described. A graphic editor is used to exemplify Magoo's architecture.

1 Introduction

Traditionally an Interactive Graphic Application is divided in an user interface and a semantics part [Pfaff, 1985]. The specification and implementation of each part is usually different although both pose common requirements including sophisticated graphics, commands given at any time, different ways to give the same command, multiple input and output devices, complex dialogues, fast and continuous prompt/feedback and non static interfaces.

The OO-AGES [Gomes and Fernandes, 1991] is an integrated client/server based model where no distinction between semantics and user interface objects exists. The Model follows the responsibility-driven approach [Brock, 1989], where each object is responsible to perform a task and to collaborate with other objects.

The Magoo architecture [Gomes et al., 1990] is an implementation of the OO-AGES model, written in C++ and using X-Window and Motif XToolkit. For each main OO-AGES concept an abstract class was written and will be described. Magoo will be used in the ESPRIT HYPERFACE project (ESPRIT 5391).

2 Overview

The OO-AGES solves the biggest problems found in creating an application based on direct manipulation techniques: the manipulation of virtual world objects. Ideally an human operator should be able to directly manipulate any virtual world object including buttons, keys, dials, furniture, clothing, the same way he does with the real world objects. Unfortunately the most popular physical devices are only suitable to handle very simple objects. The operator visualises images (raster graphics) and manipulates keyboards (ASCII values) and mouses (location value). To solve the problem it is necessary to transform low level abstractions, at the sensor/motor level, in high level abstractions, at the application object's level. Any input data should be used to manipulate a virtual world object, the image (low level re presentation) of any virtual world object should also be visualised. To model a Interactive Graphic System is to define the virtual world objects and the transformations needed to visualise and manipulate them. In the OO-AGES model there are two main objects: the Data objects and the Transformer objects.

Data objects are divided in two main families. Some contains information about virtual world objects. Others represent the information used at the man-machine interface. A *display* object is a low level data object where output is shown and input is received. Any graphic system can be used to receive and display information. The current Magoo implementation includes an encapsulation of X-Window and Motif Xtoolkit.

The transformers are usually organised in a pipeline. They are also divided in two main classes. Each object of an output pipeline, *a driver*, is responsible for the creation of a data object image. The inverse transformation is performed by an input pipeline, where each object is called a *dialog*. An output pipeline has the responsibility of transforming the data objects running through the several pipeline stages until an image is created. An input pipeline is responsible for managing (creating, editing and destroying) objects. In Magoo the first input pipeline stage is a generic event handler that can subscribe several basic event types, for instance, a button down.

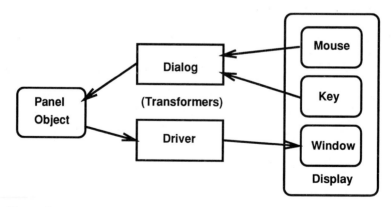

Figure 1: An application model

In Figure 1 the mouse and keyboard are used to direct manipulate a panel object. The dialog is responsible for the mapping between physical devices manipulation and panel manipulation. The driver is responsible for the creation of the panel's image. The communication between objects can be synchronous or asynchronous. In the Magoo implementation only synchronous communication is used. In summary, an application is a set of linked objects managing virtual world entities (the panel object). The main programmer's responsibility is to create dialog objects that deal with an application's dynamic.

3   Magoo Classes

In Magoo each OO-AGES main concept is implemented by a C++ abstract class. There are two main Data classes and two main Transformer classes. The most important ones will be introduced and described.

3.1   Graphic Objects

The managing of virtual world objects is the main goal of a Direct Manipulation based Interactive Graphic Application. With these applications it is possible to create, destroy and modify virtual world objects including their geometry and attributes (colour, physical attributes,..).

Many direct manipulation based applications were implemented on top of graphic systems, including GKS [ISO, 1985], PHIGS [ISO, 1988] and X-Window [Scheifler and Gettys, 1986], which were used to create graphic object images. But the main problem is not to visualise a virtual world objects but to manipulate it. Unfortunately no support is given, by those graphic systems, to modify an object, for instance to insert or delete a point in a polyline or to change a circle's radius.

In Magoo any data object can be created, destroyed or modified. The creation of an object's image is a driver's responsibility and the managing of any object is a dialog's responsibility. In Magoo there are graphic objects, GO, composed of a set of components (other data objects) and a set of methods to define and inquire the value of each component. Each GO is defined in its own coordinates space and composed of a geometric part and an attribute part. The geometric part includes all the components necessary to define a specific GO class. Polylines, Polygons, Splines, Circles, Arcs and Rectangles are available and a transformation matrix is used to define the object's coordinate space.

Attributes are used to define a GO's appearance. Font, DrawMode, Pattern, Line-Width, LineStyle, Visibility, Detectability, Foreground (Colour), Background (Colour) are available and grouped in a Graphic Context. It is possible to change a GO geometry and to rotate, shift and scale it. Several methods for points editing are available as well as specific GO dependent methods. For example it will be possible to inquire and define the radius, the centre coordinates, the starting angle and the ending angle of a arc.

Most of a virtual world entities are complex objects. Magoo copes with this requirement with the introduction of the Composite Graphic Object, CGO, concept. Those objects are composed by an editable set of GO, a transformation matrix and attributes. A GO's coordinate space is defined in its father coordinate space. If a GO has not all the graphic attributes, the missing information will be inherited from its father. Methods to inquire and define a GO's father are also available.

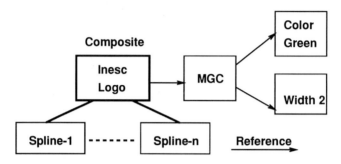

Figure 2: A tree of Graphic Objects and attributes

Figure 2 shows a composite graphic object, the "Inesc Logo" composed by a set of spline graphic objects. Two attributes were created, the foreground object "Colour Green" and the line width object "Width 2". They are grouped together in the graphic context object "MGC".

4   Magoo Display Objects

After the definition of virtual world objects it is necessary to define the sensor/motor interface that will be used. Any graphic system can be used to create images and to receive input data objects. In current Magoo's implementation a C++ Motif XToolkit encapsulation is available. There is a 1:1 relation between a Magoo display and a widget.

A homogeneous interface with the Motif XToolkit is implemented by the **MXtDisplay** class enabling the use of any widget's window to create an virtual world object's image. Displays are organised in trees and it is possible to change and inquire the relations between displays or to define and inquire any attribute value (widget resource).

In Figure 3 a tree of displays was created. The image of a virtual world graphic object can be created inside one or more displays.

5   Driver Objects

Both the virtual world and sensor/motor objects were already described. It is time to introduce the Transformer objects. To compute a low level representations of a GO, one or more **Drivers** must be created and linked with a display. To create an image inside a window a specialised driver, the **MXtDriver** must be used and linked with a **MXtDisplay** object.

Any driver manages a display list. The relative position of two GO's in a display list will define the sequence of the lower level GO creation. Methods to insert, in-

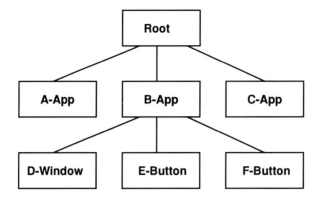

Figure 3: A simplified example of a display tree

sert before, insert after, update, remove or inquire a display list are available. A message must be sent to the driver if an update of the lower level GO representation is explicitly needed, for example its new image (graphic representation). If a graphic object is defined **active**, the drivers will be informed whenever the object is modified. Any driver can use its display list to automatically repair the contents of a window it is connected with. Thus, the lowest level objects are transparent to the application's programmer. Within Magoo it is possible to use pre-programmed interaction techniques, the XToolkit widgets, extending their graphic capabilities without any special knowledge.

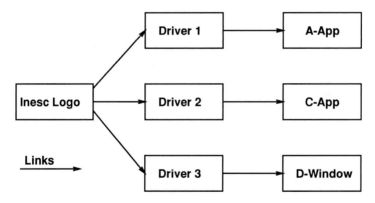

Figure 4: One Composite Graphic Object with 3 images

Figure 4 show the necessary links to obtain three different images of a Composite Graphic Object, the "Inesc Logo". The three images are computed by three drivers (MXtDriver) in three displays. Any "Inesc Logo" modification will be visible inside the three windows.

6   Dialog Objects

Until now it was possible to create GOs, to display them in several displays and to modify them. Any modification of a GO will automatically impose the modification of all its images. But most of Magoo applications are interactive and, by definition, the human operator will be responsible for the GO modifications. Magoo copes with this requirement by introducing the dialog objects.

An **MDialog**, DiO, is an object responsible for implementing the application dynamics. Most of the DiOs are responsible for the creation/management of a predefined class of GO. To receive low level events a specialised dialog is required, the **MEventHandler**. For the communication with a X dependent display an **MXtEventHandler** can be used and will be responsible for managing X window dependent events. The communication with a dialog is a two step process. First an object subscribes the service. For example, if a client wants to be informed of any button pressed the following message must be sent:

```
server -> subscribe (this, butdown);
```

as soon as a "button pressed event" is received the client will be informed:

```
client -> receiveEvent (this, curEvent);
```

An event is a Data object of **MEvent** class used both to define a subscription and to store a low level event message.

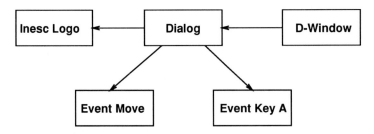

Figure 5: A Dialog managing "Inesc Logo"

Figure 5 shows a dialog responsible for the "Inesc Logo" editing. The editing operations will be based on "Move" and "Key A Press/Release" event types. In the example only "D-Window" is used for event input but the "Inesc Logo" is visible inside three different windows (figure 4).

7   Extending Magoo

It is planned to extend Magoo in different directions:

- to create new Virtual World abstractions, including 4D Objects (3D + t).
- to create new interaction techniques (Dialog classes).

- to encapsulate different graphic kernels (PHIGS++ [van Dam, 1988]).

- to use higher level physical input devices (data glove).

- to encapsulate sound devices.

With a stable model it is also possible to create new interactive tools. In Figure 2 to 5 several steps of an "Inesc Logo" editor were shown, highlighting the usefulness of an interactive application for creating Magoo applications. A similar approach as been followed by apE [Ohio, 1990] but only for Scientific Visualisation (only output).

8   Basic Extensions

Two main Magoo extensions are expected inside the HYPERFACE Project. Firstly a program that manages a Virtual World of new graphic entities. Secondly, an extension which provides new interaction techniques not available in the Motif/HYPERFACE XToolkit [Marshall, 1990] or in the Magoo classes.

To resolve the first requirements it is necessary to specify a new derived class from the GO class. For example to define an Automatic Guided Vehicle (AGV) a Composite Graphic Object with additional information about speed, and direction can be created. T he programmer will write a AGV class derived from the Magoo Composite class and will define the new components (speed, direction). Without any change, the Magoo driver Object will know how to create a lower representation of an AGV, because an AGV *is* a Composite Graphic Object [Casteleiro et al., 1991].

To fulfill the second requirement new dialog object classes will be created. Some support for this task will be available, based on a decentralised version of the GKS input model [Hubner, 1989]. The Dialogue Petri Net, DPN, formalism, proposed in [Bordegoni, 1990] will also be studied.

9   Graphic Extensions

To extend the main concepts to 3D a sub-society of three objects was also created. The display object is linked with objects of the two classes. The driver which is a 3D graphic pipeline and the dialog which supplies 3D locators.

When a 3D graphic object is created and linked to a 3D driver several 2D graphic objects are created and linked to an internal 2D driver that executed the last transformation, creating X-Window dependent graphic data objects. All the repair operations are automatically performed. Methods to change the internal attributes and to control the normalisation, visualisation and projection of 3D data objects were written.

New 3D and 4D Active Graphic Objects will be implemented. New AGO classes will be developed maintaining the main OO-AGES concepts. An encapsulation of both PHIGS+ and PostScript will be developed. Each encapsulation will consist of a driver class (MPsDriver, MPexDriver) and a dialog class, if requested (MPexEventHandler).

10   Conclusions

Magoo is an architecture suitable to fulfill Direct Manipulation requirements both at the application and at the interface level. The object-oriented nature of the architecture allows an easy integration of any kind of output graphic pipeline, interaction techniques and new physical input devices.

A first version of the Magoo Architecture, a prototype, was available before the beginning of the HYPERFACE Project and was used to implement several Man Machine interactive Graphic System based on Direct Manipulation. The key ideas were already experimentally validated but further programmer's feedback is required.

The Magoo architecture as been used to create several complex Direct Manipulation based Interactive Graphic Applications including two 3D editors.

Acknowledgements

This work was partially financed by ESPRIT, under Project HYPERFACE 5391 contract.

References

Bordegoni, M., "Theoretical Study of Hypermedia Technology", Hyperface, 2, 3, 1, December, 1990

Brock, R.W., and Wilkerson, B., "Object-Oriented Design: A Responsibility-Driven Approach", *SIGPLAN Notices*, 24, 10, pp. 71-75, October, 1989

Casteleiro, R.P., Vasconcelos, F., and Gomes, M.R., "An object-oriented Architecture for Interactive Animation and Simulation", In *Eurographics Workshop on Multimedia Systems, Applications and Interaction*, Springer-Verlag, EurographicSeminars Series, 1991

Gomes, M.R., Casteleiro, R.P., Spigelhauer, A., and Vasconcelos, F., "The Magoo Architecture", In *European X-Conference*, pp. 14-20, November, 1991

Gomes, M.R., and Fernandes, J.L., "The OO-AGES Model - An Overview", In *User Interfaces Management and Design*, pp. 307-321, Eds. D.A. Duce, M.R. Gomes, F.R. A. Hopgood, J.R. Lee, EurographicSeminars Series, Springer Verlag, January, 1991

Hubner, W., and Gomes, M.R., "Two Object-Oriented Models to Design Graphical User Interfaces", In *Eurographics'89*, pp. 63-74, Eds. W. Hansmann, F.R. A. Hopgood and W. Strasser, Elsevier Science, September, 1989

ISO, "Information Processing Systems - Computer Graphics", Graphic Kernel System (GKS) functional description, ISO, 7942, 1985

ISO, "Information Processing Systems - Computer Graphics", Programmer's Hierarchical Interactive Graphics Systems (PHIGS) functional description, ISO, 9592, 1988

Marshall, R., "The Hyperface Widget Set", Hyperface, 5, 1, 1, December, 1990

The Ohio Supercomputer Graphics Project, "apE User's Manual", Software for Visualization, Ohio University, Version 2.0, November, 1990

"User Interface Management Systems", Ed. Pfaff, G.E., Springer-Verlag, EurographicSeminars Series, 1985

Scheifler, R., and Gettys, J., "The X-Window System", *Transactions of Graphics*, 15, 2, pp. 75-109, April, 1986

van Dam, A., "PHIGS+ Functional Description Revision 3.0", *Computer Graphics*, 22, July, 1988

9

Architecture and Use of D2M2, the Delft Direct Manipulation Manager

Johan Versendaal, Willem Beekman, Marco Kruit, and Charles van der Mast

A user interface management system is presented based on an object-oriented approach to the design of both the user interface and the application semantics. The data for user interface and application semantics are stored and processed apart. However, the modelling technique is identical for both, using the same tool for semantic data modelling. The modelling technique supports most characteristics of the object-oriented paradigm: objects, classes and inheritance. The diagrams used can describe amongst others the concepts of classification, aggregation, decomposition, generalization, specialization and role attributes. Attributes of objects can be described in property forms. Transition diagrams, including pre- and post-conditions, are applied to specify the interaction possible to the end user. The concepts supported by this tool are described and discussed. This tool as well as the products it can produce are based on a graphical user interface. From these specifications a run time version of the application can be generated. A protocol is used for the communication between application and user interface manager during run time. The features of Delft Direct Manipulation Manager are demonstrated with the design and implementation of a small application with direct manipulation.

1 Introduction

The need to develop and maintain complex information systems has triggered new approaches to system design and development. The object-oriented paradigm addresses some of the main problems with the traditional life-cycle model with distinct phases. Most references, see e.g., [Korson and McGregor, 1990], eliminate the boundaries between phases of the traditional activities analysis, design and implementation. This offers alternatives to the waterfall model because all activities can be integrated within the same conceptual framework. Explicit classification structures during the analysis phase can be the base for a seamless transfer to implementation with object-oriented languages. Moreover, it seems natural that design pieces are closely identified with real-world concepts which they model. This holds both for the development of the semantics and the user interface of an application.

Therefore we insist upon regarding user interface development as a natural part of the application development when done according to the object-oriented paradigm. One of the consequences of this approach is that user interface design should be done in parallel with information analysis and application design. This approach also provides a way to cope with complexity and to reuse objects and methods. Another consequence is that user interface design, like system analysis, should start top-down, using logic diagrams. When more details concerning objects become available during the design, independent interaction tasks to be performed on a predefined set of objects by the end user could be specified. These tasks provide entries for bottom-up rapid prototyping. At this point object-oriented design of the whole system and task-oriented design of the user interface come together. This would give the redemption of the waterfall model. One main purpose of the research described in this paper is to support this top-down approach as the base of a formal description of the design.

Separation of user interface code and application code is important to support maintainable complex information systems. Many generations of solutions have been proposed and implemented in pursuit of this goal [Hix, 1990]. The separation of the user interface and the application can be considered during execution, but also during the development of the software. The user interface can be designed more or less separately, depending on the completeness of separation. This means that human factors specialists are able to bring up their experience more easily within a multi-disciplinary design team. Via this separation, reusability of the user interface components also provides consistency of user interfaces between applications.

To establish the separation of the application and its user interface, user interface management systems (UIMSs) were built. The purpose is to let the UIMS provide an environment for management of user interfaces, both during development and execution. During execution, the application simply sends requests to the UIMS and the UIMS takes care of the interaction process, checks syntax and returns the result of the user's actions to the application. The application does not know how the information is obtained from the user or how its (feedback) information is presented to the user. Therefore the user interface can be changed in appearance as well as in behavior without the application noticing it. The UIMS also encourages the reuse of existing interface modules. This provides a flexible environment for system designers and programmers as well as a comfortable and familiar working environment for the end users.

Delft Direct Manipulation Manager (D2M2) is a UIMS under development at Delft University of Technology. This UIMS manages graphical user interfaces which allow direct manipulation on Unix workstations. D2M2 consists amongst others of D2M2edit and D2M2run, the run-time part of the UIMS. In D2M2 a total separation of user interface and application is the main objective. D2M2 can be positioned within the 4th and the future generations of [Hix, 1990]. It supports maximal separation between both data and processes of user interface and application. At the same time D2M2 tries to integrate the methodologies and concepts of the user interface designer and the software engineer.

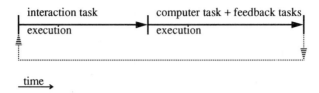

time →

Figure 1: Sequencing in human-computer interaction

2 Concepts

Applications are designed to help users in performing tasks; therefore human-computer interaction should never be an independent goal, but a means to trigger and evaluate computer actions. We define a computer action as the execution of a computer task; the triggering of a computer task is performed by an interaction task; the user can evaluate the results of the computer action by a feedback task.

We are now able to describe the sequencing in human-computer interaction for a large number of applications in terms of interaction tasks, feedback tasks and computer tasks. A user executes an interaction task; the interaction task will trigger a computer task; during and/or just after computer task execution feedback tasks can be executed.

The sequencing in human-computer interaction is depicted in Figure 1. This sequencing is not only valid for command language interaction styles, but also for Direct Manipulation and others.

During interaction task execution so called user interface data (UI data) is consulted and updated. Examples of UI data are windows, icons, scroll bars, text fields, etc. Also during feedback task execution UI data is consulted and updated. During computer task execution application semantics data (AS data) is consulted and updated. In order to achieve independence of user interface and application semantics, UI data is separated from AS data and stored independently. If AS data must be consulted during interaction task execution in order to update the UI data, we say that semantic feedback must be accomplished.

UI data is a collection of instances of UI data types. UI data types are specified by identifying classifications, generalizations and specializations: this specification process is identical to the process of semantic data modelling (see e.g., [Smith and Smith, 1977, Ter Bekke, 1991]). Further, every UI data type has to be specified in a set. Each set can be instantiated, which means that UI data of the set is visualized in a rectangular region (often a window) on screen. If sets are related to one another (e.g., in the case that if a certain set is destroyed, its related set should also be destroyed) aggregation relations are specified between them [Ter Bekke, 1991].

We distinguish interaction sets and feedback sets. During run-time, an instance of an interaction set allows for both user interaction in its rectangular region as well as output of feedback tasks; an instance of a feedback task does not allow user interaction in its rectangular region: only output of feedback tasks can be directed to the rectangular region.

Interaction tasks are specified by transition diagrams [Green, 1986], in which transitions can be traversed when a certain premise, a boolean function which consults UI data, holds. On traversing a transition UI data can be updated, so realizing lexical and syntactic feedback [Foley, et al., 1990]. We specify so-called data transfer with an interaction task in order to send the result of the user interaction to the application. Interaction tasks belong to an entry. Not the name of an interaction task, but its entry name is known to the application. If different interaction tasks produce the same data to be sent by the data transfer, we can group these tasks in the same entry. As a consequence the application could receive, during run-time, data from the user, not knowing what interaction task it came from; only knowing that it came from a certain entry. Obviously, this construction supports the emphasis on the separation of user interface and application.

Feedback tasks are specified by functions which consult and update UI data. AS data are specified by identifying AS data types, generalizations, specializations, aggregations, decompositions and attribute identification like in semantic modelling (see e.g., [Smith and Smith, 1977]). We specify computer tasks by programming code which consults and updates AS data. We support semantic feedback by semantic feedback functions which consult AS data.

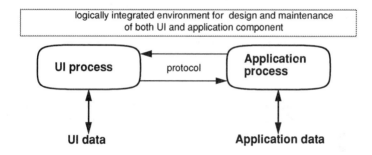

Figure 2: Separation of processes and data, the main goal of D2M2

Concluding, we can summarize that as a goal for this research we have chosen to develop concepts and architecture which separate the components "UI" and "application" completely, both for design and at run-time. And, for run-time a communication protocol has to be defined between both components which also supports semantic feedback. While the design process and the storage of both components are separated, at the same time the developing environment supporting this architecture should be suitable for multidisciplinary design teams of UI designers and software developers (see Figure 2).

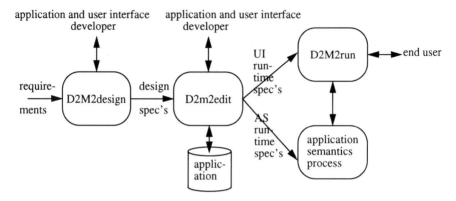

Figure 3: The main components of D2M2 and its relations

3 Architecture

D2M2 is a tool set which allows for designing, implementing, interpretation and maintaining applications with a separated user interface. The interpreting part of D2M2 is D2M2run; it executes the user interface by interpreting the UI data and takes care of the communication with the application semantics. In principle, D2M2run can manage the user interface of more than one application at the same time. The implementation and maintainence part of D2M2 is the tool D2M2edit; it allows for defining and editing of both the user interface (consisting of UI data, sets, feedback tasks and interaction tasks) as well as the application semantics (consisting of AS data, computer tasks and semantic feedback functions). The design part (D2M2design), not discussed further in this article, allows for designing the user interface and the application semantics from formal requirements according to certain methods and techniques. In Figure 3 the relations between D2M2design, D2M2edit, D2M2run and their environment is depicted.

3.1 D2M2edit

The main functions D2M2edit provides for can be summed up as follows:

- *Specification of programs*
  The major part of D2M2edit; this includes specification of the user interface elements, the application elements and the communication between these two in the run-time environment.

- *Management of reusable interface components*
  Through extensive reuse of user interface components from previous projects, substantial savings in designing, building, testing and training can be made. D2M2edit offers a user interface library for storage and retrieval of user interface elements.

- *Support for documentation and administrative tasks*
  By providing simple and efficient documentation facilities, concise and fault-

less reports can be generated, while support for project management, like authorization, can ease administration.

- *Conversion of designer specifications to run-time specifications*
  To be able to run an application, specified with D2M2edit, these designer specifications can be transformed to specifications which can be interpreted by the D2M2run run-time environment.

Since D2M2edit will frequently be used by non-programming designers and administrators, it offers a graphical interface, based on Sun's OPEN LOOK standard [Sun, 1989]. By using a mouse to manipulate windows, buttons, menus, etc. and only requiring the keyboard when strictly necessary, the environment is easy to learn and use for every kind of user.

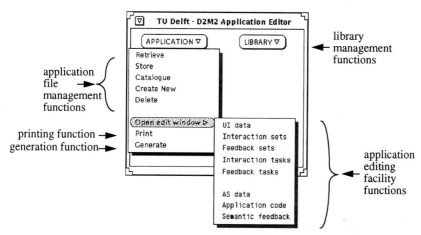

Figure 4: Main command window of D2M2edit with selected submenu "Open edit window" containing several "views" on the application

The main functions of D2M2edit are shown in the editor window after starting up. Figure 4 depicts the editor window with the major pull down menus to activate the main functions of D2M2edit.

One can choose between library maintenance and application (project) management. Only the latter will be presented, for this is the prime function of the development environment. Selecting application management brings up its menu, offering:

- Application file management, which comprises retrieval, storage, cataloging, creation and deletion of applications under implementation.

- Application editing facilities, the creation and manipulation of the user interface and application elements through the use of "views" (see below).

- Printing of documentation of the application being edited.

- Generation of run-time specifications from the user interface and application designer specifications.

Of these, the application editing best shows the graphical interactive character of D2M2edit. As explained before, a set of specifications under D2M2 consists of user interface elements (the UI data types, interaction sets, feedback sets, interaction tasks and feedback tasks) and application elements (AS data types, application code and semantic feedback functions), together with the parts required for communication (entries to group interaction tasks, data transfer code to return results of interactions and creation code for instantiation of an interaction or feedback set). All these can be edited, to which end several views are available. A view displays a small portion of the specifications of one type of element, and allows easy and manageable creation and manipulation of user interface and application, giving all information required and retaining consistency without bothering the designer with irrelevant details or distracting relationships.

An example of such a view is the "UI data type view". Through such a view, the designer can specify the hierarchy of data types comprising the interface and their behavior. Since D2M2 is based on semantic data modelling the specification of the data types is realized with a graphical interpretation of this model [Ter Bekke, 1991]. The basic UI data types, offered by the relevant window manager and available through the built-in library, are always present and called "native" types. A special UI data type "native" is ever present in an application: every UI data type directly related to the window manager is directly or indirectly derived from "native" by specialization, inheriting its basic properties and methods, but adding some of its own. UI data types not related to the window manager are specializations of the ever present UI data type "own".

Graphically, in this view two objects can be distinguished: UI data types, represented by labeled rectangles, and specialization relationships, shown as labeled lines connecting the UI data types. Figure 5 depicts the way UI data types and their relationships are represented in D2M2edit.

Buttons in the view window are used to *Add* new types, *Include* types created earlier, but not visible in this view, *Retrieve* types from a library and *Derive* a subtype (i.e., create a specialization between types). These are all functions that place data types in the view. All other functions to be performed on these graphical objects are invoked through manipulation of the objects themselves, as dictated by the concept of direct manipulation interaction. They fall into two categories: functions which merely change the appearance of the view and functions changing the UI data type specifications.

In the first category are, for example, actions to move objects around the view's graphics canvas by dragging (conforming to the OPEN LOOK standard), automatically redrawing all connected objects. Another feature of D2M2edit which serves to keep the views as clear as possible is the "expanding" of graphical data types. When an existing UI data type is added to a view, it probably has several relationships with other types. To show these as well would result in a cascade of inclusions, cluttering up the display. Only showing the single type would misinform the designer. D2M2edit displays such a type as a double-edged rectangle (see UI data type "canvas" in Figure 5). When the designer requires more information the type

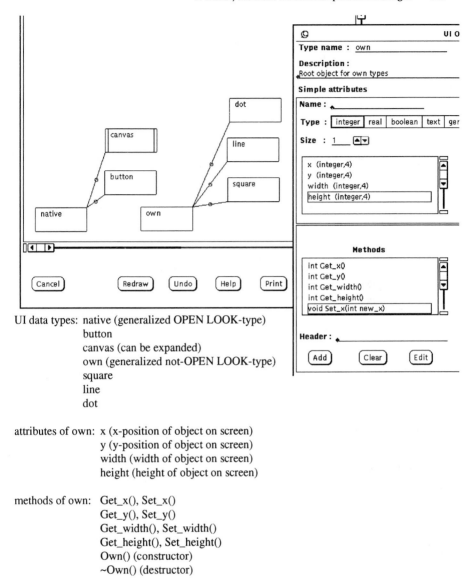

UI data types: native (generalized OPEN LOOK-type)
button
canvas (can be expanded)
own (generalized not-OPEN LOOK-type)
square
line
dot

attributes of own: x (x-position of object on screen)
y (y-position of object on screen)
width (width of object on screen)
height (height of object on screen)

methods of own: Get_x(), Set_x()
Get_y(), Set_y()
Get_width(), Set_width()
Get_height(), Set_height()
Own() (constructor)
~Own() (destructor)

Figure 5: Snapshot of UI data view and property window of D2M2edit

can be "expanded", causing D2M2edit to arrange all directly related types in the view as well.

The second category of functions actually edits the specifications of the UI data types. Examples are: copying and deleting types (with their connected relationships) and editing the properties of data types and specializations. A special property window is placed on screen when the designer clicks on the object, displaying all properties and allowing them to be edited. E.g., in the case of UI data types there are the name, description, attributes (each with a name, data type and size) and methods (each with a return type, parameter list and body). In Figure 5 a snapshot of D2M2edit of the UI data property window is depicted.

Analogous to the previous view, there are the (interaction and feedback) "set views". These allow the designer to create or edit interaction sets and feedback sets. A set consists of a collection of UI data types created earlier on or retrieved from the library, and parent-child relationships between some of these types, indicating their hierarchy when used together in an application. A child is always displayed inside its parent.

Again, the types are displayed as rectangles, while the relationships are represented by connecting lines. Within a set, no changes can be made to the actual data types used; this must be done in UI data type views.

The third view of interest is the "interaction task view". After having selected an interaction set, the designer can create or edit an interaction task. Such a task is graphically displayed as a state-transition diagram, where one creates and places the states (circles) and the connecting transitions (directed arcs). Pre- and post-conditions for the transitions are regarded as their properties, and so can be edited through a property window. The layout of the diagram can simply be changed by moving the graphical objects. Functions are furthermore provided to specify data transfer code and the entry to which this task belongs, and to check the validity of the transition diagram (determinism, islands, initial/final states, etc.).

The above represents a brief impression of part of the facilities offered by D2M2edit. Consistent use of intuitive interaction mechanisms and graphical displays makes it likely that D2M2edit is a suitable environment, in particular for user interface designers, not accustomed to heavily text-based programming environments [Versendaal, 1991].

3.2 D2M2run

D2M2run manages the user interface for the application during run-time. We recall that the static part of the user interface is implemented as a semantic data model in D2M2edit. The dynamic part of the user interface is implemented as state transition diagrams. The static part is translated into C++-classes, which can be interpreted by D2M2run directly; state transition diagrams are processed by D2M2run, according to the user input and pre- and post-conditions within the application.

During run-time, D2M2run and the application communicate with each other using a special protocol. This protocol allows the application to specify the type of user interface by enabling entries. After this enabling D2M2run activates the user interface and starts waiting for the user input. Details of the protocol and the implementation are described in [Kruit, 1990].

During the human-computer interaction, D2M2run handles all input and output until the user completes a command or data input sequence. D2M2run takes care of lexical, syntactic and semantic feedback [Foley, et al., 1990]. However, when during run-time, D2M2run needs information from the application semantics in order to produce semantic feedback, it sends a request to the application to give it the required information. It cannot access the application semantics data itself.

When the user completes an input sequence, D2M2run notifies the application by telling it what type of input has been retrieved from the user, via the entry name, along with the appropriate data. The application interprets the input sequence and executes a relevant computer task; during and after computer task execution requests for feedback task execution can be sent. At no time does either the application semantics process or D2M2run have access to each other's process data.

Thus, the application requests D2M2run to manage its user interface of which it only knows its functionality. D2M2run only manages the user interface as it was told to do by the specifications in D2M2edit, sending complete input sequences, commands and/or input data and leaving the interpretation to the application. The application does not know *how* the input was retrieved from the user and *how* its output and feedback is presented to the user, while D2M2run does not know what the semantic meaning of the data is which it sends and what the objects it manages mean to the user or the application. The only thing they know is how to communicate with one another.

Since the communication channel can vary from a local message passing mechanism to a satellite connection, D2M2run and the application semantics process may run on any machine. As long as they use the protocol they can communicate, thus allowing D2M2run to handle the application's user interface.

4   Example

The design (with D2M2design) of an application roughly consists of three (related) steps. The first step is to determine the functionality of the application and the application data types. The second step is to determine what functional regions the user interface of an application needs and what commands the user can give. The third step is to precisely determine the user interface data types and lay-outs. As an example of these steps we present a simple file manager.

The file manager must perform the following commands:

1. a group of selected files may be deleted;

2. a file may be copied to another file or directory;

3. a group of selected files may be copied to another directory;

4. the working directory may be changed;

5. the file manager can be quitted.

These requirements result, via D2M2design, in the specifications of the application semantics data types (see Figure 6) and the functional region (interaction set) (see Figure 7). They are implemented in D2M2edit.

The user can change the working directory (requirement 4) by clicking a *ui_dir* object of the file manager. The transition diagram for this interaction task is, shown

AS data types: dir (directory in file system)
                   file (file in file system)

Figure 6: Application semantics data types of file manager

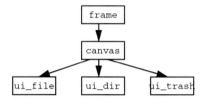

Figure 7: UI data types and relations in the one and only interaction set of the file manager

in Figure 8. The lay-out of the file manager as produced by D2M2run is shown in Figure 9.

t0: button clicked on ui_dir

Figure 8: Button clicked on ui_dir

The implementation presented results in the following entry identifications, which are the identifiers with which the application can activate the commands mentioned above and with which D2M2run can indicate what command the user has given.

- FM_ENTRY_FILES_DELETE
- FM_ENTRY_FILES_COPY
- FM_ENTRY_DIR_CHANGE
- FM_ENTRY_QUIT

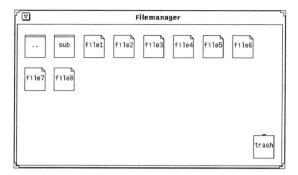

Figure 9: Lay-out of the file manager as produced by D2M2run

Notice that the second and third command (of the requirement list) are joined into one entry identification, since they are semantically the same. In the second command the group simply consists of one file. The application must have the possibility to add instances of user interface data types to the functional region, delete them and tell D2M2run it is terminating. To establish that, the following feedback task identifiers in D2M2run can be distinguished:

- FM_CREATE_UI_FILE

- FM_CREATE_UI_DIR

- FM_DELETE_UI_FILE

- FM_DELETE_UI_DIR

- FM_DELETE_ALL

- FM_QUIT

Of course the file manager must have a functional region in which the instances of user interface data types representing files and directories are placed and manipulated by the user. The function region is placed within a frame. The identifier in D2M2run for this functional region is:

- FILEMANAGER

These are all identifiers needed for the communication between the file manager application and D2M2run.

5 Conclusions

D2M2 aims to separate the user interface data (UI data) and the application semantics data (AS data). This separation proved possible during run-time using a well defined protocol for triggering and communication at the technical level. Another advantage of separation is that, during design, human factors specialists and information engineers can focus on their own view and expertise. By using the same object-oriented modelling paradigm the understanding and the co-operation within a multidisciplinary design team may be improved. An important result may be that not only creation of some kinds of interfaces will be shortened dramatically but that the creation of the whole application including user interface and application semantics will become more efficient. Moreover, D2M2 provides a basis to alter the user interface in a rather easy way, because the user interface is not highly intermingled with the application semantics. As long as the protocol between user interface and application are obeyed, user interface changes do not affect the application semantics.

Currently some realistic applications with graphical user interface are being designed in order to explore these advantages [Versendaal, 1991]. Later, controlled experiments are needed to prove this hypothesis on object-oriented design in different application domains. The current version of D2M2 supports only some of the trajectory during the design and maintenance of applications and their user interface. Future research is planned for prototyping the lay-out and generating more efficient run-time code.

References

Foley, J.D., Van Dam, A., Feiner, S.K. and Hughes, J.F. (1990). *Computer Graphics*, Addison-Wesley, Reading, MA, 1990.

Green, M., (1986). A Survey of Three Dialogue Models. *ACM Transactions on Graphics,*, 5(3):244 – 275.

Hix, D., (1990). Generations of User Interface Management Systems. *IEEE Software*, 7(5):77 – 87.

Korson, T. and McGregor, J.D., (1990). Understanding Object-Oriented: a Unifying Paradigm. *Communications of the ACM*, 33(9):40 – 60.

Kruit, M.. (1990). *D2M2run*, Master's Thesis Report, Faculty of Technical Mathematics and Informatics, Delft University of Technology, Delft, The Netherlands.

Smith, J.M. and Smith, D.C.P. (1977). Database Abstractions: Aggregation and Generalization. *ACM Transactions on Database Systems*, 2(2):105 – 133.

Sun Microsystems, OPEN LOOK Graphical User Interface Functional Description, Sun Microsystems, August 1989.

Ter Bekke, J.H., (1991). *Semantic Data Modelling in Relational Environments*, Academic Dissertation, Delft University of Technology, Delft, The Netherlands.

Versendaal, J.M., (1991). *Separation of the User Interface and Application*, Academic Dissertation, Delft University of Technology, Delft, The Netherlands.

Appendix

Semantic Data Modelling (for an extensive discussion see (Ter Bekke, 1991)) Semantic data modelling is a fairly new way of structuring and manipulating data, overcoming lots of problems encountered in other data models such as the relation model. In semantic data models identification and properties of data types are strictly separated. The model is based on the semantics of the type and their relations: they reflect the reality as it is. No real transformation is necessary, no rules have to be satisfied. All that is needed is careful representation of reality. Ambiguities and inconsistencies are then excluded.

In semantic models a data type can be represented by a rectangle with its name inside (see Figure 10).

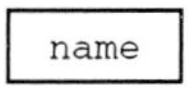

$$\boxed{\text{name}}$$

Figure 10: A representation of a data type in a semantic model

ABSTRACTIONS
The semantic data model knows just two abstractions which have a very strong relation with natural languages. They correspond with the two verbs to have and to be. Every object in reality can be described by telling what it has and what it is. The designers of databases only have to describe reality this way. In database design we distinguish: classification, aggregation and generalization.

CLASSIFICATION
Classification is cutting reality up in properties of types. For instance "name" and "number" are classifications. They simply state the existence of certain properties and lack the relation between data. They represent data, not information.

AGGREGATION
Aggregation is defined as the collection of certain properties into a type. Such a type can also be a property of another type. The name of the type represents the relation of the properties in reality. So an aggregation contains data and forms information. For example, "name" and "number could be aggregated into "directory entry" (see Figure 11). Aggregations can be expressed by the verb to have: a 'directory entry" has a "name" and a "number". In the semantic data model aggregations are represented by connecting the lower edge of the aggregating type with the upper edges of the aggregated types.

Name and number are definite properties of entry: every entry has exactly one name and one number. Entry is a variable property of name and number: both name and number can belong to any number of entries. Aggregation also has a reverse. The description of a type by a collection of properties is called "decomposition". The type "entry" can be decomposed into "name" and "number".

GENERALIZATION
Lots of problems can be described just with aggregations. However, aggregations

type entry = name, number

Figure 11: Example of an aggregation-decomposition

alone may not do the job. For instance, "name", "address" and "phonenumber" could be aggregated into a type called "person". In an organization, however, a person could be an employee or a client. Employees could have properties that client do not have, like "salary" and "function". Clients could have properties like "client number" and "credit". The model would be unnecessary complex when only aggregations would be used: every aggregation 'person" has, will be duplicated. Trouble really emerges when "person" is a property of another type. That type would have both "client" and 'employee" as a property, while these types are mutual exclusive. A person is either a client or an employee.

In reality a client is a person and an employee is a person. They inherit the properties of person. In the semantic data model this relation is called generalization. Generalization can be defined as the collection of common properties from different types into one new type. The type "person" is a generalization of "employee" and "client". These new types are specializations of the type "person". Specialization is the reverse of generalization.

In the type definition the generalization is placed between brackets. In the semantic data model a specialization is represented by a connection of an upper corner of the generalized data type with a lower corner of the specialized data type.

The specializations of person as shown in Figure 12 mutually exclude each other: a person is either an employee or a client. If they could be both, each specialization should have a connection with person. Mutually excluding specializations are stacked upon each other as in Figure 12.

```
type person = name, address, phonenumber
type employee = [person], salary, function
type client = [person], client_number, credit
```

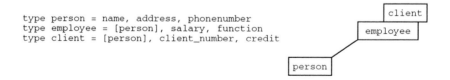

Figure 12: Example of a generalization-specialization

INTEGRITY RULES
Models need a fixed interpretation. To achieve this there are integrity rules to be upheld. Semantic data models have two integrity rules, which do not have to be specified separately. Ter Bekke (1991) distinguishes:

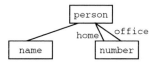

Figure 13: Example of role attributes

- Relatability: every property that occurs in a type definition is related to exactly one type with the same name. Every type may correspond with several properties.

- Reversibility: every type definition is unique. There are no different type definitions having the same name or having the same collection of properties.

ROLE ATTRIBUTES

Role attributes are used when a type has more than one attribute of the same type and when a type is a generalization of non-mutual excluding types. When a type definition contains two properties of the same type, role attributes are used to distinguish them. Role attributes can be identified by a prefix followed by an underscore. For instance, when a person has two phonenumbers, one of his office and one of his home, the roles may be "home" and "office":

type person = name, home_number, office_number

These roles are added to the model by placing them near the connection (see Figure 13).

Role attributes may also be used to distinguish between mutual exclusive and non-mutual exclusive specializations. A group of specializations which are mutual exclusive have the same role. Specializations of different groups have different roles.

Part IV

Rendering

10

An Object-Oriented Testbed for Global Illumination

Shenchang Eric Chen, Kenneth Turkowski, and Douglass Turner

Global illumination rendering involves the simulation of light interreflections between emitting and reflecting surfaces. Accounting for global illumination is necessary in the quest to generate images indistinguishable from real photographs. However, computing global illumination effects is a difficult problem and no algorithm published so far is capable of simulating all the effects in a reasonable amount of time. In this paper, we present a research testbed designed to facilitate experimentation on new global illumination algorithms. The testbed is object-oriented and encapsulates the basic components of rendering into classes that can be derived and overridden easily. The testbed allows new geometry, shading methods and display architecture to be added orthogonally. We have implemented a number of new rendering algorithms with the testbed and results are demonstrated.

1   Introduction

Realistic image synthesis is the process of creating computer synthesized images with the goal to make the images indistinguishable from real photographs. The process involves the simulation of light interacting between the surfaces in an imaginary scene. This type of image synthesis is usually referred to as the rendering of "global illumination", because the illumination of a surface cannot be determined alone without knowing the illumination and geometry of the other surfaces. Well known examples of global illumination effects include shadows, specular reflection and refraction, etc. Less well known examples are color bleeding and caustic effects.

Global illumination is generally much more expensive to compute than the "local illumination" effects, which only involve the interaction between light sources and the illuminated surface. However, global illumination is necessary in creating realistic images. Traditionally, global illumination effects are computed with renderers specialized in some of the effects, such as ray tracing for shadows, specular reflection and refraction, and radiosity for color bleeding. In most cases, these specialized renderers are not capable of rendering all the effects. In fact, the problem of computing global illumination is an on-going research area that has received much attention in recent years. To facilitate the research and development of new rendering algorithms, we present an object-oriented rendering testbed designed with this purpose in mind.

Although rendering systems are generally complex, they all contain three basic components: geometry, display architecture and shading methods. Geometry refers to geometrical primitives that a renderer can handle directly. Many renderers require diverse primitives to be converted to a common representation such as polygons before they can be rendered. The display architecture includes the projection and hidden surface algorithm that a renderer uses to display a scene from a camera setting. Commonly used display algorithms include z-buffer [Catmull, 1974] and scan-line [Watkins, 1970] methods. Ray tracing also can be used as visible surface determination method. Shading methods include illumination models that a renderer uses to compute the intensity at a point in space. Simple shading models such as Gouraud [Gouraud, 1971] and Phong [Phong, 1975] only need information about the light sources and the point to be shaded. Therefore, they are not capable of generating shadows or simulating materials such as glass. More sophisticated shading models such as ray tracing [Whitted, 1980] allows a wider range of materials to be simulated more realistically.

Since the above components are fundamental to most rendering research, we encapsulate them into three basic object classes in our testbed. The *Geometry* class serves as the base class from which all the renderable geometry is derived. All the geometry objects are parametrizable and have some common operations such as geometrical transformation and responding to geometry queries, etc. The *Scene* class encapsulates the display architecture and contains all the global information such as cameras, lights and all the renderable geometry. The Scene is the driving force of the renderer. The *Shader* class encapsulates the materials and the shading models. The common operation of shaders is to evaluate the intensity at a point. By deriving and overriding these classes, different renderers or rendering styles can be developed and experimented with quickly.

Most previously published rendering testbeds are more limited than ours in the range of rendering properties that can be experimented with. Whitted and Weimer presented a software testbed designed for experimenting with shaders and geometry in a generalized polygon scan converter [Whitted and Weimer, 1981]. Hall and Greenberg presented a testbed which applied an improved illumination model to a fixed set of geometry [Hall and Greenberg, 1983]. Although the pictures created by them were realistic at the time, the testbed was not flexible enough to allow new algorithms to be built upon because the illumination model and geometry were fixed. Grant et. al. [Grant et al., 1986] addressed the problem of displaying diverse types of geometry in an object-oriented system. In their design, each geometry and its derived classes know how to subdivide themselves into polygons that can be displayed. The shading and global illumination problem was not addressed. Potmesil and Hoffert presented a set of software tools which act as UNIX filters and can be combined together in a pipe sequence [Potmesil and Hoffert, 1987]. The pipe is unidirectional and is not quite suitable for global illumination computation, which is often iterative. Nadas and Fournier extended the pipe to a more general directed acyclic data flow system [Nadas and Fournier, 1987]. The data flow system provides a nice user interface to perform dynamic binding of display processes. However, it is still not appropriate to prototype global illumination algorithms because of its acyclic nature. The Reyes image rendering architecture presented by Cook et. al. is not really a rendering testbed[Cook et al., 1987]. However, its use of programmable shaders (i.e., shade tree [Cook, 1987]) makes it flexible enough to incorporate new shading algorithms. The disadvantage of Reyes' approach is that it is a fixed display architecture and requires all the geometrical primitives to be reduced to micropolygons. Therefore, algorithms such as radiosity are very hard to implement in this framework.

In the following sections, we present in details the basic object classes in our testbed. Example applications of the testbed in ray tracing and radiosity research are also illustrated.

2   Class Overview

The object-oriented terminologies we use throughout the paper are consistent with those in [Stroustrup, 1987]. *Class* is an abstract data type that contains both data and functions that operate on the data. Classes can be *derived* to create new classes that *inherit* the properties of the parent classes. The derived classes can modify the parent classes by defining new functions or *overriding* the parent's functions. *Object* is an instance of a class (i.e., we also use *object* to refer to the geometrical entities that comprise a 3D world. The different usage should be obvious from the context). *Virtual functions* allow functions to be called without type information. They enable objects of various types to be treated in a uniform manner.

A basic object in our testbed is Scene. The Scene object is the global structure that organizes the 3D world. It includes a place to store the resulting image, the camera, the lights and the *Renderable* objects. All of the elements of the Scene are accessible to any other objects.

Each Renderable object contains instances of two objects: Geometry and Shader. Geometry describes the shape of a geometrical entity. Shader describes how light interacts with the entity. The communication between Shader and Geometry is accomplished through *Neighborhood*, an abstraction of the differential geometry at a point on the entity (e.g., local normal or tangent vectors).

2.1   Geometry

It is desirable to support a variety of geometrical primitives such as polygons, quadrics, and patches, and to accommodate new ones in an orthogonal manner. The essential requirements of a geometrical primitive were abstracted into the base class Geometry, which are listed below:

- To transform the geometry (rotate, scale, translate).

- To determine rough spatial bounds (box, sphere, etc.).

- To tessellate into a mesh of polygons.

- To evaluate differential properties (normal, curvature, etc.) at a point.

- To intersect with a ray.

- To classify a point (in, out) with respect to the surface.

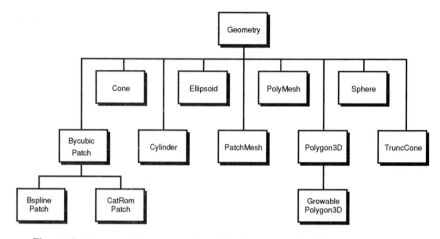

Figure 1: The current implementation of the Geometry class hierarchy

Some of these functions can be supplied directly by the base class Geometry. For example, many geometrical primitives are represented by a set of points, and transformations on those points yields a similar transformation of the geometrical primitive. The *bounding volume* of a set of points sometimes also bounds a geometrical primitive defined by those points (e.g. polygon, B- spline surface). Similarly, if surfaces are parametrized by ($0 \leq 1u \leq q$ and $0 \leq v \leq q 1$), then a generic tessellation procedure need only evaluate (x, y, z) at a grid of points (u, v). The Geometry class provides these capabilities as a default. These and other methods of Geometry are virtual, however, so that subclasses can override them if the assumptions donUt hold true.

Each primitive needs to implement its own ray-intersection routine. It is up to the primitive to cache any special information that may accelerate this process.

With a closed surface, a point is classified as either inside or outside the surface. For an open surface, the point is either on one side or another of the extension of the surface. This capability is useful for spatial decomposition, which can in turn accelerate global illumination computations.

The current Geometry class hierarchy is shown in Figure 1.

For shading purposes, it suffices to approximate geometry at a point to first or second order, i.e. normal, derivatives, curvature. Shaders can be easily decoupled from Geometry by communicating through a Neighborhood object. Each geometrical primitive can evaluate its Neighborhood, which is described in more details in the next section.

2.2   Neighborhood

A point on a surface can either be represented in the world space (x, y, z) or the parametric space (u, v). A sphere, for example, can be parametrized in terms of two angles θ and ϕ:

x = cos θ sin ϕ, y = sin θ sin ϕ, z = cos ϕ

The inverse parametrization, (x, y, z) → (θ, φ), is a projection (i.e., taking a 3-space point onto the parametric space), which is well-defined when the point is on the surface, and hopefully tolerant when the point is not exactly on the surface. A geometrical primitive is able to convert back and forth between these 2- and 3-dimensional spaces.

Once a function is established, we can ask about derivatives. The first partial derivatives, $\delta(x,y,z)/\delta(u,v)$, otherwise known as tangent vectors, can be useful for anisotropic shading [blinn, 1978] and bump mapping [Kajiya, 1985]. The cross product of the partials yields a normal. The first partials can be combined into a metric tensor, which can be used to measure length and area on a surface. The second partial derivatives can be combined into a curvature tensor, which is useful for anti-aliasing in reflection mapping [Blinn and Newell, 1976] and pencil tracing [Shinya et al., 1987]. Each geometrical primitive is able to calculate its first and second partial derivatives; the Neighborhood object itself can compute the metric and curvature tensors if necessary.

A point on a surface, along with its tangents and normal, establishes a coordinate frame. The Neighborhood object can convert between this frame and others. For example, it can project a pixel onto a surface, and measure its area in parametric units for anti-aliasing texture maps.

2.3 Shader

Our approach to shading is to hide in the shader the functionality that traditionally resides in the renderer, such as ray tracing, radiosity and caustic computation. We believe this approach is both flexible and powerful because it separates the shading computation from the rest of the rendering.

The main difference between our shaders and the shade trees [Cook, 1987] used in Reyes [Cook et al., 1987] and RenderMan [Upstill, 1990] is that our shaders are bidirectional. They not only can evaluate the intensity at a point on a surface but also can deposit energy to a surface. The Shader class has two virtual functions: *Collect* and *Deposit*. Collect takes a Neighborhood of a point on a surface, evaluates the intensity at that point and returns the intensity to the caller. The shader can be evaluated recursively to yield ray tracing style of rendering. Deposit performs the reciprocal operation to Collect. Deposit takes an incoming energy and direction, deposits some of the energy to the surface and reflects the rest of the energy to the outgoing directions based on the reflectance function of the surface. The function can be evaluated recursively to yield "backward ray tracing" style of rendering [Arvo, 1986] to compute caustic effects by tracing rays from the light.

Shaders are called when evaluating intensity or depositing energy is necessary. A typical scenario of shader invocation follows:

- Determine the nearest entity at a sample on an image plane. This could be done via ray casting, z-buffer scan conversion, or some other method that is decided by the Scene class. Note that the image plane could be associated either with the eye or with a light in the case of backward ray tracing.

- Load a Neighborhood object with relevant information by querying the Geometry object associated with the nearest entity.

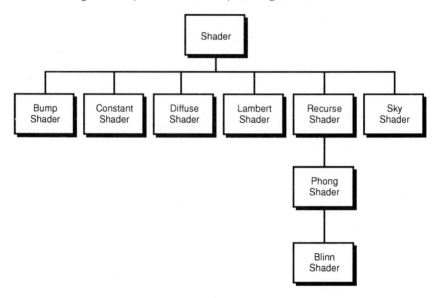

Figure 2: The current implementation of the Shader class hierarchy

- Pass the Neighborhood object to the Shader object associated with the nearest entity. Call the Collect method of the Shader if the intent is to compute reflected intensity or the Deposit method if the intent is to deposit energy on a surface.

We have implemented some basic shading models such as Phong [Phong, 1975] and Blinn [Blinn, 1977]. Both tabular or procedural texture mapping can be accommodated with our shaders. We also have a recursive shader which basically implements a ray tracer. The current shader hierarchy is shown in Figure 2.

We have developed an interpretive object-based language that allows users to write expressions to create shaders [Turner, 1991].

2.4   Scene

The Scene class has two purposes. First, it bundles all the global information into an object accessible to any other object. The global information is briefly listed below:

- Camera: the viewing parameters and transformation between world and view space.

- Buffer: the place to hold the resulting image. It could contain color, z, or any other values that the renderer generates.

- Renderables: the objects that comprise the scene.

- Lights: the light sources illuminating the scene. The Light class has a virtual function *GetIntensity*, which returns the intensity of the light arriving at a

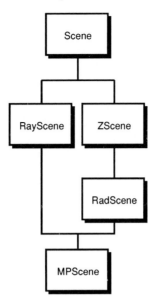

Figure 3: The current implementation of the Scene class hierarchy

point in space. The Light also contains a Renderable, which allows the light to be visible.

Second, it encapsulates the display architecture in it. Each Scene object has a virtual function *Render*. The Render function traverses all the Renderables and projects them onto the image plane. For each visible Renderable on the image plane, it calls the shader in the Renderable to collect or deposit energy. A derived class of Scene can override the Render function to implement different hidden surface or display methods. Figure 3 shows the current Scene class hierarchy. The *ZScene* class implements a z-buffer type method. The *RayScene* and *RadScene* classes encapsulate the ray tracing and the progressive radiosity methods [Cohen et al., 1988] respectively. Note that since we already can implement a ray tracer in a shader, RayScene mainly refers to using ray casting to perform the visibility calculation (i.e., shooting rays from the eye to see which object is visible). Conversely, a ZScene can generate a ray- traced image by simply invoking a recursive ray tracing shader (i.e., this approach is similar to using item buffer preprocessing for ray tracing [Weghorst et al., 1984]). A multi-pass rendering approach [Chen et al., 1991] which combines ray tracing, caustics tracing and progressive radiosity was implemented in the *MPScene* class.

We have implemented various renderers which perform z-buffer, ray tracing and radiosity using the testbed. A user of the renderer will simply need to set up a scene and call the Render method of the scene as demonstrated in the following C++ style pseudo code.

```
ARayTracer()
{
    Scene* aRayScene = new RayScene;
    // construct the scene (camera, renderables,
    // lights, etc.) from a file
    aRayScene->Read(afile);
    aRayScene->Render();
}
```

The Render method of a typical ray tracer implemented in our testbed looks like
the following:

```
RayScene:Render()
{
    for each pixel in Buffer
    {
        // find the nearst Renderable and Neighborhood
        construct a ray from the eye to the pixel;
        for each Renderable in the scene
        {
            Renderable->Geometry->Intersect(ray);
            if Renderable is the nearest intersection so far
            {
                nearestRenderable=Renderable;
                nearestNeighborhood=Renderable->Geometry->Neighborhood();
            }
        }

        // evaluate the intensity at the nearest intersection
        intensity =
            nearestRenderable->Shader->Collect(nearestNeighborhood);
        Buffer[pixel] = intensity;
    }
}
```

For a user who wants to implement a new renderer, s/he will need to derive from
the Scene class or any of its derived classes and override the Render method:

```
ANewRenderer: public Scene()
{
    public:
    virtual void Render();
}

ANewRenderer::Render()
{
    // implement the renderer here
}
```

Since the functionality to access the renderables, lights and image etc., is inherited
in the derived classes, the user can concentrate on implementing the difference
between the derived class and the base class. Similarly, we can create new Geometry
or Shader classes by deriving and overriding.

Figure 4 shows an image created from our multi-pass renderer MPScene. The color bleeding, caustics, shadows, specular reflection and refraction effects in the image were computed in separate passes. The rendering process involved ray tracing from the light as well as from the eye. A radiosity pass was used to compute the radiosity of each surface and created a radiosity map for each of the surfaces. The radiosity maps provided an accurate approximation to the diffuse interreflection. They were used to replace the constant ambient term that most shading models use. A caustic pass was used to create a caustic map for each surface by tracing rays from the lights to the specular surface. The rays stopped at diffuse surface and deposited energy to the caustic maps. The final pass involved ray tracing from the eye to create an image. A special kind of shader which knows how to obtain radiosity and caustic from the maps was used to perform the final shading. Since MPScene was derived from RadScene and RayScene, the functions to shoot rays and compute radiosity were inherited. The following pseudo code shows the process. The same process was used to compute Figure 5, which shows a shadow of a stick created by a wall acting as a secondary light sources. Details about the multi- pass rendering can be found in [Chen et al., 1991].

```
MPScene::Render()
{
    // the radiosity pass: it computes a radiosity map for
    // each surface
    RadScene::Render();

    // caustic pass: it computes a caustic map for each surface by
    // shooting rays from the lights to specular surfaces. The rays
    // stop at diffuse surfaces
    for each light
    {
        set camera at light;
        for each direction from the light to the scene
        {
            find the nearestRenderable and
            nearestGeometry as in RayScene;
            nearestRenderable->Shader->Deposit(nearestNeighborhood);
        }
    }

    // ray tracing pass: it computes the final image
    // the shaders know how to get the caustic and radiosity
    // from the maps
    set camera at eye;
    RayScene::Render();
}
```

3 Conclusions and Future Directions

We have presented a flexible rendering testbed designed for experimenting with global illumination algorithms. The testbed is composed of three basic classes: Geometry, Shader and Scene. They correspond to the basic components in most renderers. By deriving and overriding the classes, different rendering components can be modified orthogonally.

The main advantage of our testbed is that it allows fast prototyping of new rendering capabilities. For example, adding a new primitive to a renderer is usually considered a major task. In our testbed, it only requires overriding some functions in the Geometry class. The same is true for adding new shaders or display methods. The concept of bi-directional shaders proves to be very useful in exploring different styles of rendering.

We have both compiled and interpretive shaders. The compiled shaders are the basic nodes of hierarchical shaders that can be specified with an interpretive language. This approach gives us both flexibility and performance. Work is underway to build a graphical shader editor and a shader library. Dynamic linking of the shaders is also desirable in the future.

Further research is required to solve the problem of *context sensitive* shaders. Some shaders are context sensitive because they expect specific global scene data to exist in the scene(e.g., the spatial decomposition data for a ray tracing shader). This kind of shaders makes the scene and the shaders inter- dependent on each other.

Currently, only parametrizable primitives are supported. More research is needed to integrate implicit surfaces to our testbed.

References

Arvo, J., "Backward Ray Tracing," SIGGRAPH '86 *Developments in Ray Tracing seminar notes*, 12, Aug. 1986.

Blinn, J.F., and Newell, M.E., "Texture and Reflection in Computer Generated Images," *Communication of ACM*, 19, 10, October 1976, 542-547.

Blinn, J.F., "Models of Light Reflection for Computer Synthesized Pictures," *Computer Graphics* (SIGGRAPH '77 Proceedings), 11, 2, 192-198.

Blinn, J.F., "Simulation of Wrinkled Surfaces," *Computer Graphics* (SIGGRAPH '78 Proceedings), 286-292.

Catmull, E., *A Subdivision Algorithm for Computer Display of Curved Surfaces*, Ph.D. Thesis, Report UTEC-CSc-74-133, Computer Science Department, University of Utah, Salt Lake City, UT, December 1974.

Chen, S.E., Rushmeier, H.E., Miller, G., and Turner, D., "A Progressive Multi-Pass Method for Global Illumination," *Computer Graphics* (SIGGRAPH'91 Proceedings.), Las Vegas, August 1991.

Cohen, M., Greenberg, D.P., "The Hemi-cube: A Radiosity Solution for Complex Environments," *Computer Graphics* (SIGGRAPH '85 Proceedings), 19, 3, July 1985, 31-40.

Cohen, M., Chen, E.S., Wallace, J.R., Greenberg, D.P., "A Progressive Refinement Approach to Fast Radiosity Image Generation," *Computer Graphics* (SIGGRAPH '88 Proceedings), 22, 4, Aug. 1988, 75-84.

Cook, R.L., "Shade Trees," *Computer Graphics* (SIGGRAPH '84 Proceedings), 18, 3, July 1984, 223-231.

Cook, R.L., Carpenter, L., and Catmull, E., "The Reyes Image Rendering Architecture," *Computer Graphics* (SIGGRAPH '87 Proceedings), 21, 4, July 1987, 95-102.

Gouraud, H., "Continuous Shading of Curved Surfaces," *IEEE Transactions on Computers*, 20, 6, June 1971, 623-628.

Grant, E., Amburn, P., and Whitted, T., "Exploiting Classes in Modeling and Display Software," *IEEE Computer Graphics and Applications*, November 1986, 13-20.

Hall, R.A. and Greenberg, D.P., "A Testbed for Realistic Image Synthesis," *IEEE Computer Graphics and Applications*, November 1983, 10-20.

Kajiya, J. T., "Anisotropic Reflection Models," *Computer Graphics* (SIGGRAPH '85 Proceedings), 19, 3, July 1985, 15-21.

Nadas, T., and Alain, F., "GRAPE: An Environment to Build Display Processes," *Computer Graphics* (SIGGRAPH '87 Proceedings), 21, 4, July 1987, 85-93.

Phong, B.-T., "Illumination for Computer Generated Pictures," *Communications of the ACM*, 18, 6, June 1975, 311-317.

Potmesil, M. and Hoffert, E.M., "FRAMES: Software Tools for Modeling Rendering and Animation of 3D Scenes,", *Computer Graphics* (SIGGRAPH '87 Proceedings), 21, 4, July 1987, 85-93.

Shinya, M., Takahashi, T., and Naito, S., "Principles and Applications of Pencil Tracing," *Computer Graphics* (SIGGRAPH '87) Proceedings, 21, 4, July 1987, 45-54.

Stroustrup, B., *C++ Programming Language*, ISBN 0-201-12078-X, Addison-Wesley, 1987.

Turner, D., "A Small Object-Based Interpretive Language for Computer Graphics", to be published.

Upstill, S., *The RenderMan Companion*, ISBN 0-201-50868-0, Addison-Wesley, 1990.

Watkins, G.S., *A Real-Time Visible Surface Algorithm*, Univ. Utah Computer Science Dept. UTEC-CSc-70-101, June 1970.

Weghorst, H., Hooper, G., and Greenberg, D.P., "Improved Computational Methods for Ray Tracing," *ACM Transactions on Graphics*, 3, 1, January 1984, 52-69.

Whitted, T., "An Improved Illumination Model for Shaded Display," *Communication of the ACM*, 23, 6, 343-349.

Whitted, T. and Weimer, D.M., "A Software Test-Bed for the Development of 3-D Raster Graphics Systems," *Communication of the ACM*, 23, 6, 343-349.

Figure 4: An image created with a multi-pass method that accounts for shadows, color bleeding, caustics, specular reflection and refraction [Chen et al., 1991]

Figure 5: Soft shadows created by indirect lighting

Volume II

The Third Eurographics Workshop on Object-Oriented Graphics

Co-Chairs

Vicki de Mey, University of Geneva, Switzerland
Xavier Pintado, University of Geneva, Switzerland

Programme Committee

C. Bass (USA).
E. Blake (South Africa).
J. van den Bos (Netherlands).
N. Craighill (USA).
S. Cunningham (USA).
A. van Dam (USA).
E. Fiume (Canada).
B. Freeman-Benson (Canada).
M. Kaplan (USA).
M. Katevenis (Greece).
C. Laffra (USA).
N. Magnenat Thalmann (Switzerland).
A. Pavanello (USA).
J. Rankin (Australia).
T. Takala (Finland).
K. Turkowski (USA).
R. Turner (Switzerland).
P. Wisskirschen (Germany).

Part V

Modeling II

11

Sharing Between Graphical Objects Using Delegation

D. Brookshire Conner and Andries van Dam

We investigate the suitability of object-oriented paradigms for graphics by comparing a variety of object-oriented graphics systems and noting which of their features are readily modeled by class-instance systems and which by delegation systems. We examine how these systems establish patterns of sharing of data and behavior, and note that these patterns are established in a remarkably consistent fashion. We conclude that these patterns of sharing are more naturally modeled in a delegation system than in a class-instance system.

1 Introduction

The movement towards object-oriented programming has influenced all application areas, including 2D and 3D interactive graphics. While traditional graphics subroutine libraries are not object-oriented [GL manual, Howard et al., 1991, Upstill, 1990], newer graphical 2D user-interface (GUI) toolkits are [Myers, 1989], and object-oriented 3D graphics libraries are emerging [Strauss and Carey, 1992]. While these toolkits and libraries use the class-instance model of object-oriented programming, our experience with our delegation-based interactive modeling and animation system [Zeleznik et al., 1991] has convinced us that the newer delegation model of object-oriented programming is better suited to the demands of interactive graphics. This paper provides a somewhat more formal demonstration of this conviction.

This paper analyzes existing object-oriented graphics systems, showing that many features of graphics systems are more readily represented in a delegation model. We begin with a general description of the organization of most graphics systems, then compare the class-instance paradigm with the delegation paradigm. We then present an abstract discussion of how objects can share information in object-oriented systems, noting the kinds of sharing graphics systems allow. This brings us to the heart of the paper, where we examine how several graphics systems allow their objects to share information. We conclude by showing that sharing in object-oriented graphics has more characteristics in common with sharing in delegation systems than with sharing in class-instance systems.

2   The Generic Object-Oriented Graphics System

2.1   What is "object-oriented"?

Object-oriented literature is rarely precise about what makes something "object-oriented" and advertisements for "object-oriented" systems are even less so. We must therefore state what we mean by "object-oriented," especially in graphics, where the application domain includes many concrete "objects." Certainly, the mere existence of objects is not enough to constitute object-orientation.

We see two key aspects as necessary to being object-oriented. The first is the ability to define and create entities that encapsulate both data and behavior, typically called "objects." By this definition, a C procedure is not an object, because it usually does not encapsulate data. A C `struct` is also not an object, because it does not encapsulate behavior. Lisp closures and Modula-2 or Ada modules do encapsulate both data and behavior, but do not fully provide the second aspect of object-orientation. This second and more important aspect is the ability to provide sharing of behavior and data between entities. This sort of sharing is usually called inheritance. Our two-part definition is broader than some [Wegner, 1987], in not requiring classes, since we would like to include paradigms such as delegation and actor-based paradigms that are ruled out by stricter definitions.

Let us examine the second aspect of object-orientation, inheritance, a little more closely. The discussion must remain somewhat abstract — a more concrete example might use ideas unique to a particular object-oriented paradigm. We would like to avoid such prejudices, since the primary goal of this paper is to objectively determine what object-oriented paradigm is best suited to computer graphics.

Consider two objects, A and B. If B is sent the message m, B may draw on its own resources (e.g., code or data) to respond to m, or it may draw on the resources of another object, such as A. If B were to use A's resources, A and B would be sharing some part of the response to m. B can be said to inherit some of its response to m from A. This sharing can occur to greater or lesser degrees. B might use A's resources exclusively. Alternatively, it might use some of A's and some of its own. For example, A's response to m might be to send the message n to the original recipient of m (usually itself). B might not share n with A. Thus, sending m to B would enact B's response to n, and sending m to A would enact A's response to n.

We can thus see how within a system, there can be degrees of object-orientation, depending on the extent to which objects and inheritance are supported by a system. Some parts of a system may provide better support than others — a particular object-oriented system could be very object-oriented in one part of the system, and only barely object-oriented in another part. For example, in a graphics system, just having primitives is not enough. PHIGS+ is clearly not object-oriented with respect to its drawing primitives: they are not objects because they don't encapsulate both data and behavior, although PHIGS+ structures do encapsulate data in the form of geometry and attributes within structures, and attributes can be inherited from a parent structure by a child [Gaskins, 1992]. The Doré system [Doré, 1992] is somewhat object-oriented — the programmer can add new primitives, but the implementation of new primitives cannot be shared with earlier ones (i.e., inherited). The Inventor system is clearly object-oriented in its provisions for drawing primitives [Strauss and Carey, 1992], since the programmer can provide a new node type by subclassing from any pre-existing node type and choosing to share all or some part of the pre-existing node's behavior.

2.2 Components of Graphics Systems

Let's now examine common components of a generic object-oriented graphics system. These components give us a starting point for comparisons of actual systems. For simplicity, we include both application-side and device-side portions of a graphics system. In the future, we intend to investigate this boundary in closer detail, looking at what features are supported on the device side and in the implementation language, and what features are utilized on the application side provided by the graphics system, and how extensibility relates to both sides.

Most graphics systems provide support for two hierarchies, a class hierarchy and a directed acyclic graph (DAG) of instances of the classes in the class hierarchy (this is often called a *part* hierarchy, although it is often used for more than just part-subpart relationships, as will be discussed later.) The class hierarchy is typically used to support sharing of code, whereas the DAG is usually used to support sharing of attributes. Most often, the class hierarchy is a static code construct provided by the graphics system and is usually extended only at compile time. The DAG, on the other hand, is a more dynamic construct that is almost always built at run time.

The class hierarchy

The class hierarchy in a graphics system typically provides modeling primitives such as geometric objects like rectangles, polygons, polyhedra, quadrics, and spline patches. Systems that emphasize interaction (such as most 2D systems) provide interaction tools such as pulldown menus, text fields, and scroll bars. The class hierarchy is always a taxonometric hierarchy, in which items near the top are more general kinds of objects and items lower in the hierarchy more specialized. This hierarchy is used to share implementation, which is especially important in graphics, since many fundamental operations, e.g. clipping, scan-conversion, and shading, can be difficult to implement correctly. In addition, the class hierarchy provides some measure of procedural abstraction, since common actions, like drawing a primitive or performing a pick test, are provided as abstract methods of a base class.

The DAG

The runtime DAG implements the scene hierarchy, the collection of objects that comprise the model that the programmer is representing or that the interactive end-user is constructing. It is built from objects instanced from the classes in the class hierarchy. As a DAG, it implements Sutherland's master-instance hierarchy [Sutherland, 1963]. In 2D systems, especially ones for user interfaces, this hierarchy is usually a conceptual hierarchy of controls and feedback, with conceptually related controls grouped into a subhierarchy. In 3D systems, which tend to be geared more towards geometric modeling, the hierarchy usually represents a parts breakdown of the model.

A few systems provide multiple DAGs, allowing different DAGs to specify different attributes. For a model of a building, say, one DAG can represent the building on a floor-by-floor basis, one the plumbing, and one the electrical system. Objects in more than one DAG, such as a faucet on a particular floor, would inherit attributes from both DAGs. Some systems provide mechanisms to accomplish some of the same things that multiple DAGs would do. The PHIGS+ name set mechanism can be used to specify pickability, highlightability, and visibility. By using filters on the name set, these special attributes can be set as if they were attributes in their own DAG and represented a different hierarchy from the parts hierarchy in the Central Structure Store DAG.

The DAG provides several additional features. If a single instance is referenced several times, i.e., there is more than one path from the root to a particular instance, then one instance is in effect being used several times, perhaps in several contexts. In addition, the DAG can factor out commonality. Since graphical attributes are usually propagated along the edges of the DAG, i.e. from parent to child, setting attributes high in the graph effectively sets the attributes for the entire subgraph. This operation bears a striking similarity to inheritance in the class hierarchy, where changing a method high in the class tree potentially affects classes in the entire subtree.

Similarity of the DAG and the class hierarchy

A further similarity between the DAG and the class hierarchy can be found in their purposes. These two hierarchies are meant to accomplish two distinctly different tasks: the class hierarchy provides a taxonomy of the kinds of objects available in the system, and the DAG provides a parts-subparts breakdown of the run-time application model. However, in practice, the separation is usually far from orthogonal. Graphics systems are often used for interactive applications, such as drawing programs or CAD/CAM systems, in which the user is incrementally building or modifying an object. Users naturally want to try several variations, perhaps by building a rough model, for example, a simple automobile, then refining several different copies, so as to produce cars with different headlights or fenders. Thus, the DAG is often used to model a taxonometric hierarchy, even though that is not its purpose.

Thus, we see two different hierarchies designed with two different purposes in mind, but with distinctions not as precise as we might have thought. A delegation system, being well-suited to exploratory programming [Stein et al., 1989, Ungar and Smith, 1987, Ungar and Smith, 1991], is also well-suited to the taxonometric-like characteristics of the DAG. The remainder of the paper will investigate the inheritance and sharing found in the DAG and show that a delegation model better represents both the dynamic taxonomy and run-time sharing found in graphics than a traditional class-instance model.

3   Two Models for Object-Orientation

There are two predominant paradigms for objects in object-oriented programming: the class-instance paradigm and the delegation paradigm [Borning, 1986, Halperin and Nguyen, 1987, Wegner, 1987]. In a class-instance system, all objects are instances of a class. Classes can inherit from other classes. When an object is sent a message, the method used to respond to that message is the version of the message in the object's class. If the class does not contain a suitable method, then the method used is the one in the nearest superclass. A search for a method can either be done at runtime, as in SMALLTALK, which, in principle, actually searches through runtime class objects, or at compile time, as in C++, which builds up a table of function pointers, producing a single table index at runtime instead of a complete search. Thus, there are two relationships, that between an object and its class and that between a class and any class it inherits from. The classic example of a class-based language is SMALLTALK. In contrast, delegation systems, such as SELF have only one relationship [Ungar and Smith, 1991] between an object and any object it inherits from. In a delegation system, when an object receives a message, it looks for a method in *itself* rather than in its class. If no suitable method is present, the search continues recursively in objects, called parents, that this object inherits from.

3.1 Which to Choose?

The tradeoffs between a class-instance system and a delegation system are the subject of some debate. In general, delegation is seen as being more suited to exploratory, developmental programming, whereas class-instance systems seem to provide better support for guaranteed reliability.

Pros of delegation

In particular, delegation systems are seen as more flexible and easier to learn [Borning, 1986]. A delegation model is a strict superset of class-instance models, since delegation can model class-instance relations but classes and instances cannot model delegation without additional constructs [Halperin and Nguyen, 1987]. This makes delegation systems more flexible, in that the programmer is not bound to the class-instance paradigm and can use more open-ended constructs, and this greater flexibility makes some problems simpler to model. Two such problems are unique instances and extended instances. With a unique instance, only a single example of a particular object exists, like the proverbial perfect cup of tea. Defining a second class object to correspond to this unique object is clumsy. Extended instances are a related problem. A group of objects has similar behavior, but one or two instances support behavior the others don't, like Dumbo, the elephant who could fly. Making a completely unrelated object is inappropriate, since Dumbo is still an elephant. However, a normal class-instance system does not provide support for the possibility that Dumbo can fly, unless Dumbo is an instance of the new class of flying elephants.

Eliminating classes also makes delegation systems simpler in two ways. First, the confusing construct of metaclasses is seen as the hardest part of SMALLTALK to learn [O'Shea, 1986], and delegation systems have no need for metaclasses. Since all objects must be instances of a class in a class-instance system, systems that support classes as runtime objects, as SMALLTALK does, must have objects for classes to be instances of, hence metaclasses. However, what class are metaclasses instances of? Note that not all class-instance systems suffer from this problem of infinite regress: any system that does not support classes as runtime objects, such as C++, does not run into this problem.

Delegation paradigms also simplify the possible relationships between objects. Class-instance systems have two object relations, that between a class and a derived class and that between a class and an instance of the class. Delegation systems, however, have only one relationship, that between an object and its parent. Users of a delegation system thus have fewer concepts to learn with a delegation system.

Perhaps the most compelling reasons for using a delegation paradigm arise when delegation is examined in the context of graphics, as we are doing in this paper. A delegation system is an inherently exploratory world, amenable to easy, flexible, incremental modification and creation, filled with actual concrete objects, not abstractions. An interactive graphics program is, ideally, similarly easy and flexible, with easily created and modified concrete objects. Indeed, we believe future graphics applications will provide progressively more flexible and modifiable objects, allowing modification of what is typically thought of as the object's "type" (such as whether it is a sphere or cone) [Zeleznik et al., 1991]. Historically, this approach to graphical programs has been around as long as there have been interactive graphical programs [Sutherland, 1963]. Users of drawing programs do not think of the objects they manipulate as instances of abstract categories, whose parameters they are modifying. Users see the objects they manipulate as independent objects, an approach that is much closer in feel to delegation than to class-instance paradigms.

Cons of delegation

On the other hand, delegation systems have some distinct disadvantages. They tend to produce even more message sends than traditional class-instance relations, in part because delegation's greater flexibility seems to preclude some obvious compiler optimizations (such as flattening the inheritance hierarchy for a particular object to eliminate method searches). However, the SELF compiler seems to tackle this problem remarkably well, reportedly performing better than SMALLTALK and comparably to optimized C code, at least for integer computation [Chambers, 1992, Chambers and Ungar, 1991]. A second drawback is that the objects in a delegation system are even more concrete than instances in a class-instance system, so that delegation becomes somewhat unnatural for inherently abstract entities like integers. For example, what is the prototypical integer? Zero, one, and infinity all seem likely candidates, but their behavior is far too specialized. However, graphics applications are inherently concrete, since, by definition, they want to *show* their objects.

Finally, the greater flexibility of delegation systems is very much a double-edged sword — the same flexibility that makes rapid prototyping possible makes it easy to change the wrong thing inadvertently. This touches directly on an old and vehement programming language battle: flexibility versus security. For large projects, security becomes extremely important. In programming languages, more flexible constructs are often seen as encouraging poor code structuring (e.g., the well-known *goto* versus *while, repeat, for* debate).

However, the flexibility provided by delegation systems is exactly the kind of flexibility that most object-oriented graphics systems try to support, as the analysis in Section 5 demonstrates. Previous analyses of delegation for graphics also suggest that delegation is more suited for graphics [Borning, 1986, Wisskirchen, 1990]. Wisskirchen goes so far as to provide a short example [Wisskirchen, 1990] and point out that it is "simpler and more natural to program." He did not pursue this direction, however, choosing instead to base his GEO++ system on a class-instance system because it is "in wider use and has been more strongly standardized."

In what follows, we provide additional arguments in favor of delegation by analyzing how existing graphics systems share information (e.g., attributes). We survey a variety of object-oriented graphics systems and show that the sharing inherent in a delegation system can handle the capabilities graphics systems provide more readily than a class-instance system can.

4 Sharing

A series of concrete examples can give a straight-forward demonstration of a system's capabilities. However, careful choice of the examples can make the worst systems look good and the best systems look bad. We thus begin with an abstract description of sharing in object-oriented systems. We use this abstract basis as a framework to describe the general abilities of a variety of graphics systems. Due to space limitations, we will not be able to discuss all aspects of the abstract framework in relation to all aspects of graphics systems.

4.1 An Abstract Description of Sharing

We frame our discussion in terms of the Treaty of Orlando [Stein et al., 1989], which discusses how objects share information in object-oriented languages. In particular, what are the patterns of this sharing and how is it established? This is a very generic approach, designed to avoid language-centric questions by specifically avoiding terms or structures in any particular language or paradigm.

Points to consider about mechanisms supporting sharing include the following:

- *How* is sharing established?

  implicit Sharing is a mechanism provided by the system and applied uniformly for all objects.

  explicit Sharing is an operation allowing the programmer to control the patterns of sharing.

- *When* is sharing established?

  static Sharing is established at or before object creation and cannot be changed thereafter.

  dynamic Sharing is established at any time and can be changed at any time.

- *For what* objects is sharing established?

  per group Sharing is established for a group of objects all at once (e.g., using a class to establish sharing among all its instances).

  per object Sharing is established on an object-by-object basis. Individual objects can thus have idiosyncratic behavior.

Patterns of sharing, i.e. how inheritance or delegation is established between objects, comprise half of the difference between class-instance models and delegation models. To avoid any confusion, we call this form of sharing, in which objects borrow information from each other, *empathy* [Stein et al., 1989] rather than *inheritance*, which could refer to a particular language construct. Different choices about how the patterns of empathy work yield different object models. Class-instance systems typically provide a form of empathy that is *static, implicit,* and *per-group*: static, since the class tree usually doesn't change; implicit, since sharing between instances and between classes is automatically provided as a uniform feature by the system; and per-group, since sharing is specified for all instances of a class at once. Delegation systems are usually *dynamic,* either *implicit* or *explicit,* and *per-object*: dynamic, since delegation relations between objects are typically allowed to change; implicit in systems like SELF and explicit in systems like Actors; and per-object, since each object has its own parent slot.

The other half of the difference between class-instance systems and delegation systems deals with *templating*: how new objects are made (as opposed to empathy, which concerns how existing objects borrow information from other objects). Class-instance systems embed a template for an object within a class. This template produces objects with instance variables and a pointer to the object's class. Delegation systems such as Actors have no templates — objects are made anew every time, while delegation systems such as SELF allow any object to be a template — objects are made by copying other objects. Note that different systems share different information during templating. In most class-instance systems, there is a sharp line between what is shared by all instances of a class (i.e., the methods) and what is not (i.e., the instance variables). In systems like SELF, a new object doesn't share any information with its template since the new object is a copy of the old one.

4.2 Empathy in Graphics

In graphics, objects share information in an empathic fashion through both the class hierarchy *and* through the run-time DAG, sharing code using the class hierarchy, sharing attributes through the DAG. As noted in Section 2, attributes such as surface properties, geometric transformations, and geometry are usually propagated along the edges of the DAG. Although most graphics systems use the equivalent of a DAG structure, empathic sharing of attributes is done by a variety of mechanisms. Each graphics system accomplishes this sharing in its own way and calls the mechanisms involved by different names. Learning a new graphics system thus means learning a new way of doing things, so that most graphics systems have steep learning curves.

Sharing, as realized both by empathy and by templating, can be used to greater or lesser extents for many different aspects of an object, including an object's protocol (what messages it understands), an object's implementation (how it responds to messages), and an object's data. We focus on sharing in general, without worrying about exactly which graphical attributes, objects, and methods are shared through empathy, and which through templating, since in general, no two systems support exactly the same kinds of information as either attributes or objects. Certainly, there are differences between 2D and 3D systems. However, we are concerned here with how objects share information, regardless of exactly the kinds of objects supported by a particular system.

In the next section, we will analyze how graphics systems use sharing. As noted before, it is not feasible to cover all aspects of sharing in a paper this size, especially for the number of graphics systems discussed. We will instead focus on a particular part of the graphics system, the application's model of the system (i.e., how the application programmer thinks of the graphics system), and a particular kind of sharing, namely empathy. It could also be fruitful to consider internals of graphics systems, either at the device driver or graphics library level. Alternatively, one could investigate the ramifications of how templating is performed in graphics systems. Thus, we can consider a simple space of topics for analysis of object-oriented graphics systems: the two kinds of sharing along one axis, and the various layers of implementation and abstraction of the graphics system along the other axis. In such a space, this paper remains in "empathy for application abstractions" corner. Future papers might investigate other regions of this space, and the effects of kinds of object-orientation on topics such as performance, reliability, and extensibility.

5   Analysis of Existing Object-Oriented Graphics Systems

Here we survey some well-known graphics systems (the X Toolkit, and PHIGS+) and a variety of systems that call themselves "object-oriented," giving a brief description of how each establishes empathic sharing of information between objects. We first discuss systems that perform templating using more traditional class-instance-like mechanism and then systems that use the more unusual prototype mechanism found in most delegation systems. While we don't otherwise analyze these systems with respect to templating, this categorization serves to provide an overview of the general approaches involved. A summary of the following discussion may be found in Table 1 at the end of the section.

5.1   Class-Instance Systems

The X Toolkit

The X Toolkit is an object-oriented system implemented in C that provides a framework for toolkits of interaction techniques [Myers, 1989, Nye and O'Reilly, 1990] (It does not provide the interaction techniques themselves, merely the framework to implement them). For example, the OSF/Motif Toolkit is implemented on top of the X Toolkit [Heller, 1991]. Since it is freely distributed with the X Window System, the X Toolkit is quite widespread, and has had a large influence on other 2D graphics systems.

Instances in the X Toolkit called *widgets* are arranged in a strict tree (in contrast to many other graphics systems that, as noted in Section 2, allow instances to be arranged in a DAG). Parents can be established only when a widget is created — a widget cannot be moved around in the hierarchy, but must instead be destroyed and recreated.

A widget's attributes are termed *resources*, and particular classes of widgets support different resources. For example, scrollbars support attributes related to the appearance of the thumb of the scrollbar, attributes that would be meaningless for pushbuttons. If a resource is set on or requested from a widget that is inappropriate, it is ignored. If a widget has no specified value for a resource, it gets the value from its parent in the instance hierarchy, although most widget classes provide default values.

Sharing is thus *static*, since there is no reparenting, *implicit*, since it is established by the parent-child relationship, and *per-object*, since different widgets have different parent widgets and thus inherit resource values differently, even if the widgets are instances of the same class.

InterViews

The InterViews toolkit has a similar functionality to the X Toolkit along with a widget set (such as Motif). It is, however, written in C++, making it cleaner, since it need not implement mechanisms to support the class hierarchy and instancing from it [Linton et al., 1989]. In addition, it tends to have higher-level classes (e.g., tree viewer vs. drawing area) than an X Toolkit widget set.

In addition to objects equivalent to X Toolkit widgets, which InterViews calls *interactors*, InterViews supports objects called *glyphs*, lighter-weight, more dynamic versions of interactors [Calder and Linton, 1990]. Unlike interactors, glyphs can be shared among several parent glyphs or interactors. Thus, unlike the X Toolkit, InterViews sharing is *dynamic*, since the parent-child relationships for glyphs can change. Other than glyphs, however, sharing is quite similar, being *implicitly* established by parent-child relationships and different on a *per-object* basis.

PHIGS+

PHIGS+ is a graphics system to perform 3D rendering at interactive speeds with rudimentary interaction techniques [Howard et al., 1991, Gaskins, 1992], but it is not an object-oriented graphics system. It does not provide the ability to make new classes of objects. However, it is a standard graphics system, and, because of its age and widespread availability, has widely influenced the design of subsequent graphics systems.

Like most graphics systems, PHIGS+ provides a run-time DAG hierarchy. Indeed, the PHIGS+ DAG is the exemplar for 3D graphics systems. Many systems use duplication of a PHIGS+ hierarchy as an example of how useful the system is. In terms of the DAG, many systems do not provide much more functionality than PHIGS+. However, the PHIGS+ equivalent of a class hierarchy is merely a subroutine library with calls to create a variety of primitives. Thus, users cannot extend the system with new primitive types.

The PHIGS+ model provides structures containing ordered primitives, attributes, and references to substructures. Attributes inserted into a structure before a primitive affect the primitive's rendering, and structures inherit or share attributes with their parent. Attributes set in the parent structure (before the child) have the same effects as if they had been specified at the beginning of the child structure. The PHIGS+ name set, as discussed in Section 2.2, is an exception to the attribute sharing provided by the DAG.

Sharing in PHIGS+ is *dynamic*, since one can move structures around, removing them from one parent structure and placing them in another, or reference them several times. Attribute sharing is *implicitly* provided by order in the structure and the parent/child relationship between structures, again with the exception of the name set mechanism. Finally, sharing is *per-object*, since each structure has a different parent.

Mirage

Mirage is a system for building interactive 3D applications that makes use of both object-oriented programming and knowledge representation techniques [Tarlton and Tarlton, 1989, Tarlton and Tarlton, 1992]. It provides three major class hierarchies, Forms, Activities, and Events, to model geometry, time-dependent behavior, and interactivity, respectively.

Hierarchical arrangement of instances of Form and its subclasses provides a runtime hierarchy quite similar to the PHIGS+ DAG, except for two significant differences. First, Mirage hierarchies are strictly trees, not DAGs, in order to prevent ambiguities when cameras are multiply instanced. Second, order of attributes set on Forms is not important, so that using Forms is a more declarative style of modeling than found in PHIGS+. Like structures in a PHIGS+ hierarchy, instances of Forms inherit attributes set on their parent. Instances of Activities can be hierarchically composed, much like Forms, and attributes such as duration and speed are inherited. Events are handled in a somewhat different manner, since Events, being inherently discrete, are not hierarchically composed.

Sharing is *dynamic*, since the hierarchy of either Forms or Activities can be changed. These hierarchies provide an *implicit* and *per-object* sharing of their attributes.

Inventor

The Inventor system from Silicon Graphics is a system for building interactive 3D graphics applications [IRIS, Strauss and Carey, 1992]. As a C++ class library, it can be extended rather easily, although supporting some features in a new class, such as automatic file I/O, requires a fair amount of work, as C++ does not support these features especially well.

Subclasses of the base class SoNode provide modeling primitives, including spheres, patches, various attributes, and grouping primitives. Subclasses of SoNode also include interactive objects called manipulators that can be used to move and resize objects and control lights and cameras. Grouping primitives arrange SoNodes into the familiar DAG. As in PHIGS+, both order of nodes that specify attributes and attributes specified in parent nodes are relevant. Attribute values are changed either by editing nodes or by changing the execution DAG, e.g., moving, adding, or removing nodes. This can be done at runtime.

Inventor also provides classes to perform actions on the entire DAG, build supplementary 2D interfaces, and handle user events. It is also straightforward for one portion of the DAG to monitor changes in another portion, making it relatively easy to implement simple constraints.

Sharing of attributes is *dynamic*, because the DAG can change, and *implicitly* provided by order and grouping. Like other graphics systems, sharing is also *per-object*, being unrelated to an object's class.

GEO++

The GEO++ system is quite similar to PHIGS+, although it is implemented in SMALLTALK [Wisskirchen, 1990]. Like Mirage it limits its hierarchies to strict trees. In GEO++ terminology, *Groups* contain *Parts*. A Part can be another group or an output primitive. Attributes can be set anywhere along the tree, and propagate down the hierarchy in a manner quite similar to PHIGS+. Thus, like PHIGS+, GEO++ is a *dynamic, implicit, per-object* environment.

TBAG

TBAG is a somewhat different system that uses functional programming to provide interactive 3D applications [Elliott et al., 1991, Elliott, 1992], and thus it has a unique approach to modeling. The class hierarchy here serves as data types that functions can operate on. Rather than a runtime DAG, TBAG programmers write functions that return geometric objects. Composing functions provides hierarchical models. True to the functional programming tradition, rather than modifying models passed into them, TBAG functions return completely new objects.

Sharing is therefore *static*, since functional composition is not changed at runtime. Note that conditionals within a function do not change this, since a conditional function returns a static object. Functional composition is also an *implicit* means to share information between objects. TBAG functions are generic, operating uniformly on geometric objects regardless of their actual class, making sharing *per-object*.

5.2   Delegation-Based Systems

Delegation-based programming languages are not as widespread or standardized as class-based languages. Most class-instance systems discussed use an existing class-instance programming language, usually C++. The two delegation systems described below use two non-object-oriented programming languages (C and Lisp) and implement their own delegation systems.

Garnet

The GARNET system from Carnegie Mellon University is designed to build highly interactive 2D interfaces [Myers et al., 1990]. GARNET's fundamental object model, KR, is very similar to SELF's. There are objects called *schemata*, and slots which contain values (e.g., other schemata and Lisp atomic types) [Guise, 1989]. Sending a message to a schema looks for the slot with the same name. A special :IS-A slot acts as a parent slot — searching for a slot continues in the parent schema if the slot is not found in the child. *Formula*s are one-way constraints that can be established between schemata.

GARNET's basic support for graphical objects is found in the Opal package [Pervin et al., 1990]. Packages built on top of Opal provide interactive behavior and more sophisticated grouping abilities. We focus on Opal and KR, since the higher-level packages do not significantly affect GARNET objects' ability to share information. In some ways, GARNET's sharing abilities are more limited than SELF's, since GARNET disallows multiple inheritance. However, the presence of constraints at a fundamental level, even one-way constraints, provides an even greater flexibility, giving GARNET the ability to *explicitly* share attributes. As a SELF-like delegation system, it of course provides *per-object* sharing. Although its hierarchy is a strict tree, it does allow subtrees to be moved around, providing *dynamic* sharing.

UGA

The UGA system, developed at Brown University, is designed to build interactive 3D animations [Zeleznik et al., 1991]. In UGA, objects are described in the scripting language FLESH and can have their attributes set by time-varying functions called *chops* (for change operation). These "attributes" include normal graphics attributes, such as geometry and surface properties, as well as more sophisticated attributes, such as dynamic properties like inertia and velocity. Responses to user actions can also be specified as an attribute. One particular attribute is a parent object. The initial value for an attribute is the object's parent's value for that object, with a default for objects without parents. When an object is asked for an attribute, its chops can affect the value obtained from the parent. Thus, parent chops provide a basic delegation mechanism within FLESH.

An additional attribute is a members list for objects that represent groups. Objects can be members of and inherit attributes from multiple groups, allowing a flexible combination of attribute organization. In addition, one-way constraints called *dependencies* provide another mechanism to share attribute values. Dependencies allow an object to explicitly choose which attributes to inherit, rather than inheriting all attributes, as with a group or a parent.

Sharing in UGA is *dynamic*, since group member lists and parents are both attributes, and can thus change. It is *implicitly* provided by parents and groups, but *explicitly* provided by dependencies, in both cases on a *per-object* basis.

5.3 Constraints

Constraints are a way to add explicit sharing controls to an otherwise implicit system, as we have seen in both UGA and GARNET. If one object depends on another (a one-way constraint), the two objects are sharing information. However, constraints are usually between particular fields of an object, especially in a user interface, where objects lay themselves out by lining up their boundaries with one another. Since the constraints thus apply to individual attributes, it becomes an explicit sharing, rather than the implicit sharing of inheritance, which specifies that all parts of an object are shared at once.

Multiway constraints entail sharing of data that is smart enough to know how to modify itself to maintain a constraint when one or the other of the constrained objects tries to assign a value to the constraint. Both the constrained objects share the constrained values. This is a local constraint-satisfaction technique, and it easily falls into local minima. This gets a bit messier with a global constraint system, where, in some sense, all objects that are constrained are sharing information together.

Inheritance can be understood and implemented as a one-way constraint [Borning, 1986]. The child object is constrained to support some of the same things as the parent, e.g., slot names, behavior, and protocol. This approach works to some extent, but constraints, being a declarative construct, have more of a *static* feel than a *dynamic* one, although certainly constraint systems commonly allow constraints to be changed, added, and removed.

GARNET and UGA provide one-way constraints as a system primitive. Inventor provides easy ways to write code that implements one-way constraints through the use of *Sensor* objects that perform a callback when a particular piece of data changes. Finally, function composition in TBAG provides the equivalent of a one-way constraint. Objects returned by functions effectively depend on the argument objects passed into the function.

System	Language	When	How	For
Class-Instance Systems:				
X Toolkit	C	static	implicit	per object
InterViews	C++	dynamic	implicit	per object
PHIGS+	C	dynamic	implicit	per object
Mirage	C++	dynamic	implicit	per object
Inventor	C++	dynamic	implicit	per object
GEO++	SMALLTALK	dynamic	implicit	per object
Functional Systems:				
TBAG	C++	static	implicit	per object
Delegation Systems:				
UGA	C / FLESH	dynamic	explicit	per object
GARNET	Lisp/ KR	dynamic	explicit	per object

Table 1: Object-oriented graphics systems, the paradigms they use, and the kind of sharing they provide. Note that all provide sharing of graphics attributes that is per-object. Most use dynamic, implicit sharing, derived from notions of PHIGS-like hierarchy. Systems that support constraints support explicit sharing.

6   Implications for Object-Oriented Graphics

6.1 Observations

From our analysis in Section 5, we can make several observations. First, we can note some features of the problems graphics systems are trying to solve, and the ways they try to solve them. Interactive graphics applications are flexible, exploratory kinds of environments, and graphics systems are designed to support this – almost all systems allowed editing of the models they built, and most built these models in a hierarchy allowing sweeping changes in the objects. A few systems, such as PHIGS+, Inventor, and UGA, made use of ordering as well as hierarchy, providing an additional mechanism to specify and modify models.

We can also discuss how these systems share information among objects, irrespective of their intended application. For example, all systems, without exception, support *per-object* sharing. The class of an object only specifies default attribute values, never where an object obtains attribute values. Further, almost all systems have exactly the same kinds of sharing: *dynamic*, *implicit*, and *per-object*. This kind of sharing supports flexible, exploratory environments [Stein et al., 1989], which should come as no surprise, considering the flexibility required by an interactive graphics application. The addition of *explicit* sharing in systems supporting constraints only increases the flexibility of the system.

A little thought can explain why the systems that are not classified as dynamic, implicit, and per object are different. The X Toolkit is a static system because the fundamental X object (the X Window) doesn't allow reparenting without a great deal of effort. Other systems implemented on top of X, such as InterViews, circumvent this by not having X Windows and objects in the DAG in a one-to-one correspondence. TBAG is static because it is functional. Rather than editing an object, functions take graphical objects and return new ones. Since the functions can be arbitrarily complex, this does not limit TBAG's abilities — TBAG simply chooses that geometry and attributes should be treated in as formal a fashion as entities like integers or floating point numbers.

Most of the graphics systems covered were implemented in a class-instance language, C++. Such a language supports *static, implicit, per-group* sharing — orthogonal to the kind of sharing provided by the graphics system itself. A few systems weren't even implemented in an object-oriented programming language. Clearly, graphics systems are not making extensive use of the sharing provided by the programming languages they are implemented in. This is not because they are badly implemented — most of the C++ systems make extensive use of C++'s classing mechanisms in the class hierarchy. Rather, it is because the operations required by a graphics system, namely dynamically building individual objects, is not supported by a class-instance paradigm.

6.2 Object-Oriented Graphics is Not Re-using Code

Thus, every graphics system implements its own method of sharing, in its own particular fashion. Each system is idiosyncratic in particular details, even though, as we have seen, all systems are trying to provide remarkably similar and consistent ways for objects to share information. This seems to contradict one of the fundamental strengths of object-oriented programming, namely the ability to share code when the functionality required is similar. So why are graphics programmers using object-oriented programming languages that don't provide the kind of sharing interactive graphics needs? The most compelling answer we can come up with is Wisskirchen's: class-instance models are simply more standard [Wisskirchen, 1990].

While most graphics systems provide implicit sharing, certain examples indicate that explicit sharing is more suitable. Constraints are an example of explicit sharing. Since common programming languages do not provide the kinds of sharing graphics programmers need, we feel that the graphics community should begin to advocate programming languages that *do* provide this sharing, lest we continue to reimplement the dynamic environments needed for graphics.

6.3 Delegation is Better for Graphics

From our analysis in Section 5, it is clear that a delegation system models the sharing required by graphics systems better than a class-instance system. In addition, delegation models common problems in graphics, such as unique instances, better than classes, and appears to simply produce cleaner solutions to graphics problems in general, providing more concrete objects that map more cleanly to the inherently concrete objects of graphics [Borning, 1986, Wisskirchen, 1990].

Arguments against delegation are being weakened by current research, such as the supposition that delegation is inherently inefficient when the SELF compiler indicates that this may not be the case. Other arguments against delegation, while weaknesses in one problem domain, are strengths in graphics. Delegation's inherent flexibility, while perhaps inappropriate for situations requiring guaranteed behavior, is especially important for graphics. Delegation's objects are more concrete, making them less appropriate for abstract entities, but even more appropriate for the concrete, visible objects of graphics.

We wish to investigate delegation and its applicability further, and feel that other researchers working on object-oriented graphics systems should consider delegation as well. Delegation is a general and powerful mechanism well-suited to the problems of graphics.

7 Future Work

As noted before, this paper analyzes a particular area in the space of sharing as it appears in graphics systems. Further analysis of this space can proceed in two fruitful ways. First, this work can benefit from analysis of additional graphics systems, and in greater depth than allowed in a paper of this length. Second, analysis should be performed on additional areas of the space of sharing in graphics systems. How is templating used and/or implemented across graphics systems? How is templating and empathy used and implemented in various parts of graphics systems? Is sharing affected by where the boundary between internal representation and external abstraction falls? These and other questions would provide a deeper, more rigorous understanding of graphics, a field that has traditionally been too much a "hacker's" domain.

Acknowledgments

This work was supported in part by NSF/DARPA, IBM, Sun Microsystems, NCR, Hewlett Packard and Digital Equipment Corporation. The authors would also like to thank Carl Bass and Wm Leler of Ithaca Software and Conal Elliot of Sun Microsystems for helpful discussions about this paper.

References

Borning, A. H. (1986).   Classes versus prototypes in object-oriented languages.   In *IEEE/ACM Fall Joint Computer Conference*, pages 36–40.

Calder, P. R. and Linton, M. A. (1990). Glyphs: Flyweight objects for user interfaces. In *Proceedings of ACM Third Annual Symposium on User Interface Software and Technology*, pages 92–101.

Chambers, C. (1992). *The Design and Implementation of the SELF Compiler, an Optimizing Compiler for Object-Oriented Progamming Languages*. PhD thesis, Stanford University.

Chambers, C. and Ungar, D. (1991). Making pure object-oriented languages practical. In *OOPSLA '91 Proceedings*, pages 1–15. Published as *SIGPLAN Notices* 26(10), October

1991.

(1992). *Doré Programmer's Manual*. Kubota Pacific, Inc.

Elliott, C. (1992). TBAG via C++. Unpublished handout.

Elliott, C., Schechter, G., Abi-Ezzi, S., and Deering, M. (1991). *TBAG: Time, Behavior, and Geometry*. Unpublished. Sun Microsystems internal document.

Gaskins, T. (1992). *PHIGS Programming Manual*. O'Reilly and Associates, Inc.

GL Programmer's Manual. Silicon Graphics, Inc.

Guise, D. (1989). KR: Constraint-based knowledge representation. Technical Report CMU-CS-89-142, Carnegie Mellon Univeristy.

Halperin, B. and Nguyen, V. (1987).   A model for object-based inheritance.   In [Wegner and Shriver, 1987].

Heller, D. (1991). *Motif Programming Manual*, volume 6 of *The X Window System Series*. O'Reilly & Associates, Inc.

Howard, T. L. J., Hewitt, W. T., Hubbold, R. J., and Wyrwas, K. M. (1991). *A Practical Introduction to PHIGS and PHIGS PLUS*. Addison Wesley.

IRIS Inventor Programming Guide. Silicon Graphics, Inc., 2nd draft edition.

Kim, W. and Lochovsky, F. H., editors (1989). *Object-Oriented Concepts, Databases, and Applications*. ACM Press Frontier Series. ACM Press.

Linton, M. A., Vlissides, J. M., and Calder, P. R. (1989). Composing user interfaces with InterViews. *IEEE Computer*, 22(2):8–22.

Myers, B. A. (1989). User-interface tools: Introduction and survey. *IEEE Software*, pages 15–23.

Myers, B. A., Guise, D. A., Dannenberg, R. B., Zanden, B. V., Kosbie, D. S., Pervin, E., Mickish, A., and Marchal, P. (1990). Garnet: Comprehensive support for graphical, highly interactive user interfaces. *IEEE Computer*, pages 71–85.

Nye, A. and O'Reilly, T. (1990). *X Toolkit Intrinsics Programming Manual*, volume 4 of *The X Window System Series*. O'Reilly & Associates, Inc.

O'Shea, T. (1986). Why object-oriented programming systems are hard to learn. In *OOPSLA '86 Conference Proceedings*.

Pervin, E., Myers, B. A., Kosbie, D., and Kolojejchick, J. A. (1990). *Opal Reference Manual: The Garnet Graphical Object System*. Carnegie Mellon University.

Stein, L. A., Lieberman, H., and Ungar, D. (1989). A shared view of sharing: *The Treaty of Orlando*. In [Kim and Lochovsky, 1989].

Strauss, P. S. and Carey, R. (1992). An object-oriented 3D graphics toolkit. In Catmull, E. E., editor, *SIGGRAPH '92 Conference Proceedings*, pages 341–349. ACM SIGGRAPH, Addison-Wesley.

Sutherland, I. E. (1963). Sketchpad: A man-machine graphical communication system. In *Proceedings of the Spring Joint Computer Conference*, pages 329–346, Baltimore, MD. Spartan Books.

Tarlton, M. A. and Tarlton, P. N. (1989). Pogo: A declarative representation system for graphics. In [Kim and Lochovsky, 1989], chapter 7, pages 151–176.

Tarlton, M. A. and Tarlton, P. N. (1992). A framework for dynamic visual applications. In Levoy, M. and Catmull, E. E., editors, *Proceedings of the 1992 Symposium on Interactive Three-Dimensional Graphics*, pages 161–164. ACM SIGGRAPH.

Ungar, D. and Smith, R. B. (1987). SELF: The power of simplicity. In *OOPSLA '87 Conference Proceedings*, pages 227–241. Published as *SIGPLAN Notices*, 22, 12 (1987).

Ungar, D. and Smith, R. B. (1991). SELF: The power of simplicity. *Lisp and Symbolic Computation*, 4(3).

Upstill, S. (1990). *The RenderMan Companion*. Addison-Wesley.

Wegner, P. (1987). The object-oriented classification paradigm. In [Wegner and Shriver, 1987].

Wegner, P. and Shriver, B., editors (1987). *Research Directions in Object-Oriented Programming*. The MIT Press.

Wisskirchen, P. (1990). *Object-Oriented Graphics*. Springer-Verlag.

Zeleznik, R. C., Conner, D. B., Wloka, M. W., Aliaga, D. G., Huang, N., Hubbard, P. M., Knep, B., Kaufman, H., Hughes, J. F., and van Dam, A. (1991). An object-oriented framework for the integration of interactive animation techniques. In Sederberg, T. W., editor, *SIGGRAPH '91 Conference Proceedings*, pages 105–112. ACM SIGGRAPH, Addison-Wesley.

12

Acting on Inheritance Hierarchies

Adelino F. da Silva

A visual programming system is presented in which an object-based framework is imposed on a strongly typed object-oriented language. Active objects in this framework are viewed as a network of cooperating agents subject to mechanisms of behaviour replacement and delegation. Since these mechanisms are effective in a structured organization they tend to increase the active object's responsibilities and push delegation to a higher level in the design process. The framework is intended to provide, at a coarser level, the flexibility and dynamic characteristic of delegation-based languages without sacrificing the structural design and the efficiency enabled by strongly typed languages.

1 Introduction

Knowledge sharing is a powerful feature of object-oriented design. In many object-oriented languages inheritance is the main mechanism used for sharing code and behaviour. Inheritance hierarchies provide the supporting structure for the sharing of knowledge specified in base classes by derived classes. In class-based inheritance all objects of a class share a common interface. This inheritance uniformity promotes modularity and simplifies modification since changes made to a class may affect all its members [Wirfs-Brock and Johnson, 1990, Silva and Duarte-Ramos, 1991]. Class hierarchies may, however, constrain evolution. The links between base classes and derived classes enforce a static structure which may be difficult to modify without extensive re-design. Run-time changes are not easily supported by inheritance-based languages. On the other hand, differential inheritance in which behaviour is shared at the level of objects may be required for a flexible design. Delegation-based languages focus on behaviour sharing at the level of objects [Lieberman, 1986]. Run- time change is supported in the implementation of delegation through message passing between objects. Therefore, concurrency is naturally incorporated in the concept of objects. Delegation allows an object receiving a request message to forward it to some other object for processing. By focusing on the individual object, flexibility and dynamicism is gained at the expense of structural design [Stein, 1991].

In this paper, a visual programming system is presented (see [Myers, 1990]) in which an object-based framework is imposed on a strongly-typed object-oriented language [Ellis and Stroustrup, 1990]. A clear-cut distinction between active and passive objects is made. Passive objects are perceived as resources used by active objects. This distinction has led to two kinds of inheritance hierarchies. Active objects in this framework are viewed as a network of cooperating agents subject to mechanisms of behaviour replacement and delegation. Since these mechanisms are effective in a structured organization they tend to increase the active object's responsibilities and push delegation to a higher level in the design process. As in actor systems, locality laws restrict the number of possible interactions between objects. The framework intends to provide, at a coarser-level, the flexibility and dynamicism characteristic of delegation-based languages without sacrificing the structural design and the efficiency enabled by strongly-typed languages. The domain of application of the present platform has been originally directed to the design and implementation of visual programming concurrent systems. It is supposed that the fields of parallel programming [Suhler, 1990], and discrete-event simulation [Misra, 1986] could benefit from the present approach as well.

2 Object-Oriented Concurrent Model

Similarly to some actor systems [Yonezawa, 1990, Agha, 1986], we are interested in designing a system in which computations are performed by a collection of independent concurrent computational units or agents. Agents manifest their behaviour in response to a finite set of incoming communications. Agents may create new agents to whom they can delegate behaviour. A communication mechanism provides the required interaction between cooperating agents. The agents exist in an environment having some hierarchical structure, and are controlled by a master agent which supervises common resources and manages allocation of finite space. Our approach emphasizes the development of a visual language for programming the network of agents and their interactions. In addition, agents are perceived as independent entities or objects existing in a particular environment having some specific hierarchical structure. Therefore, their behaviour may be modelled after class-based inheritance mechanisms.

An agent is an active object with a structure consisting of state variables, a set of member-functions and a message queue. Each agent has a single serial processing power or thread. The communication between agents is local, in the sense that messages may be sent only to the sender's acquaintances, and asynchronous [Wegner, 1990]. No handshaking to send/receive messages takes place. Each agent has a unique queue in which incoming messages are put in the order of arrival. These messages are perceived as communicating objects, created by the sender, and passed through local shared memory to the receiver agent. The receiver will be, in general, responsible for destroying the message-object but it can also pass the message to other agents. Each agent is connected to other agents located in a finite two-dimensional space. These connections define the agent's acquaintances. The topology of connections is dynamic. An agent may be required to be connected to, or disconnected from, some other existing agent. In terms of delegation, three forms are considered: direct, private and hierarchical. In direct delegation, an agent requires the creation of a new agent to be integrated in the main network of agents. The new agent may then communicate with existing agents, reporting directly to the master agent. In private delegation a specific agent controls the new agents it creates in a tree-like manner. The new agents are allowed to communicate only with the parent, being invisible to the base network. In hierarchical delegation, the agent constructs its own network of agents, modelled after the main network, and eventually reporting to it in the end.

3 Implementation Model

The concurrent capabilities of the system are integrated in the framework of object-oriented computing [Nierstrasz and Stadelmann, 1991, Nierstrasz, 1991]. The behaviour of the active objects is implemented by a set of cooperating lightweight processes, which are threads of execution or tasks that share a single address space within the framework [Axford, 1989]. When an active object or agent is first created it enters the ready state. After it is scheduled for execution, as determined by its priority and the scheduling policy, it enters the running state. If a running object needs to await the arrival of a resource it enters the blocked state; it returns to the ready state when another agent unblocks it by supplying it the awaited resource. It may unblock automatically if a time interval expires. If a running object is pre-empted, by another active object or by an interrupt handler, it returns to the ready state. An active object can voluntarily sleep for a desired time interval. It returns to the ready state when the time interval expires or when it is explicitly awakened by another agent. An object which ends its own execution enters the terminated state until its resources are released. An agent in any state enters the terminated state if it is killed by another agent. The agent's set of possible states and transitions is represented in Figure 1. Each active object has a priority associated with it. Active objects are scheduled for execution according to the their priority so that the one having highest priority is always executed first. Those objects having the same priority are scheduled in the order that they become ready to run. An object can also change its own priority. Two scheduling methods are supported: event-driven scheduling and real-time scheduling. In the former, the system time automatically advances when all active objects are either blocked or sleeping. The scheduler exits when no active objects exist or can be awakened by advancing the time. In real-time scheduling, one can advance the system's clock using an interrupt source in order to synchronize it with the passage of time.

Inter-object communication is done through shared memory instead of mailboxes. The double copying of messages into the mailbox and into the active object is thus avoided. The main facility used by the interface for inter-object communication is the blocking queue. Each active object automatically receives its own built-in blocking queue implemented as a doubly linked list. Messages are themselves objects passed between active objects by placing them into queues. An active object can enqueue message-objects into another object's blocking queue using the active object's identifier. Message-objects are passed by reference, that is the queue maintains references to the enqueued items. The blocking queue has the capability of synchronizing the activities of multiple objects. If an object attempts to dequeue a message-object from an empty blocking queue, it suspends execution awaiting the arrival of a message. When another active object places a message-object into an empty queue it unblocks the waiting active object, which then dequeues the message-object after resuming execution. On the other hand, a single object may

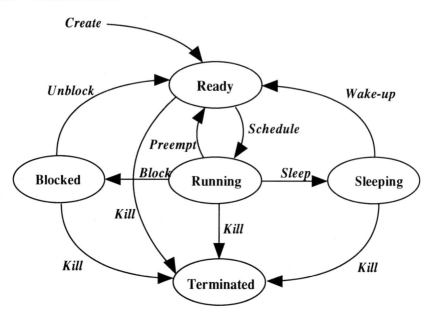

Figure 1: Agent's states and transitions

serve a blocking queue to which requests are submitted by other objects. A time-out interval may be defined for active objects kept waiting in the blocking queue. Semaphores can be used to control access to shared data structures.

To deal with active objects, a set of C++ classes has been built to introduce con-currency at the object-level. One fundamental class is the Thread base class (as partially defined in Figure 2). The public member functions of class Thread are inherited by all classes involving objects eligible for running. Therefore, a class of objects is declared active by deriving it from the Thread base class. By default, the Thread class constructor initializes the object and puts it in the ready state. Class Thread also manages the object's built-in queue by supplying member func-tions which encapsulate the behaviour of enqueueing and dequeueing of message-objects. All enqueued objects are instances of the same Qelement class. They serve as standard carriers which reference the actual message-objects containing the in-formation to be communicated. A link field in class Qelement enables the linking of Qelement objects into a queue. The actual behaviour of the active object is encapsu-lated in member functions subject to redefinition in derived classes. The behaviour of an active object can be modified by other active objects or by the master agent.

4 Visual Programming

Agents live in a visual programming environment [Chang, 1990, Glinert, 1990]. The environment simulates a discrete two-dimensional space. Each agent has a visual signature represented by an icon, and an address specified by the 2D co-ordinates where the agent's visual signature resides. When an agent is created it

```
class Thread {                                  // Concurrent base class
public:
   friend class NetworkManager;                 // network manager is a friend
   virtual void process();                      // main active behaviour
// enqueue objects in receiver agent's queue having identifier TaskId
   virtual void enqueue(void*,char*,TaskId );
// dequeued object's class name is passed to external function
   virtual void *dequeue(char *nm);
   virtual void task() { process(); }           // default active member-function
   Thread(char*, int, int );                    // constructor
   static TaskId tid[MAXTASKNUMBER];            // task identifiers
// ... other member-functions
protected:
   char *pname;                                 // Thread name
   int pnum;                                    // Thread id
   int priority;                                // Thread priority
// ... other member-variables
};
```

```
class Qelement {  // Double linked list objects reference enqueued objects
public:
// ... other member-functions
private:
   LINK ni_link;                                // Qelement's link
   void *pobj;                                  // pointer to enqueued object
   char *objNm;                                 // enqueued object's name
// ... other member-variables
};
```

Figure 2: Definition of queue elements and threads

is assigned a non-occupied location in the environment. In the current implementation, each agent is limited to having at most four acquaintances, one for each side of the rectangular icon box, with whom it can communicate at any given moment. The channels of communication between the agent and its acquaintances are visualized by directed links. Together, the icons and the links form a dynamic dataflow diagram. This diagram can be set up and modified interactively by the user, or it can evolve as a result of the actions of the agents in the environment. In interactive mode, the agents are created by dragging icons from an icon table to the proper screen locations. By default, this action automatically activates the object which the icon represents by putting the object in the ready state. Each agent has the possibility of managing an attached window object. The window object permits the visualization of the agent's operations as well as the querying of information related to its integration in the network.

As regards the active object's responsibilities, the main issues are the assignment of replacement behaviour, the definition of the communication and synchronization mechanisms, and the specification of delegation. Each active object has a set of member functions which account for the behaviour characteristics of the class (Figure 3). If desired they can be activated as tasks. Since these member functions have to be defined at compile time they model a static behaviour. The object's replacement behaviour is implemented by an external function, called visiting function, which is passed to the object and is made eligible for concurrent execution. This function can be run as a task in accordance with the schedule set up by the task manager. This external function is an application in its own right which can be coded and tested independently. Since the visiting function can be substituted at run-time it accounts for the dynamic capabilities of the framework. The function specifying the new behaviour can be passed to the active object by other active objects, or by the network manager responsible for operating the platform. Moreover, by acting on the dataflow diagram, the user can interactively re-assign functions to the objects from a pre-defined function table.

```
class Agent : public Thread {            // Definition of agents as active objects
public:
// enqueue object "name" in channel ic
   int EnqOne(void *, char *name, int ic);
// dequeue one validated object (irrespective of incoming channel)
   void* DeqOne(char **AllowedInputObjNames, int nInput, int i, int &id);
// substitution of agent's active function
   void set_proc(void (*Icfunction)(void*)) { icfn = Icfunction; }
   void process();                       // process main active function
// Icfunction is an external function
   Agent(NetworkManager *, void (*Icfunction)(void*) = NULL,...);
// ... other member-functions
private:
   friend class NetworkManager;          // network manager is a friend
   NetworkManager *pmnger;               // network manager's services may be required
   void (* icfn)(void *);                // replaceable agent-specific-function
   Agent *in[4];                         // connections from (4) acquaintances
   Agent *out[4];                        // connections to (4) acquaintances
   WndX *wic;                            // agent's attached window
   int ix,iy;                            // handle point
// ... other member-variables
};
```

Figure 3: Class of active objects

An important design issue is to separate the specification of the communication and synchronization from the specification of the units of computation. Each active object has a fixed number of channels of communication, and a queue for receiving incoming messages. Once defined, the object's channels are maintained and operated by the network manager. Each object is visually linked to its acquaintances. For inter-object communication purposes each external function or application manipulates input and output objects which must be taken into account in a proper dataflow setting. In order to separate the definition of the active object's behaviour from the definition of the message-objects acceptable to it, the active object has the possibility of enqueueing and dequeueing messages which are not directly interpreted by the object but passed back to the external function manipulating them. Therefore, the active object is not bound to a static set of acceptable input/output objects. On the other hand, the behavioural specification carried by the external function may be coded independently.

5   Framework Management

The framework (or network) manager is the entity controlling the network of agents and their inter-object communications. The data structure operated on by the manager must fulfill some design specifications as regards to its prospective responsibilities. The data structure must be dynamic in order to enable efficient updates. Insertions, deletions as well as node searching are often executed operations. In addition, the data structure must serve a visual programming environment supporting interactive re-specification. On the other hand, following the active objects' delegation assignments, the structure must permit the dynamic redefinition of the objects' attributes. A modified pseudo-point-quadtree has been introduced [Overmars, 1982, Samet, 1990]. The data structure is a hierarchical quaternary tree whose leaves store 2D handle points associated with the screen locations of the active objects' signatures or icons. The leaves of the quadtree structure do not store the active objects themselves but hold pointers to arbitrary data types which can be customized by the application. The quadtree structure was defined as a generalized class (Figure 4). The member functions implement the required dynamic operations of node insertion, node deletion, node searching, etc. The generalization of the class to objects of any type is implemented through macros. Another important feature is the possibility of having an external user-defined function to be passed to the generic quadtree structure. This visiting function effectively enables the dynamic substitution of global operations acting upon the quadtree structure. Hence, the dynamic reassignment of replacement behaviour for the structure parallels and complements the one for active objects.

In order to build an application, a default table of icons representing active objects is presented to the user. A network of active objects may be visually programmed by moving instances of the icons to specific screen locations and dragging lines between them, according to the communication pattern of the corresponding active objects. For active objects referenced in the icon-table, the introduction of new active objects in the network amounts to the insertion of new icons and respective links in the data structure. This introduction must nevertheless satisfy proper layout requirements. Redefinition or substitution of active objects' functions is supported by the interface as well. Redefining an object's function involves two aspects: the redefinition of the function, i.e., the (textual) code, and the redefinition of its visual (iconic) content, presentation and textual-to-visual correspondence. For dealing with these matters a class was defined (class FnArr). The class manages operations on an array of pointers to functions. Operations such as add, remove and replace care for the maintenance of a set of basic functions. An external user defined function, for instance, may be added to the basic function set and thus be made available to the designer. The class deals with the textual to visual mapping as well. Each icon function has a unique visual signature which evokes its code contents. The function's visual signature must then be incorporated in the icon table to be presented to the user. To deal with the manipulation of information as described above, the

```
typedef void (* VISIT)(void *);

class Knode {                                 // Node of quadtree structure
private:
  friend class Ktree;
  Knode* pk[4];                               // four sons
  int ox, oy;                                 // point coordinates
  void* body;                                 // pointer to active object
// ... other member-variables
};
class Ktree {                                 // Modified pseudo-point-quadtree
public:
  int insert(int ,int, void* );               // node insertion
  Knode* seek(int ,int );                      // node searching (by coordinates)
  void remove(int ,int );                      // node deletion
  void set_process(VISIT what_to_do) { visit = what_to_do; }
  Ktree(VISIT what_to_do = NULL);
  ~Ktree(void) { cleanup(); }
// ... other member-functions
private:
  Knode* root;
  void (* visit)(void*);                       // global visiting function for Ktree
  void cleanup(Knode*n = NULL, int first=1);
// ... other member-variables
};
// Example of macro declaration
#define mkdtree(type) name2(mkdtree,type)
#define mkdtreedeclare(type)\
struct mkdtree(type) : Ktree {\
  mkdtree(type)(void (*what_to_do)(type *) = NULL) : (what_to_do) {}\
// ... other declarations
}
declare(mkdtree,Agent);                        // tree of pointers to Agents
```

Figure 4: Defining elements of the quadtree structure

tools provided by the main interface for text and icon editing may be used. The objects of class FnArr are used by the framework manager to make the interface more dynamic (see Figure 5).

6   Delegation

6.1   Characterization

Inheritance allows incremental definition of classes. All instances of a class use the definitions of attributes stored in the class. The grouping properties of the hierarchy account for the structure of all instances of a class. Therefore, any change

```
class NetworkManager : public Window {
public:                            // the manager operates in a visual environment
    void mesh();                   // introduce in dataflow graph
    void link(Agent *p);           // establishing connections with acquaintances
    Agent* fetch();                // find agent
    Agent* seek(int , int );       // search agent's handle
// pre-defined functions and icons are passed to the manager
    NetworkManager(FnArr* , ... );
    ~NetworkManager();
// ... other member-functions
private:
    mkdtree(Agent) *tree;          // tree of pointers to agents
    FnArr *xfni;                   // referencing external functions and their icons
    VISIT fn0;                     // structural visiting function set to xfni[0];
// ... other member-variables
};
```

Figure 5: Features of the network manager

made to a class attribute will affect all of the instances. Moreover, instances in strict inheritance are independent since changing the state of one instance does not affect other instances. Delegation, on the other hand, allows incremental definition of all objects. Any object can serve as a prototype. An extension object is constructed by defining a list of objects sharing knowledge with the new object (its prototypes), and a personal behaviour pertaining to the object itself. When an extension object receives a message it may try to respond by itself, or rely on the prototypes by forwarding (delegating) the message. In many cases the object being delegated to can be perceived as performing a service for the original object. In these circumstances, a reply mechanism must be provided. For an analysis of the main paradigms used in existing object-oriented graphics systems see Conner et al. [Conner and van Dam, 1993].

In our model we have used inheritance to model the structural properties of the active objects (agents). The agents' basic common attributes, in the sense that they are not subject to change, are shared by inheritance. Passive objects are mainly thought of as resources, being modelled by inheritance as well. We have implemented active objects as objects belonging to the same class. This would be overly restrictive in a strict hierarchical system. However, we have previously introduced some mechanisms for modelling differential behaviour among instances of a class structure. The replacement behaviour mechanism allows the modelling of agents sharing a common structure and having specialized behaviour defined at the instance level. It is this specialized behaviour, not provided by the instance template and subject to dynamic modification, which permits the flexibility that inheritance lacks. Since we end up with objects having different attributes it makes sense to consider ways of playing with their inter-dependences.

By implementing dynamic behaviour replacement, we have achieved differential behaviour at the instance level but not yet for the dependence of instances which goes with delegation. The forward and reply features must be supported as well.

In order to support message passing among objects, an environment supervised by a manager has been introduced. As referred to before, "the physical environment" is a discrete 2D space in which each agent has its own mail address. Dependences between objects are maintained in this space, subject to the limitations imposed on the number of connections per active object. These connections are visually supported by the network. There are, however, other dependences between objects which may occur as a result of the private activity of an agent which may not have direct visible support within the original network. This mechanism is characterized below under the name 'private delegation'.

6.2 Mechanisms

Active objects wanting to implement delegation have several alternatives. (Several other possibilities, such as broadcasting and forwarding unacceptable messages, are not considered here). At the active object level, a script may reference other active objects responsible for implementing some specialized service. This can be achieved by associating a mail address with an available service within the network. The agent's script here is roughly equivalent to the list of prototypes in delegation languages. Nevertheless, in order to allow for full flexibility the agent's scripts should be dynamic. Another possibility is to query the manager for services and mail addresses associated with the network of agents. Suppose that an agent does not know who can provide a certain service. He may query the manager for this purpose and implement delegation afterwards. Once the mail address of the delegated object becomes known, links between delegating and delegated objects can be established. Therefore, under this assumption, delegation uses the resources and environment control functions assigned to the manager. Yet another dimension of flexibility worth mentioning is provided by delegation preceded by creation. An agent may require the manager's services to incorporate a new agent in the network. After assigning some behaviour to the new agent, delegation follows the usual mechanisms.

The reply mechanism is implemented through the specification of a destination address. A reply mail address is passed to the delegate object, which may well be the mail address of the delegating object itself. Furthermore, the explicit use of destination addresses enables the composition of delegation in a chain of delegating agents. The implicit form of delegation supposes that some service will be provided by an agent on behalf of the delegating agent with no need to return a reply.

As implied above, delegation is implemented by asynchronous message passing between agents. Therefore, the concurrent model of computation described earlier is used for this purpose. The basic synchronization mechanisms at our disposal are the blocking queues and the assignment of priorities. Messages are dequeued in the order in which they arrive to the blocking queue. Blocking queues provide mutual exclusion which allows them to be safely called by multiple agents. Priorities associated with the agents' threads can be changed in order to fit an appropriate schedule. An agent can also change its own priority. Re-scheduling of the agents' activities is controlled by the manager. The user can control the re-scheduling mechanism by interacting with the graphical user interface.

6.3 Composition

We now consider some forms of delegation for composing applications with different requirements namely, direct, private, and hierarchical delegation mechanisms.

In direct delegation the new object is to be linked to the existing network. The delegating object then requests the manager's services for settling the new object in the environment and linking it to its specified acquaintances. A behavioural function is passed to the created object by the delegating object. As usual, once created the new object enters the ready state until it is scheduled for execution according to the priority assigned to it. Of course, the new object's task may depend on objects whose tasks have been executed earlier, thus leading eventually to deadlock. Active objects have, however, the possibility of requesting the re-scheduling of tasks and the re-assignment of priorities. In order to allow for runtime modifications, these actions are typically programmed within the visiting function passed to the active object, and executed by the object's active member-function associated with that function.

Private delegation means that the active object directly controls the execution of the objects it delegates to in a parent-child relationship. The new objects are not integrated in the global framework of active objects. In addition, the parent blocks until the completion of its children. Private delegation activities are not visually supported by the graphical interface. The private agent bears total responsibility for the agents it may have created as well as for the activities delegated to them. It may, however, depend on the operating system for thread creation within the global task system, provided appropriate restrictions on priority assignments are met.

In hierarchical delegation the active object has the possibility of acting as manager of its own network of active objects. The top-level network is suspended and control is passed to the assigned sub-manager. The top-level structural pattern is replicated by instantiating a new manager class object at the new hierarchical level. In particular, the user can interactively define a new dataflow diagram representing a close-up of the behaviour of some active object (Figure 6). Except for the initialization and information transfer after completion, interaction between hierarchical diagrams is not allowed. As soon as the sub-network has finished execution the upper manager resumes operation according to the scheduler. The scheduling policy followed has maintained the overall task space flat and assigned higher priority to the tasks down the hierarchy. As before, active operations may be defined at run-time by the external function passed to the active object concerned.

7 Conclusion

The inheritance relation is an important object-oriented concept supporting reuse and extensibility. Inheritance relationships permit the modelling of abstractions as part of the design phase by identifying commonality among abstractions. Inheritance in combination with polymorphism are design features providing strong support for the extension of existing systems. On the other hand, concurrent object-oriented design often calls for loosely coupled systems, leading to models of computation based on dynamically interacting objects. The tradeoff between flexibility and inheritance has led to the emergence of a large variety of object-oriented lan-

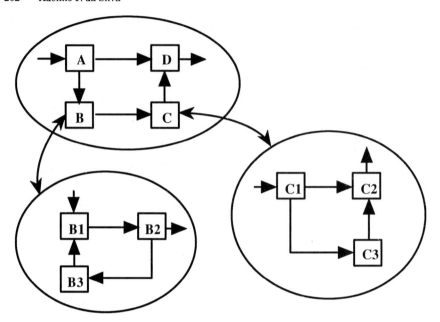

Figure 6: Hierarchical delegation in a dataflow setting

guages. The design approach presented in this paper introduces concurrency in the framework of the C++ language. Classes have been introduced to model processes as objects having their own thread of execution. Communication among active objects has been developed in a structured visual programming framework. Several delegation mechanisms have been conceived and implemented to support highly interactive software development. The structural characteristics of the framework, in conjunction with the delegation patterns of the active objects, effectively enabled the reconfiguration of the interface and the dynamization of the intercommunication mechanisms. The adequacy of the present framework to model animation and discrete event simulation problems will be evaluated in the future.

References

Agha, G. (1986). *ACTORS: A Model of Concurrent Computation in Distributed Systems*. The MIT Press, Cambridge, Mass.

Axford, T. (1989). *Concurrent Programming: Fundamental Techniques for Real-Time and Parallel Software Design*. John Wiley & Sons.

Chang, S.-K. (1990). *Principles of Visual Programming Systems*. Prentice-Hall.

Conner, D. B. and van Dam, A. (1993). "Sharing Between Graphical Objects Using Delegation". In *this volume*. Springer-Verlag.

Ellis, M. and Stroustrup, B. (1990). *The Annotated C++ Reference Manual*. Addison-Wesley.

Glinert, E.P., et al., (1990). "Exploring the General-Purpose Visual Alternative". *Journal of Visual Languages and Computing*, 1:3–39.

Lieberman, H. (1986). "Using Prototypical Objects to Implement Shared Behavior in Object-Oriented Systems". In *Proceedings of OOPSLA'86*, pages 214–223. ACM.

Misra, J. (1986). "Distributed Discrete-Event Simulation". *ACM Computing Surveys*, 18(1):39–65.

Myers, B. A. (1990). "Taxonomies of Visual Programming and Program Visualization". *Journal of Visual Languages and Computing*, 1:97–123.

Nierstrasz, O. (1991). "The Next 700 Concurrent Object-Oriented Language". In *Object Composition*, pages 165–187. Université de Genève.

Nierstrasz, O., Tsichritzis, D., de Mey, V., and Stadelmann, M. (1991). "Objects + Scripts = Applications". In *Object Composition*, pages 11–29. Université de Genève.

Overmars, M. H. (1982). *The Design of Dynamic Data Structures*. Lecture Notes in Computer Science, no. 156, Springer-Verlag.

Samet, H. (1990). *The Design and Analysis of Spatial Data Structures*. Addison-Wesley.

Silva, A. and Duarte-Ramos (1991). "Building User-Interface Support for Object-Oriented Design". In *Proceedings of the First Int. Conf. on Computer Graphics and Visualization Techniques, Compugraphics'91*, pages 371–380.

Stein, L. A. (1991). A unified methodology for object-oriented programming. In *Inheritance Hierarchies in Knowledge Representation and Programming Languages*, pages 211–222. John Wiley & Sons.

Suhler, P. A. (1990). "TDFL: A Task-Level Dataflow Language". *Journal of Parallel and Distributed Computing*, 9:103–115.

Wegner, P. (1990). "Concepts and Paradigms of Object-Oriented Programming". *ACM OOPS Messenger*, 1(1):7–87.

Wirfs-Brock, R. and Johnson, R. (1990). "Surveying Current Research in Object-Oriented Design". *Communications of the ACM*, 33(9):104–124.

Yonezawa, A. (1990). *ABCL: An Object-Oriented Concurrent System*. The MIT Press, Cambridge, Mass.

13

The PREMO Framework: Object-Oriented Issues

Peter Wisskirchen

The need for a coordinated method for addressing all aspects of the construction of, presentation of, and interaction with multi-media objects has lead to the need for the standardization of a Presentation Environment for Multi-Media Objects (PREMO). In this paper the state of discussions inside the DIN working group is reported focusing on object-oriented aspects of the PREMO framework.

1 Introduction

Efforts towards a second generation of graphics standards have led to the formulation of a New Work Item Proposal [ISO, 1992a] formulated by an ISO Working Group arguing for a Programming Environment for Graphics Objects. As a reaction to this proposal, a working group of the German Standardization Body DIN (DIN working group) has worked out a document describing the overall architecture and kernel functionality of a coming family of standards. On the basis of this work, Version 1 of an Initial Draft for a *Presentation Environment for Multi-Media Objects* (PREMO) was composed during an ISO/IEC JTC 1/SC 24/WG 1 meeting at Gut Ising, Chiemsee, Germany in October 1992 [ISO, 1992b].

In this paper the state of discussions inside the DIN working group is reported focusing on the object-oriented aspects of the PREMO framework. It should be noted, however, that this paper is influenced by personal opinions of the author and it should therefore not be misinterpreted as the official DIN view.

In [Kansy and Wisskirchen, 1991] it was argued that the complexity of graphics and the vast diversity of constituencies with differing requirements could not be fulfilled by one standard. On the other side, it is not desirable to provide a separate standard for each constituency as this would be too expensive for developers of graphics system, too difficult for educating graphics programmers, and it would destroy the benefit of portability of programs.

Therefore, a new effort has been started to generate a second generation graphics standard which comprises the capabilities of existing standards, avoids the errors and pitfalls of the first generation standards, is sufficiently flexible to be adapted to the needs of a variety of applications, and provides all these capabilities in a well-structured way. To achieve this goal, PREMO will be defined as a multi-part standard of closely related, configurable components, open for extensions whenever new development has to be taken into consideration by standardization bodies, and using the potential of object-oriented programming to achieve modularity as well as flexibility.

Examples of intended PREMO components are class libraries for 2-D and 3-D basic systems, different renderers including photorealistic presentations, animation systems and geometric modellers. In particular, the intended components shall play a key role in multi-media applications by providing, in a standard way, the main functionality for computer based modelling, display and animation of information.

The framework is based on a *hybrid* model, allowing the use of different *modelling paradigms* concurrently. Thus single output primitives, part hierarchies, explicit and implicit functional representations, as well as complex rules and constraints to describe complex object dependencies can be used to create one single graphics scene.

A PREMO system consists of a set of components each described as a class library. Specific rules describe how single components may be combined to build up a valid configuration.

2   Overall Architecture of PREMO

The architecture of PREMO is based on the definition of a framework and sets of components. Components consist of a set of related objects. Components encapsulate related sets of functionality (data and operations) while the framework gives rules for both individual components (as sets of related objects), and between components (in terms of allowed interrelationships and interfaces). The architecture also contains rules describing criteria for the development of components as well as how to configure, extend and customize existing components to generate a specific system for some application area. PREMO is based on a specialization of the Computer Graphics Reference Model (CGRM), a draft international standard [ISO, 1991]. In PREMO, the five environments of the CGRM are grouped into three PREMO environments as shown in Figure 1. This grouping was done because, at this level of abstraction, PREMO is concerned only with the interface to the lower three CGRM environments and is not concerned with a finer level of detail. These three environments are:

- *modelling environment* (construction environment),
- *virtual environment* with the scene as a collection of primitives to be displayed,
- *presentation environment* (comprising viewing, logical, and realization environment).

The modelling environment accomodates the application-oriented modelling components; the presentation environment contains the different presentation techniques; the scene is the mediator between different modelling and presentation components (see Figure 2).

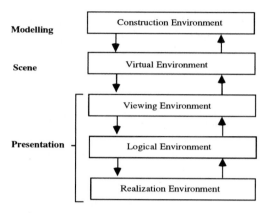

Figure 1: Environments of the CGRM as seen in PREMO

3   Modelling (Construction Environment)

An application program interfaces primarily with modelling components (modeller) which create scenes. Such modellers consist of a family of related producers capable of creating the desired output objects and inserting them into scenes. Different modellers allow the generation of models of different complexity. Examples include geometric modelling, animation, physically based modelling, data visualization, and music composition. Different modellers can contribute to one scene and one modeller can contribute to several scenes. The modellers provide rich and application specific functionality to build up a model according to the needs of an existing constituency. The model may be described as an arbitrary structure of objects, e.g., as a part-of-hierarchy or a group of moving objects' constraints by forces. Objects may depend on some mathematical calculation (scientific visualization) or on other objects (constraints). Any value may be expressed by a constant value or a time function for animation purposes. Properties may specify graphical and application specific aspects intermixed. Geometry is a property which is defined in application specific coordinates. Modelling transformations are properties which position objects within a common reference coordinate system used in the virtual environment, called world coordinates (WC).

4   Scene (Virtual Environment)

The scene in the virtual environment of the Computer Graphics Reference Model is a central concept used in PREMO. The scene is a collection of output objects delivered by one or several modelling systems to be processed by one or more producers. Functions on the scene include addition and deletion of output objects. The scene serves as mediator between modelling systems and renderers. It supports the output primitives in the most general form. As it does not use or manipulate the content of output objects, it should not be seriously affected when new modellers and producers are developed which introduce new output objects and properties. The scene does not support structure. Structure belongs to the modelling domain as such structure describes a decomposition at the modelling level rather than a

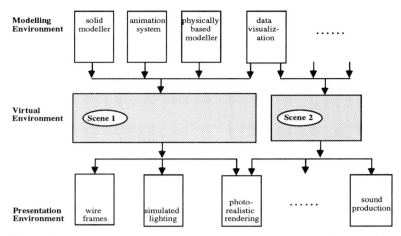

Figure 2: The scene as mediator between different modelling and presentation components

graphical decomposition of a scene. All values of output objects (its properties) may be defined as time dependent information. The time information is maintained in the scene. The scene is therefore not a snapshot, a single frame, but describes the scene over a finite or infinite time interval. This enables the system to optimize the computation of successive images; sufficient information for generation of special effects like motion blur and temporal anti-aliasing is available at this level and can be given to producers. A scene can be animated by producers in two different ways. In synchronous time mode, the scene is evaluated by a producer at times strictly dictated by an external clock (e.g., real time or slow motion). In event driven mode, one or more producers evaluate a scene at fixed (simulated) instants prescribed by the application. The progression of time is controlled by events like "production finished" or by application specific events. Sound is supported as an object which can be used as either an output object or a property object.

5   Presentation

In PREMO, producers, such as renderers, determine the way and the quality of processed scenes. They use different algorithms for generating output objects including flat shading, ray tracing, radiosity based methods, MIDI sound etc. Therefore, producers are organized into different classes.

Producers have different requirements about what kind of output objects they can handle. Applications may use analytically defined bodies like spheres and boolean conjunctions of bodies. A producer may expect simple basic output objects like triangles, lines, text, and sound segments or it may require complex primitives with specific surface attributes to calculate reflected and refracted rays. For doing this, a producer asks the output objects to describe themselves in these terms. This makes producers independent of specific modellers and their output objects; it requires that a set of methods is defined which has to be served by all output objects processed. We call these methods that are a prerequisit for the definition of extensible renderers "rendering capabilities". A simple producer may ask for a triangulation of an object with simple colour values at the corners, whereas a high performance producer may demand an analytic description of the object and material properties like green velvet.

A producer knows the characteristics of the destination objects which may be objects such as pix-maps, z-buffers, two-dimensional primitives, or video frames. In the latter case, this knowledge is required to generate an adequate display optimally (e.g., filling a frame buffer with regard to the appropriate resolution and colour calibration or generating PostScript output). Application relevant characteristics can be inquired by the application from the producer.

For camera objects, properties control the viewing (camera parameters). When one object is to be viewed from different positions, two camera objects with different camera properties have to be generated.

PREMO is formulated in a language independent way by using object-oriented terminology based on the class-instance paradigm. Some problems in finding a language independent functional description which is precise enough but gives enough room to come to convenient language bindings for the different object-oriented languages currently in use, were already mentioned in [Kansy and Wisskirchen, 1991]. As a first approach, at the Chiemsee meeting in October 1992, an adaptation of the OMG Basic Object Model was included in the Initial Draft [ISO, 1992b].

6   How to Extend and Customize PREMO?

Presently, different ideas are being discussed to extend and customize PREMO by adding new renderers, modelling paradigms, or sets of output primitives. By extension we mean the integration of new standard components by respective committees. By customization we mean the integration of non-standard components into a pre-manufactured kernel by the application programmer or by a third party.

6.1   Extension

As mentioned, the model's entities are evaluated to produce or change the state of a scene purely focusing on graphics aspects. To support the specification and integration of a new modelling paradigm, a scene description interface (SDI) will be standardized. SDI is defined by a set of methods provided by a class Scene, and it consists more or less of the usual methods to edit a set oriented graphics collection consisting of single output primitives. Each modelling component introduced as a new standard component must be described by using the SDI as far as the communication between model and scene is concerned. New output components, including renderers, can be introduced in the sense of extensions by describing their effects on a given scene. This is possible because the scene is transparently defined as a set of output primitives.

6.2   Customizing by Adding Non-Standard Components

Based on a standard SDI, non-standard modelling components, e.g., procedural descriptions [Upstill, 1990] can be plugged in. Such a component may be realized by a third party and can then be integrated into PREMO provided that it communicates via the SDI interface (cf. Figure 2, right). Procedural descriptions can be used for many purposes, for example, to define fractals and other recursive models, or to introduce composed primitives with new editing methods [Amburn et al., 1986].

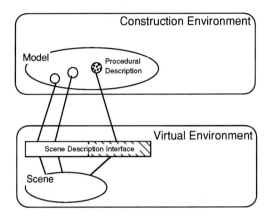

Figure 3: Scene description interface

A given configuration may be customized, for example, by adding non-standard output primitives as part of a modelling component. This is quite simple as long as these objects are able to produce lower level primitives that can be understood by the scene and the renderers evaluating it. These possibilities are described in [Egbert and Kubitz, 1992] for an object-oriented environment.

6.3   Using the Potential of Inheritance

Up to this point, we have mainly argued that the definition of interfaces between different environments allows adding new components as long as their interfaces are compatible with the definitions prescribed by the standard. The main potential of an object-oriented standard, however, can be seen in offering the use of inheritance in an appropriate way. In the following, we give two examples showing overriding of default behavior and the use of abstract classes in connection with the proposed standard.

6.4   Overriding Default Behavior

Inheritance supports incremental program development and modification by introducing subclasses with methods overriding predefined behavior. Overriding methods is one of the central concepts of object-oriented application frameworks based on the idea of a generic application such as MacApp [Schmucker, 1986], ET++ [Weinand et al., 1989] or GINA [Spenke et al., 1991] and it is extensively used in current object-oriented graphics systems to modify default behavior.

Overriding an existing method is not strictly against information hiding because the implementation of the method being overridden is not used in this process.

Nevertheless, overriding requires both the name (pattern) of the method in question and its class to be revealed. In the field of standardization, there are strong arguments against revealing to many classes and method-patterns in a standard document because this would limit the freedom for a manufacturer to realize his own implementation. Therefore, the selection of classes and methods to be revealed and mentioned in the standard as candidates for customization requires some sensitiveness and fine tuning.

Examples of methods which can be overridden may be reactions to pick-operations, definition of pick-sensitive areas, interaction feedback and other methods where experiences with existing standards have shown a demand to achieve higher flexibility.

6.5   Generic Renderers

An important example for using object-oriented approaches is the definition of an extensible ray tracer. By an extensible ray tracer, we understand a raytracer which can handle newly introduced (user defined) types of primitives as long as they are defined as subclasses of a predefined abstract class. To reach the goal of extensibility, the division of functionality between the raytracer and the scene objects (primitives) to be rendered must be defined in an appropriate way. The basic idea is the concept of a raytracer which can do without precoded knowledge about specific primitives types by sending appropriate inquiries to scene objects when accessing them. In this case, all knowledge required by the renderer is (and must be) provided by respective methods of the primitives (rendering capabilities). For raytracing, these methods are essentially methods to inquire the primitive's bounding box, ray intersection point for a given ray, normal vector and material properties at the intersection point. Note that the basic idea of an extensible ray tracer, although somewhat limited by using just plain C, was already suggested by Heckbert's hints on writing a ray tracer [Heckbert, 1991]. Rendering capabilities, in the sense that a user-defined object replies to a drawing protocol message with a collection of base objects that can be drawn by a predefined renderer, are described in [Bahrs, et al., 1992].

How can the idea of extensible renderers be used for the coming graphics standard? A standard will focus on a few well understood rendering paradigms. These rendering paradigms have to be analyzed carefully to define a minimal set of rendering capabilities the primitives must provide for each type of renderer. To organize these methods, one should note that some methods, for example, the calculation of a normal vector, are required by different types of renderers, whereas some other methods (mesh approximation) may be irrelevant for some renderers (ray tracers). Therefore, in order to organize the rendering capabilities in a way that duplications of methods with the same functionality are avoided, a class hierarchy (using multiple inheritance) is proposed as part of the coming standard document.

In analogy to rendering capabilities, we suggest as well to assign additional methods, e.g., for geometric modelling, interaction, deformation, reading and writing metafiles, to primitives and to organize them by abstract classes. Consequently, a primitive, e.g., a sphere, can be considered as an object whose type is rather dynamic. When porting an application using spheres across different platforms it depends on the specific renderers found on the platforms as to what capabilities must be installed (maybe by mixing them into the sphere's class hierarchy). Thus, the class hierarchy for primitives will be installation dependent which sounds to be a rather complicated concept. But nevertheless, the advantage of this rather dynamic approach is that tailorability will be supported and over-specification is avoided by exclusively adding capabilities that are really used on a given platform. For this to happen, how the different object-oriented languages will support flexible adding and removing of methods needs to be examined.

7   Type and Object Identity

One specific problem discussed in animation concerns the deformation of graphics entities in time. Such an object could (and should) be seen as an item with stable identity but with changing behavior. With such a concept, it is understandable that a prototype-delegation model with some very specific characteristics was proposed in [Zeleznik et al., 1991].

In PREMO, the following approximation to handle this problem, without leaving the class-instance based model, is currently discussed:

- See all time varying graphics output objects as instances of a very general primitive type, for example, a nurb. Then deforming, for example, a circle into a quadrangle could be interpreted as a deformation of one nurb by changing its parameters in time. Although nurbs cannot be handled very easily by the application programmer and not all cases can be modelled in this way, the requirements of object deformations should not have the consequence of selecting an alternative programming paradigm when defining an object-oriented graphics standard.

- Define deformation objects with changing geometry by introducing a special class where time dependent geometry is modelled by information "contained" in these objects. Such an object could provide methods to assign, for example, a circle at time t0, and a square at time t1, together with a deformation rule. Problems with this model are that the usual methods to handle a circle or a square are not part of the deformation object itself. The question is whether this should be seen as a serious disadvantage in practical applications.

8   Further Problems

Not all modelling paradigms presently used in computer graphics have been analyzed by our working group concerning their compatibility and affinity with the object-oriented programming paradigm. Is the object-oriented paradigm well suited to formulate the time dependent relations of n graphics entities by a set of differential equations? Is the set of equations itself modelled as an object in a natural way? Similar questions seem to be open in relation to constraints.

Constraints have been used for a long time in connection with object-oriented systems. Some recent publications propose and discuss a smooth integration of the constraint mechanism into object-oriented systems [Wilk, 1991, Laffra, 1992]. Nevertheless, as presented by E. Blake at the Third EuroGraphics Workshop on

Object-Oriented Graphics, powerful constraint mechanisms violate encapsulation and thus compromise important goals of object-orientation. Thus, it may cause problems for a standard committe – obliged to rely on existing programming languages, such as C++ – to include a constraint mechanism in a convenient way into an object-oriented standard.

9 Acknowledgement

The author thanks his colleagues from the DIN Working Group on PREMO for helpful ideas, discussions, and comments.

References

Amburn, P., Grant, E., and Whitted, T., Managing geometric complexity with enhanced procedural models. In *Computer Graphics, 18 (3)*, pages 129–135, 1986.

P. Bahrs and W. Dominick and D. Moreau, GOII: An Object-Oriented Framework for Computer Graphics In *Computer Graphics Using Object-Oriented Programming*, Cunningham, S., Knolle-Craighill, N., Fong, M.W., and Brown, J.R., pages 111–136, J. Wiley and Sons, New York, 1992.

Egbert, P. and Kubitz, W., The graphical presentation support system. In *Computer Graphics Using Object-Oriented Programming*, Cunningham, S., Knolle-Craighill, N., Fong, M.W., and Brown, J.R., pages 137–164, J. Wiley and Sons, New York, 1992.

Heckbert, P.S., Writing a Ray Tracer, In Glassner, A.S., editor, *Writing a Ray Tracer*, pages 263–293. Academic Press, London, 1991.

ISO, *Computer graphics P Reference model*. Draft International Standard ISO/IEC DIS 11072, 1991.

ISO, *Attachment to NP for a Programming Environment for Graphical Objects (Prego)*. Document ISO/IEC JTC1/SC24 N712, 1992.

ISO, *Initial Draft PREMO (Presentation Environment for Multi-Media Objects)*. Document ISO/IEC JTC1/SC24 N847, 1992.

Kansy, K. and Wisskirchen, P., The new graphics standard – object-oriented. In Blake, E. and Wisskirchen, P., editors, *Advances in Object-Oriented Graphics I (Proceedings of the Eurographics Workshop on Object-Oriented Graphics, 1990)*, EurographicSeminars Series, pages 199–215. Springer-Verlag, 1991.

Laffra, C., *PROCOL – A Concurrent Object-Oriented Language with Protocols, Delegation, Persistence, and Constraints*. PhD-Thesis, Erasmus University, Rotterdam, 1992.

Schmucker, K., *Object-Oriented Programming for the Macintosh*. Hayden Book Company, Hasbrouck Heights, New Jersey, 1986.

Spenke, M., Baecker, A., Berlage, T., and Beilken, C., Gina – a user interface development environment based on osf/motif. In *Proceedings of the First International Lisp Users and Vendors Conference, Gaitherburg, Oct.* 1991.

Upstill, S., *The RenderMan Companion*. Addison-Wesley, 1990.

Weinand, A., Gamma, E., and Marty, R., Design and implementation of ET++, a seamless object-oriented application framework. In *Structured Programming 10 (2), June*, 1989.

Wilk, M., Equate: an object-oriented constraint solver. In *OOPSLA '91 Proceedings*, pages 286–298, 1991.

Zeleznik, R. et al., An object-oriented framework for the integration of interactive animation techniques. In *SIGGRAPH '91 Proceedings, Computer Graphics Vol. 25, no. 4*, pages 105–112, 1991.

Part VI

Constraints II

14

An Object-Oriented Architecture for Constraint-Based Graphical Editing

Richard Helm, Tien Huynh, Kim Marriott, and John Vlissides

Direct-manipulation graphics editors are useful tools for a wide variety of domains such as technical drawing, computer-aided design, application building, and music composition. Constraints can be a powerful mechanism for specifying complex semantics declaratively in these domains. To date, few domain-specific graphics editors have provided constraint-based specification and manipulation facilities. Part of the reason is that graphical editors are hard enough to develop without implementing a constraint system as well. Even though graphical editing frameworks can reduce the difficulty of constructing domain specific graphical editors, a fundamental problem remains: there do not exist general constraint solving architectures that are efficient enough to support highly interactive editing, yet suitably flexible and extensible to adapt to different editing domains.

Addressing this problem, we present an object-oriented architecture that integrates the graphical editing framework Unidraw with QOCA, a powerful new constraint solving toolkit. QOCA leverages recent advances in symbolic computation and geometry to support efficient incremental solving of simultaneous equations and inequations, while optimizing convex quadratic objective functions. QOCA also supports new kinds of constraint manipulation that have novel applications to graphical editing. QOCA exploits the implementation language to provide a convenient, object-oriented syntax for expressing constraints in the framework. The result is a generic and easily extended architecture for constraint-based, direct-manipulation graphical editing.

1   Introduction

Constraints are a powerful formalism in graphical user interfaces, both as an aid in interface development and as an interaction paradigm. Constraints can specify spatial and semantic relationships declaratively between objects in a user interface, while an underlying constraint solver will ensure that interface meets the specification. Previous work [Borning, 1981, Borning and Duisberg, 1986, Epstein and Lalonde, 1988 Maloney et al., 1989, Nelson, 1985, Jr. and Allan, 1990, Sutherland, 1963, Szekely and Myers, 1988] has established that constraint systems need at least the following capabilities to be effective in graphical user interfaces:

- multi-way constraints that can express at least simultaneous linear equations and inequations [Freeman-Benson and Borning, 1992, Helm et al., 1992a].

- low latency and high-bandwidth feedback during direct manipulation [Maloney et al., 1989].

- incremental addition and deletion of constraints [Helm et al., 1992a, Maloney et al., 1990].

- the ability to detect causes of unsatisfiability for debugging inconsistent systems of constraints [Helm et al., 1992a].

- semantic feedback during direct manipulation to indicate valid ranges for variables and movements of objects [Hudson, 1990].

- graceful handling of underconstrained systems [Maloney et al., 1989, Freeman-Benson, 1990].

Drawing packages, CAD systems, application builders, and diagrammatic editors are representative of a class of applications that could benefit particularly from constraints. These direct-manipulation graphics editors let a user manipulate visual manifestations of familiar objects to convey information in a domain, and they are usually responsible for maintaining spatial and semantic relationships between objects. Constraints are a natural way to specify these relationships and to ensure their maintenance. Responsibility can thus be transferred from the user to the constraint system, freeing the user to focus on more creative aspects of his task.

Yet few graphical editing systems employ constraints to any degree; those that do are research prototypes [Bier and Stone, 1986, Nelson, 1985, Borning, 1981, Sutherland, 1963]. Perhaps one reason is that graphical editors are notoriously difficult to implement, even with conventional user interface toolkits. Several frameworks for building graphical editors have been reported recently [Tarumi et al., 1990, GECK, 1990, Vlissides and Linton, 1990] that address this problem. These frameworks provide a generic software architecture that typically supports the following:

- the definition of domain-specific graphical components and their semantics

- mechanisms for composing and structuring components

- (reversible) operations on components

- specialized direct manipulation techniques

- persistence and externalization of application data

Experience with graphical editing frameworks [Vlissides, 1990] has shown that they simplify editor development for different domains compared with traditional user interface toolkits, which support only the controlling elements of an application (e.g., buttons, scroll bars, and menus). Unfortunately, current frameworks take little or no advantage of the power of constraints. This deficiency reflects the fact that constraint capabilities are absent from most hand-built graphics editors. Therefore combining the capabilities of a graphical editing framework with a general-purpose constraint system can make domain-specific, constraint-based graphical editing systems far simpler to develop.

Integrating graphical editing frameworks and constraint systems raises new issues and challenges. Some problems stem from the nature of constraint-based editing in a highly interactive environment: every component may be constrained, and the entire constraint system may need to be re-solved on every input event (e.g., mouse motion). Other problems concern the integration itself: constraints can be so basic to the operation of framework objects but so closely coupled with the constraint system that integrating them requires a rewrite of the framework, the constraint system, or both. Consequently, the integration strategy requires a careful design and implementation effort to minimize modifications to the existing systems.

This paper presents an architecture for constraint-based, direct-manipulation graphical editing that addresses these issues. The architecture integrates Unidraw [Vlissides and Linton, 1990] a graphical editing framework developed at Stanford University, and QOCA (Quadratic Optimization Constraint Architecture), a new object-oriented constraint-solving toolkit developed at IBM Research. Unidraw is an established graphical editing framework that already has limited constraint-solving capabilities. QOCA leverages recent results in symbolic computation and geometry to support efficient incremental and interactive constraint manipulation. Our goal is to combine these systems to provide a generic and easily extended architecture for constraint-based, direct-manipulation graphical editing.

This paper offers an overview of the integrated architecture and its subsystems. We begin by presenting examples of constraint-based editing that demonstrate the power and desirability of this paradigm in general and the advanced capabilities of QOCA in particular. Then we describe the Unidraw framework and how we integrated it with QOCA toolkit objects to allow constraint specification. Next we provide details of the QOCA implementation and the algorithms on which it is based. We conclude the paper with a summary of the architecture and discussion of future directions for this work.

2 Sample Applications

QOCA is an extensible constraint solving toolkit that supports incremental solving of simultaneous (in)equations and optimizes convex quadratic objective functions. QOCA also supports new kinds of constraint manipulation that have novel applications to graphical editing. The following examples illustrate how graphical user interfaces can benefit from this technology, both in implementing commonplace functionality and in providing new, constraint-based capabilities.

2.1 Graphical Connectivity

A simple application of constraints in user interfaces is to maintain connectivity between graphical objects. The top of Figure 1 depicts rectangle objects A and C and an arrowheaded line B. We wish to link the rectangles with the line so that the arrows and rectangles abut regardless of their relative positions, as shown at the bottom of the figure.

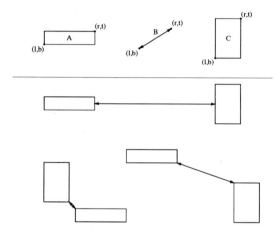

Figure 1: Boxes-and-arrows connectivity

To ensure that the endpoints of the arrows remain inside the rectangles, we begin by specifying the inequality constraints

$$l_A \leq l_B \leq r_A,\ b_A \leq b_B \leq t_A,\ l_C \leq r_B \leq r_C,\ b_C \leq t_B \leq t_C$$

over the variables defining the rectangles and line. These constraints are insufficient, however, because they do not guarantee that the arrowheads and rectangles abut properly. We can express these semantics as an optimization problem that minimizes the arrowheaded line's length:

$$minimize((l_B - r_B)^2 + (b_B - t_B)^2)$$

This expression, called an **objective function**, ensures that the line assumes the shortest distance between the rectangles. Objective functions are distinct from constraints: an objective function can only affect an underconstrained system. During constraint solving, therefore, QOCA will assign values to variables that minimize the objective functions. As the line's endpoints are constrained by the inequalities and governed by this objective function, the line will reorient and deform to accommodate the desired optimization.

2.2   Underconstrained Systems

So far we have used an objective function to specify an explicit design criterion: that the arrowheads and rectangles should abut. Less obvious is the need to clarify what happens when the user moves a rectangle, say rectangle A. Rectangle C may remain stationary and the line may stretch, for example, or the line may stay a fixed size while C moves the same distance as A. Without specifying a preference, either scenario is plausible; the system is underconstrained.

Handling underconstrained systems is a classic problem in constraint satisfaction. Stated generally, a constraint system must have a way to determine values for variables that are not constrained to take unique values. Requiring precisely constrained systems—that is, neither over- nor underconstrained—places too much responsibility on the user to create potentially complex yet error-free constraint specifications.

One way to deal with this problem is with constraint hierarchies [Borning et al., 1989], in which lower priority constraints express default behavior. The constraint solver selects (either arbitrarily or via comparators) non-required constraints to include in the solution. The primary difficulty with constraint hierarchies is in defining appropriate hierarchies (and comparators) so that, as constraints and defaults from different parts of the hierarchy are selected, the resultant solutions are continuous with respect to each other.

In contrast, the process of minimizing objective functions effectively selects values for underconstrained variables. The key idea is to continually refine the objective functions during direct manipulation so that new solutions are always as close as possible to the old. The objective functions provide a declarative way to express exactly what "closeness" means.

Returning to our connectivity example, we can make the system behave predictably when a rectangle is moved by introducing additional objective functions. Suppose we require that the rectangles deform and move as little as possible during direct manipulation. This requirement is captured via the objective functions

$$minimize(\ (l_A - l_{0A})^2 + (b_A - b_{0A})^2 + (r_A - r_{0A})^2 + (t_A - t_{0A})^2\ )$$

and

$$minimize(\ (l_C - l_{0C})^2 + (b_C - b_{0C})^2 + (r_C - r_{0C})^2 + (t_C - t_{0C})^2\ ),$$

which state that the new values for the variables defining the rectangles (l_A, r_A, ..., l_C, r_C, ...) should remain as close as possible to their current values given by the constants (l_{0A}, r_{0A}, ..., l_{0C}, r_{0C}, ...). By updating these constants at the start of each direct manipulation, we ensure that the rectangles will be deformed no more than necessary (and typically not at all).

Through objective functions, QOCA supports the "Principle of Least Astonishment": it guarantees that the rectangles will move as little as possible should the system ever be underconstrained. Moreover, because solutions are selected via objective functions, which are continuous, solutions generated by the solver during direct manipulation are likewise continuous with respect to each other. The system will not generate sudden discontinuous jumps between solutions.

2.3 Constrained Layout

Simultaneous linear constraints are a convenient way to express graphical layout. For example, Figure 2 graphically depicts constraints that left-align three small boxes and center the topmost small box horizontally in the surrounding box. Vertical constraints provide whitespace between the boxes and the surrounding box, ensuring that it is large enough to contain the smaller boxes.

Given that the dimensions of the surrounding box are $W \times H$ and the dimensions of the top most box are $w \times h$, the constraints that capture this layout are:

$$3h + 2Y_1 + 2Y_2 = H, \qquad 2X_1 + w = W, \qquad X_1 = Y_1.$$

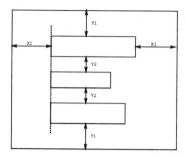

Figure 2: Example layout

These constraints form a system of simultaneous linear equations in three un-knowns, thereby demonstrating the need for a constraint solver that can solve simultaneous linear equations. In general, a constraint solver based on local prop-agation is not adequate whenever constraints express a dependency between the x and y dimensions.

Objective functions add even more power as they can express layout in terms of a "spring" metaphor, in which layouts can deform in precise and intuitive ways. The objective function measures the potential energy of a particular configuration, and the best layout is the one that minimizes this potential.

More formally, a spring S is specified by its minimum length L_{min}, its rest length L_{rest}, its maximal length L_{max}, and its energy coefficients when compressed E_{comp} and stretched E_{str}. Letting x be the extent of S, x must obey the constraints $L_{min} \leq x \leq L_{max}$, and the energy of S is:

$$e(x) = \begin{cases} E_{comp}(L_{rest} - x) & \text{if } L_{min} \leq x \leq L_{rest}; \\ E_{str}(x - L_{rest}) & \text{if } L_{rest} \leq x \leq L_{max}. \end{cases}$$

As the acronym suggests, QOCA is designed to solve quadratic optimization prob-lems. At first glance it is not clear that minimization of e can be handled by our system, because it is piecewise-linear rather than quadratic. However, we can trans-form this into a quadratic optimization problem (actually a linear optimization problem) by introducing two new variables: x_{comp}, the amount the spring is com-pressed, and x_{str}, the amount the spring is stretched. The associated constraints are

$$L_{min} \leq x \leq L_{max}, \qquad x_{comp} \geq 0, x_{str} \geq 0, \qquad x = L_{rest} - x_{comp} + x_{str}$$

and the energy of S is given by

$$e'(x, x_{comp}, x_{str}) = E_{comp}x_{comp} + E_{str}x_{str}.$$

Now for all $L_{min} \leq x \leq L_{max}$, the minimum value of $e'(x, x_{comp}, x_{str})$ is the same as that of $e(x)$—the minimum value of e' occurs when both x_{comp} or x_{str} is zero. Thus the two problems have the same solution.

2.4 Diagnosing Anomalies

One of the problems with declarative specifications in general and constraints in particular is that it can be difficult to ascertain the cause of unexpected behavior.

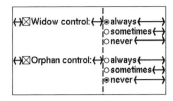

Figure 3: Dialog box with horizontal spring constraints superimposed

Figure 4: Resized dialog box with incorrect layout behavior

The larger the set of constraints, the more likely it is that the system is either over- or underconstrained, inconsistent, or otherwise at odds with desired semantics. Any system that supports nontrivial constraint specifications should also offer mechanisms for diagnosing anomalous behavior.

For example, consider interactive layout in a user interface builder. The dialog box in Figure 3 consists of check boxes and radio buttons aligned with spring constraints (arrows) and an alignment constraint (dashed vertical line). The builder is displaying only horizontal constraints for simplicity.

Now the interface designer would like the whitespace in between and around the buttons to grow and shrink equally as the dialog is resized. When the designer resizes the dialog, however, the radio buttons stay a fixed distance away from the right edge (Figure 4). To diagnose this problem, the builder can use the constraint system to determine the causes of unsatisfiability.

A natural interface to this functionality would let the user try to move a misplaced object. Then the system can provide feedback to help explain why the object cannot occupy its proper place. QOCA supports this diagnosis by providing primitive operations for testing the satisfiability of constraints and detecting the causes of their unsatisfiability.

In Figure 5 the user is trying to move one of the misplaced radio buttons. The system responds by displaying graphically the constraints that keep the button

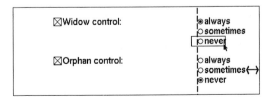

Figure 5: Diagnosing incorrect layout behavior

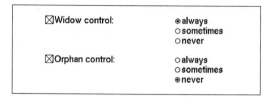

Figure 6: Corrected layout behavior

from moving: the left-alignment constraint and the spring to the right of the second "sometimes" radio button. This suggests to the user that a spring constant is incorrect. When he examines the spring's attributes he discovers that its spring constant is zero when it should be identical to that of the other springs. The user can then modify this constant in the builder, and the resulting interface exhibits the proper resize semantics (Figure 6).

3   Unidraw Framework Integration

Unidraw is an object-oriented framework for building direct-manipulation graphical editors. It is a part of InterViews [Linton et al., 1989], a comprehensive set of programming abstractions and tools for the design and implementation of workstation applications. Unidraw partitions the common functionality of graphical editors into four major class hierarchies:

1. **Components** represent the elements in a graphical editing domain, for example, geometric shapes in technical drawing, schematics of electronic parts in circuit layout, and notes in written music. Components encapsulate the appearance and semantics of these elements. The user arranges components to convey information in the domain of interest.

2. **Tools** support direct manipulation of components. Tools employ animation and other visual effects for immediate feedback to reinforce the user's perception that he is dealing with real objects. Examples include tools for selecting components for subsequent editing, for applying coordinate transformations such as translation and rotation, and for connecting components.

3. **Commands** define operations on components. Commands are similar to messages in traditional object-oriented systems in that components can receive and respond to them. Commands can also be executed in isolation to perform arbitrary computation, and they can reverse the effects of such execution to support undo. Examples include commands for changing the attributes of a component, duplicating a component, and grouping several components into a composite component.

4. **External representations** define a one-way mapping between components and their representation in an outside format. For example, a transistor component can define both a PostScript representation for printing and a netlist representation for circuit simulation; each is generated by a different class of external representation.

Partitioning editor functionality into components, commands, tools, and external representations is the foundation of the Unidraw architecture. We will introduce additional Unidraw classes as they become relevant.

3.1 Basic Integration

The obvious application of QOCA in Unidraw was as a replacement for Unidraw's special-purpose geometric constraint solver, which enforces connectivity semantics between components. However, making QOCA's full power available to the Unidraw programmer adds a new dimension to the framework's capabilities—support for constraint-based graphical editing. In this section we discuss several key aspects of the integration of these two systems.

Unidraw can leverage constraints in two ways: (1) constraints can define attributes of new user-defined components, for example, to define the center point of a rectangle in terms of its corners; and (2) constraints can appear as graphical components to be manipulated in their own right. Before describing how this is done in Unidraw, we must first consider how to specify constraints in QOCA.

Expressing Constraints in QOCA

QOCA makes constraints, objective functions, and variables first class objects, and it provides a natural syntax to define these objects directly in the programming language, in this case C++. QOCA defines constraints and variables using the arithmetic and relational operators of C++. This requires heavily overloading these operators, but the result is a natural syntax for declaring constraints.

The following example, written in C++, captures the relationship between temperature scales in Fahrenheit, Celsius, and Kelvin as constraints over variables representing these quantities. It makes use of three classes, **CVariable**, **Constant**, and **Constraint**.

```
CVariable fahr, cent, kelv;
Constant Freezing = 32.0;
Constant AbsoluteZero = -273.13;

Constraint c1 =   fahr - Freezing == cent * 1.8;
Constraint c2 =   cent == kelv + AbsoluteZero;
```

Constraints are added to the system merely by instantiating constraint objects. QOCA ensures that the values of CVariable objects adhere to the constraint specification. Through operator overloading, QOCA evaluates the expressions in the constraints and returns instances of class **Expression**. Expressions are objects that capture the abstract syntax tree of the expressions in the constraint. These structures can be then assigned as in the case above or can be manipulated symbolically by other objects.

Objective functions define expressions to be minimized or maximized. In this example, suppose we want to minimize the difference between the variable representing Fahrenheit and freezing.

We can express this requirement with an instance of class **Objective**:

```
Objective o = Minimize(fahr*fahr - 2*fahr*Freezing +
     Freezing*Freezing);
```

Minimize is a function that takes an Expression as an argument and returns an instance of class Objective. The Objective object o establishes an objective function that QOCA must consider in solving the constraint system.

It is often necessary to assign values to the variables and then have these values automatically propagate to the constrained variables via the constraint solving class **ConstraintSolver**. But the allowed values of CVariables are governed by Constraint and Objective objects. Consequently, assigning a value to a variable is not a direct assignment—the assigned value may be inconsistent with some constraints or may not satisfy some objective. Instead QOCA treats an assignment to a variable as a *request* that the CVariable take that value. Only when the constraint system is solved are the requested values considered. Then the solver propagates computed values back to the variables, notifying them that they have changed. In solving the constraints, the requested values act as parameters to the system, and all other variables will depend on them. Thus we can write

```
cent = 95;
```

and the solver will assign the correct values to `fahr` and `kelv` whenever the Solve method (i.e., `ConstraintSolver::Solve`) is called.

The classes CVariable, Constant, Constraint, Objective, and ConstraintSolver are the primary base classes visible to users in QOCA, and they do not depend on Unidraw in any way. Additional classes integrate QOCA and Unidraw without compromising their independence, as we demonstrate in subsequent sections.

Constraint State Variables

CVariable objects play a central role in the specification of constraints. Clearly if Unidraw is to support general constraint specification, it must surface CVariable to the users of the framework. Complicating the issue is Unidraw's notion of a **state variable**. State variables are persistent values that can define a graphical user interface for viewing and modification, and they can change automatically through Unidraw's support for dataflow. Components commonly have one or more state variables that store user-accessible state. For example, an inverter component in a schematic capture system may use state variables to define the logic levels at its input and output terminals.

State variables thus play some of the same roles as constraint variables, and vice versa. To avoid introducing dependencies between Unidraw and QOCA, we derive a new class, **constrained state variable**, or **CSVar**, from both the StateVar state variable base class and from CVariable. CSVar inherits both the constraint semantics of CVariable and the persistence and other Unidraw-oriented aspects of StateVars without introducing dependencies between the base classes.

The mechanism for keeping CSVars consistent with the constraint system builds upon both the QOCA and Unidraw architectures. Ordinary CVariables receive requests for change. Later they have their values updated in one pass via

`ConstraintSolver::Solve`. However, Unidraw programs do not call this operation directly. Unidraw already defines a global Update operation that synchronizes the application and the state of its constituent objects, which may involve solving connectivity constraints, repainting the screen, and so on. We simply extended this operation to invoke Solve on the constraint solver.

CSVars have the added need to notify their enclosing component (if any) whenever they change. Therefore the CSVar class adds protocol for associating one or more components with an instance. CSVar also extends CVariable's Update operation to notify its associated components of a change in its value.

3.2 Constraining Components

To place constraints on components, variables that represent attributes of components must be defined in terms of CSVars. This lets us establish constraints between an object's internal values (i.e., **internal constraints**) and across objects (**external constraints**).

Internal constraints simplify a component's definition. Code previously required to maintain relationships between member variables is now delegated to the solver through the constraints. Internal constraints also simplify alternate definitions of objects. For example a rectangle can be defined by a center point and one corner or by opposite corners. Consider the class **ConstrainedRectComp**:

```
class ConstrainedRectComp : public Component {
    CSVar _left, _right, _centerx;
    CSVar _top, _bottom, _centery;
    Constraint _Xconstraint, _Yconstraint;
...
};

ConstrainedRectComp::ConstrainedRectComp () {
    _Xconstraint = _left + _right == 2.0 * _centerx;
    _Yconstraint = _top + _bottom == 2.0 * _centery;
}
```

This class defines six member CSVars representing its opposing corner points and its center. Note how internal constraints in the constructor define the center point in terms of its corners.

To present constraints graphically as components, we derive a new base class of graphical component called **ConstraintComp**, which defines an appearance and manipulation semantics for constraints. Derived classes add semantics for particular constraints. For example, the derived class **PointEqualityComp** takes two pairs of CSVars representing two points and establishes an equality constraint between them:

```
class PointEqualityComp : public ConstraintComp {
public:
    PointEqualityComp(CSVar&, CSVar&, CSVar&, CSVar&);
    ...
private:
```

```
    Constraint _XConstraint, _YConstraint;
};

PointEqualityComp::PointEqualityComp (
    CSVar& x1, CSVar& x2, CSVar& y1, CSVar& y2
) {
    _XConstraint = _x1 == _x2;
    _YConstraint = _y1 == _y2;
...
}
```

In general, graphical components in Unidraw use structured graphics objects [Vlissides and Linton, 1988] to depict themselves graphically. PointEqualityComp maintains a structured graphic object to present its constraint to the user in an intuitive manner.

ConstraintComp objects are often constructed by tools that query components for their CSVars using Unidraw's interpreted command mechanism. The tool provides the appropriate direct manipulation semantics, such as dragging or stretching a line between two points. Once a tool has obtained the required CSVars, it returns a command that pastes the component into the drawing and establishes the proper external constraints.

For example, the tool that creates an EqualityPointComp between two points asks the two components containing these points to return the appropriate CSVar objects. Then it instantiates an EqualityPointComp, passing the CSVars to the constructor. Finally, it returns a PasteCmd object containing the new instance. Later in the paper we discuss in more detail how we exploit Unidraw's direct manipulation model to involve constraint solving and how undoable commands containing constraints work.

3.3 Supporting Undo/Redo

In integrating QOCA and Unidraw, it is important to retain full undo and redo capabilities. Two semantics are essential:

1. Constraints and optimization functions can exist without affecting the constraint system.

2. The constraint system can be queried for its current state, and it can revert to exactly that state at an arbitrary point in the future.

Enabling and Disabling

The first semantics implies that an instantiated constraint or objective does not necessarily affect the behavior of the system: only an *enabled* constraint or objective may have an affect. This is relevant to the undo model in that structural changes to the system may have to be undone.

For example, suppose the user deletes the right-hand rectangle in Figure 9. In standard Unidraw this would be accomplished via a DeleteCmd, which removes the component being deleted from its enclosing structure *but does not destroy it*.

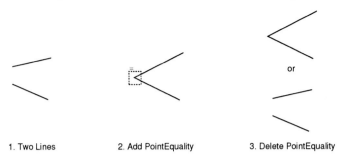

1. Two Lines   2. Add PointEquality   3. Delete PointEquality

Figure 7: Hysteresis in underconstrained systems

Instead, the command stores both the component and its position in the structure. If the DeleteCmd is later undone, it reinserts the component in the structure at the proper place. It is far easier and cheaper to save the component than to reconstruct it, since a component can be arbitrarily complex.

Similarly, it is better to disable and enable constraints and objectives than it is to destroy and recreate them. When the constrained rectangle is removed, it disables all the constraints and objectives that affect its CSVars; if it is subsequently pasted or reinserted into the display, it simply enables them again.

The Constraint class in QOCA provides protocol for enabling and disabling its instances. The ability to switch constraints on and off at will is one of the novel features of QOCA and is intrinsic to supporting undo/redo semantics. It requires efficient incremental addition and deletion of constraints. No other constraint solving system that we know of provides this capability for the class of constraints that QOCA solves.

Saving and Restoring System State

The second semantics ensures that the editor does not suffer from hysteresis or round-off errors as operations are undone and redone. There is no guarantee, for example, that undoing a state-changing operation (such as a move) by performing the inverse operation will return the system to exactly the original state. Round-off errors can accumulate even in ostensibly well-behaved systems.

Hysteresis can occur in underconstrained systems as constraints are added and deleted. Consider the scenario in Figure 7. The endpoints of two lines are constrained to coincide via an equality constraint, which is subsequently removed. Because the lines are underconstrained, the top portion of stage 3 is a valid configuration. However, to support undo and redo, the display must be restored to the configuration at the bottom of stage 3; otherwise unpredictable results will occur as the user performs additional undo commands.

To ensure stability, state-changing commands query the constraint engine for **Solution** objects both before and after they carry out their operations. A Solution object captures the state of the constraint solver at a particular instant. On undo, these commands then direct the constraint engine to adopt the original (i.e., pre-execution) solution. On redo, they set the post-execution solution. The constraint system computes the same values after arbitrarily many undo and redo operations.

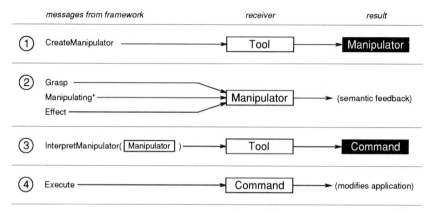

Figure 8: Basic direct manipulation sequence

3.4   Constraining Direct Manipulation

It is important to enforce constraints and to see their effects during direct manipulation. Otherwise, the result of the manipulation may not correspond to the feedback provided. For example, a drawing editor may let a user stretch an unconstrained rectangle arbitrarily. But a rectangle that is constrained to be square should stay that way as it is stretched, thereby reflecting the constraint in the manipulation. This section summarizes Unidraw's direct manipulation model and how it is integrated with QOCA to support constrained direct manipulation.

Unidraw Direct Manipulation Model

Tools are fundamental to Unidraw's direct manipulation model. The user *grasps* and *wields* a tool to achieve a desired *effect*. The effect may involve a change in component or other application object state, or it may change the way components are viewed, or there may be no effect at all (if, for example, the tool is used in an inappropriate context). Most tools generate animated effects as they are wielded to provide semantic feedback to the user.

Tools employ **Manipulator** objects and commands to handle the mechanics of the direct manipulation and enact its outcome. A manipulator abstracts and encapsulates the code that generates semantic feedback. Manipulator provides a standard interface to an abstract state machine that defines interaction semantics. Commands actually carry out the intent of the manipulation and permit its undoing and redoing.

Figure 8 depicts the four basic stages of a direct manipulation:

1. The active tool receives a CreateManipulator message from the framework in response to user input. The tool creates an appropriate manipulator and returns it to the framework.

2. The framework exercises the manipulator in response to user input:

   (a) **Grasp** instructs the manipulator to prepare to generate semantic feed-

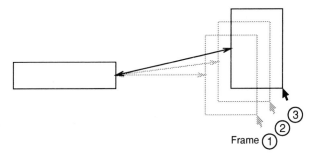

Figure 9: Animation produced by `CDragManip::Manipulating`

back. In response, the manipulator typically initializes internal state associated with the ensuing animation.

(b) The framework issues **Manipulating** messages repeatedly in response to user input until the manipulator indicates that manipulation has ceased. Each call to Manipulating usually generates a new frame of animation.

(c) **Effect** instructs the manipulator to finalize its internal state following the direct manipulation.

3. The framework asks the active tool to interpret the manipulator it had created via the InterpretManipulator message. The manipulator returns a command in response.

4. The framework executes the command to carry out the user's intent.

This discussion omits many details of Unidraw's direct manipulation model to focus on the parts that relate directly to its interplay with QOCA. See [Vlissides and Linton, 1990] for more detail.

Integrating Constraints

To enforce constraints during direct manipulation, Unidraw may solve the constraint system on every input event. The state of the system thus changes *before* manipulator interpretation at stage 3 above. This contrasts with interactions that do not involve constraints, wherein the application is affected only after manipulation has ended.

Consider the boxes-and-arrows connectivity example from Section 2.1. Figure 9 depicts three frames of animation produced when the user moves the right-hand rectangle with a **MoveTool**. In this case, each frame is generated by a call to Manipulating on an instance of **CDragManip** (short for "constrained drag manipulator"), the manipulator that the MoveTool created. MoveTool initializes the CDragManip with the CSVars that define the lower-left and upper-right corners of the rectangle being moved.

CDragManip's Grasp operation records the current values of the system's CSVars in a Solution object. Each subsequent call to Manipulating generates a frame of animation: CDragManip requests changes to the rectangle's CSVar values each time the cursor moves during manipulation. Then CDragManip calls `Unidraw::Update`, which solves the constraint system and updates the display. Unidraw thus maintains the connectivity constraints during direct manipulation simply by treating each frame of the animation as an incremental change to the constraint system.

QOCA's incremental parametric constraint solver performs each step of the manipulation efficiently. It treats the variables being manipulated (that is, those that receive requests to change value in the call to Manipulating) as parameters. The solver minimizes the manipulation of the constraints by solving parametric quadratic optimization problems incrementally. Most often it computes new values of variables that depend on the parameters directly—constraint manipulation occurs relatively infrequently.

A subtle point in this strategy concerns when to change the objective functions to reflect the rectangle's final position. Recall that the system includes objective functions (expressed via Objective objects) that minimize the distance between the rectangle's initial and final positions. After manipulation it is necessary to adjust the constants appearing in these objectives to make their values correspond to the new position.

We refer to this process as **leapfrogging** the objective functions at the end of each manipulation step to catch up to the current values of the CSVars they effect. This adjustment takes place in the command that records the overall effect of the direct manipulation. When the framework issues the InterpretManipulator message (passing the CDragManip as an argument) to the MoveTool, it responds by producing a **CMoveCmd**, or "constrained move command." This command's purpose is twofold: (1) to adjust the rectangle component's objectives, and (2) to provide a record of the manipulation should it be undone or redone later. If the command is undone (or redone), CMoveCmd moves the rectangle back to its original position (or to its new position) and adjusts the rectangle's objectives accordingly.

4   QOCA Internals

4.1   Architectural Overview

QOCA has the four main components illustrated in Figure 10:

1. A **solver**, which adds or deletes constraints while incrementally maintaining the solved form. The test for satisfiability is a byproduct of maintaining the solved form.

2. A **detector**, which takes a constraint that is inconsistent with the current constraints and identifies sources of the inconsistency.

3. A **projector**, which takes a set of variables and projects the current constraints onto those variables.

4. An **optimizer**, which recomputes the current solution given requested values for parameters. It finds values for non-parametric variables that both satisfy the constraints and minimize the optimization problems.

In addition, QOCA maintains a record of the **current constraints** and the **current optimization function**. It also maintains a **current solution**, the assignment

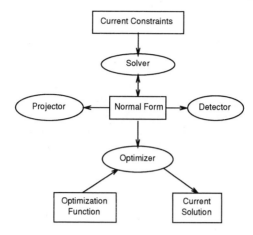

Figure 10: QOCA architecture

of variables that satisfies the current constraints and minimizes the current optimization function.

QOCA's architecture is designed to be flexible. It permits experimentation with different classes of constraints and domains (e.g., reals, booleans, etc.), different constraint solving algorithms for these domains, and different representations for objects in these domains. QOCA's object-oriented design allows parts of the system to be varied independently of others. For example, real numbers, currently represented as doubles, can be changed to infinite precision or rational representations simply by changing the definition of a single class.

Moreover, as improved algorithms and solvers are developed, existing algorithms can be replaced with minimal disturbance. This modularity highlights an advantage of using global constraint solvers such as QOCA. Systems that employ local propagation [Maloney et al., 1989, Myers et al., 1990] often distribute constraint solving methods throughout the system, relegating to each object the responsibility to solve its own constraints. This makes it difficult to exploit efficient representations and constraint solving algorithms in these systems.

4.2 Implementation

Here we describe briefly the algorithms and techniques used in the constraint system. A complete description of QOCA is forthcoming [Helm et al., 1992b], and preliminary performance measurements have already been reported [Helm et al., 1992a].

QOCA leverages the well-developed theory and efficient algorithms that have been investigated extensively in operations research for handling linear constraints. The Simplex algorithm is the key technique used in the system. The Simplex is an efficient symbolic manipulation technique for testing satisfiability and for optimizing linear constraints. QOCA also takes advantage of new results from symbolic computation, both for efficient representation of constraints and in incremental algorithms for constraint manipulation. QOCA currently supports linear arithmetic constraints, that is, linear equalities and inequalities over the real numbers, and the optimization of convex quadratic functions.

Normal Form

Almost all constraint manipulation in QOCA is on the **normal form** of the current constraints. The normal form is essentially a compiled non-redundant representation of the constraints in which as many variables as possible are eliminated. Elsewhere [Helm et al., 1992a] we discuss in detail some of the ramifications of normal forms for constraint solving. Briefly, the normal form is constructed as follows. Assume that we have a set of linear equalities and inequalities over the variables $x_1, ..., x_n$. We can rewrite them into a set of equalities by replacing each inequality

$$a_1 x_1 + a_2 x_2 + \cdots + a_n x_n \leq b$$

by

$$a_1 x_1 + a_2 x_2 + \cdots + a_n x_n + s = b$$

where s is a distinct new **slack variable** and $s \geq 0$. The normal form of this rewritten set is obtained by eliminating as many of the original variables $x_1, ..., x_n$ as possible using Gauss-Jordan elimination. The remaining equations will contain only slack variables. These equations are collected, and the Simplex algorithm is used to find their **feasible basic form**. Thus the normal form consists of two sets of equalities. The first set, called the **defining equations**, contains the equations used to eliminate the original variables $x_1, ..., x_n$. The second set, called the **slack equations**, is a basic form of the equations in slack variables.

In practice we do not explicitly compute the normal form of a constraint set C. Rather, we represent the normal form implicitly as the product MC, where M is an invertible matrix called the **quasi-inverse**. M is essentially the product of the elementary row operations used to compute a normal form from C. One advantage of this implicit representation is that M is smaller than C, which means performing a pivot on M is cheaper than performing one on C.

Adding and Deleting Constraints

The main advantage of the quasi-inverse representation, however, is that M captures how the original constraints were used to obtain the solved form. This lets the solver (re)compute a normal form efficiently when a constraint is deleted. We handle the addition of constraints and incremental computation of a new normal form with standard techniques in sensitivity analysis [Murty, 1988]. The expected cost is proportional to the cost of one pivot in M. In fact, we use the Dual Simplex, and so adding a constraint has in the worst-case exponential complexity. In practice, however, the Simplex algorithm has incremental cost proportional to the number of constraints added. In fact, the Simplex is routinely used in problems with many millions of constraints, and it is often preferred to the more complex interior point methods that have polynomial worst-case complexity. The actual cost of this pivot depends on the representation of M. With a non-sparse representation, the actual cost is $O(n^2)$, where n is the number of original constraints. The cost should be significantly less with a representation that preserves the sparseness in the original system. At present, however, the system uses a non-sparse representation for simplicity.

Causes of Unsatisfiability

Each time a constraint is added to the solver, it is first simplified using the defining equations. If the new constraint becomes a contradiction after the simplification, the causes of the unsatisfiability can be traced back immediately using the quasi-inverse—indices of the non-zero elements in the row of the quasi-inverse corresponding to the new constraint indicate the constraints that contradict it. When the simplified constraint contains only slack variables, it is added into the slack equations; then the Simplex is activated to solve the system. If this system is infeasible, one can apply the technique proposed by Gleeson and Ryan [Gleeson and Ryan, 1990] to identify the minimally infeasible subsystems and hence decide which constraints should be removed to obtain feasibility.

It follows from the construction of the normal form that the number of slack equations is less than or equal to the number of inequalities in the original system. This is critical because (except for constraint deletion and addition) all operations in the constraint system have cost proportional to the number of slack equations rather than the size of the original system. The defining equations are only used to transform solutions in terms of the slack variables to solutions in terms of the original variables.

Projection

Given a set of variables to project on, the projector first combines the defining equations for these variables with all the slack equations. Then a projection algorithm computes the actual projection. Since the projection space is assumed to be small, we use a projection algorithm called the Convex Hull Method [Lassez and Lassez, to appear], which is based on a geometric approach. For small projection spaces, it is much faster than other projection algorithms based on algebraic manipulation. It uses the Simplex algorithm repeatedly to compute the convex hull of the projected constraints.

Quadratic Optimization

The algorithm used for optimizing convex quadratic functions is a variant of the Simplex algorithm; see Murty [Murty, 1988] for details. When a new constraint is added, the optimization problem is (re)solved to find the new solution. During direct manipulation, however, a sequence of very similar optimization problems are solved in which the values of parameters change only slightly. In this case we solve the optimization problem incrementally, making use of the basis of the last solution as the starting basis for the new optimization. If the parametric values are sufficiently close, the cost of each optimization is expected to be one pivot on the slack equations. In fact, during direct manipulation we often know that the optimal solution for the initial parameter values is just the current solution. This means that the initial basis can be constructed efficiently, since we know which variables are basic.

To our knowledge, optimization functions are a new technique for handling underconstrained systems in user interface applications. This approach is related to Witkin's system for graphical animation [Witkin et al., 1990], which uses functions to define the total energy of a system. In this system a global solver tries to minimize the total energy during manipulation to control the movement of graphical objects. Our constraint toolkit can be viewed as combining an energy model approach and pure constraints.

5 Conclusion

Basic constraint technology has matured to the point that highly interactive applications can incorporate constraints in both their interface and their implementation. Concurrently, advances in reusable user interface frameworks have made graphical editing systems easier to implement. Our work has focused on combining these developments to create a powerful, object-oriented architecture for constraint-based graphical editing.

We have integrated QOCA, an extensible constraint system, with Unidraw, a framework for building direct-manipulation graphical editors. Critical to QOCA's effectiveness in supporting constraints in Unidraw-based applications are its ability to solve simultaneous equations and inequations, optimize convex quadratic objective functions, incrementally add and delete constraints, incrementally re-solve parametric quadratic optimization problems, and detect causes of unsatisfiability in inconsistent constraints. An important goal of the integration was to avoid compromising existing Unidraw capabilities such as its direct-manipulation model and unlimited undo/redo. QOCA's powerful linear arithmetic constraints, constraint manipulation techniques, and sound theoretical foundation make QOCA an advanced platform for interactive constraint-based editors.

We plan to use QOCA extensively in the future. One project will extend key glyphs in InterViews, such as trays and glue, to be implemented in terms of QOCA constraints. QOCA will also serve as a basic element in our pen-based visual language parsing system [Helm et al., 1991]. We will continue research into new algorithms for manipulating constraints, QOCA being a good vehicle for exploring new algorithms. We also hope to make QOCA freely available, thereby promoting more widespread applications for constraints.

References

Bier, E. and Stone, M. (1986). Snap-dragging. In *ACM SIGGRAPH '86 Conference Proceedings*, pages 233–240, Dallas, TX.

Borning, A. (1981). The programming language aspects of ThingLab – a constraint-oriented simulation laboratory. *ACM Transactions on Programming Languages and Systems*, 3(4):343–387.

Borning, A. and Duisberg, R. (1986). Constraint based tools for building user interfaces. *ACM Transactions on Graphics*, 4(4).

Borning, A., Maher, M., Martindale, A., and Wilson, M. (1989). Constraint hierarchies and logic programming. In *International Conference on Logic Programming*. MIT Press.

Epstein, D. and Lalonde, W. (1988). A smalltalk window system based on constraints. In *Object-Oriented Programming Systems, Languages and Applications Conference*, pages 83–94. ACM Press.

Freeman-Benson, B.N. (1990). Kaleidoscope: Mixing objects, constraints, and imperative programming. In *Object-Oriented Programming Systems, Languages and Applications Conference*, pages 77–88.

Freeman-Benson, B.N. and Borning, A. (1992). Integrating constraints with an object-oriented language. In *European Conference on Object-Oriented Programming*, pages 268–286.

(1990). *GECK User's Guide*. V.I. Corporation.

Gleeson, J. and Ryan, J. (1990). Identifying minimally infeasible subsystems of inequalities. *ORSA Journal on Computing*, 2(1):61–63.

Helm, R., Huynh, T., Lassez, C., and Marriott, K. (1992a). A linear constraint technology for user interfaces. In *Graphics Interface*, pages 301–309, Vancouver, Canada.

Helm, R., Huynh, T., Marriott, K., and Vlissides, J. (1992b). QOCA: An extensible object-oriented constraint solving toolkit. Technical Report In Preparation, IBM T.J. Watson Research Center.

Helm, R., Marriott, K., and Odersky, M. (1991). Building visual language parsers. In *Computer Human Interaction (CHI)*, pages 105–112. ACM Press.

Hudson, S.E. (1990). Adaptive semantic snapping—a technique for semantic feedback at the lexical level. In *ACM CHI '90 Conference Proceedings*, pages 65–70.

Olson, D.R., and Allan, K. (1990). Creating interactive techniques by symbolically solving geometric constraints. In *ACM User Interface Software Technologies Conference*, pages 102–107, Snowbird, Utah.

Lassez, C. and Lassez, J.-L. (To Appear). Quantifier elimination for conjunctins of linear constraints via a convex hull algorithm. In Kahn, G., MacQueen, D., and Plotkin, G., editors, *Symbolic and Numerical Computation-Towards Integration*. Springer-Verlag.

Linton, M.A., Vlissides, J.M., and Calder, P.R. (1989). Composing user interfaces with InterViews. *Computer*, 22(2):8–22.

Maloney, J., Borning, A., and Freeman-Benson, B. (1990). An incremental constraint solver. *Communications of the ACM*, 33(1):55–63.

Maloney, J.H., Borning, A.H., and Freeman-Benson, B.N. (1989). Constraint technology for user interface construction in ThingLab II. In *ACM OOPSLA '89 Conference Proceedings*, pages 381–388, New Orleans, LA.

Murty, K.G. (1988). *Linear Complementarity, Linear and Nonlinear Programming*. Heldermann Verlag, Berlin.

Myers, B.A., Guise, D.A., Dannenberg, R.B., Zanden, B.V., Kosbie, D.S., Pervin, E., Mickish, A., and Marchel, P. (1990). Comprehensive support for graphical, highly interactive user interfaces: The Garnet system. *IEEE Computer Magazine*, 23(11):71–85.

Nelson, G. (1985). Juno, a constraint-based graphics system. In *ACM SIGGRAPH '85 Conference Proceedings*, pages 235–243, San Fransisco, CA.

Sutherland, I. (1963). Sketchpad: A man-machine graphical communication system. In *Spring Joint Computer Conference*, pages 329–345.

Szekely, P. and Myers, B. (1988). A user interface toolkit based on graphical objects and constraints. In *Object-Oriented Programming Systems, Languages and Applications Conference*, pages 36–45.

Tarumi, H., Rekimoto, J., Sugai, M., Yamazake, G., Sugiyama, T., and Akiguchi, C. (1990). Canae—a user interface construction environment with editors as software parts. *NEC Research and Development*, 98:89–98.

Vlissides, J.M. (1990). *Generalized Graphical Object Editing*. PhD thesis, Stanford University.

Vlissides, J.M. and Linton, M.A. (1988). Applying object-oriented design to structured graphics. In *Proceedings of the 1988 USENIX C++ Conference*, pages 81–94, Denver, CO.

Vlissides, J.M. and Linton, M.A. (1990). Unidraw: A framework for building domain-specific graphical editors. *ACM Transactions on Information Systems*, 8(3):237–268.

Witkin, A., Gleicher, M., and Welch, W. (1990). Interactive dynamics. In *ACM/SIGRAPH Conference*.

Graphics Object-Oriented Platform for Euclidean Geometry Computations

John R. Rankin

Recent object-oriented programming languages are enabling the top level code in application programs to resemble more closely the form of the mathematical expressions that the
program is meant to be implementing. This facility is very useful for non-programmers, and
mathematicians and geometers who are not interested in the fine syntactic details of computer
programming languages. This paper describes an object-oriented platform that makes it easier
for non-professional programmers to implement and test concepts from standard Euclidean geometry on a computer graphics screen. The idea is that this platform enables one to construct
and test geometric hypotheses and theorems in a language closely resembling the way Euclid
and traditional geometry expresses geometric concepts, symbols and theorems. Although the
language used by Euclid for geometry is precise it also includes the contextual facilities of
natural languages saveing one from having to spell out every characteristic and attribute in detail. It is this demand for completeness in specifying details that has made standard computer
programming languages laborious and tedious to deal with. The graphics object-oriented platform described in this paper incorporates the facility for handling incompleteness in a natural
and visually acceptable way. Additionally the platform incorporates constraint resolution by an
improved iteration technique. Finally, the platform contains the hierarchy of geometrical shapes
to which the geometer needs immediate access. Here it is pointed out that the object-oriented
programming object hierarchy is properly the inverse of the conceptual geometrical hierarchy
of shapes.

1 Introduction

Traditional high level programming languages, while providing powerful features
for improved programming, have still left a very wide gap between themselves and
natural languages. This means that programming still remains the domain of the
computer software expert. The need to make computer programming more accessible to the general public is an on-going one, and from this thrust we have newer
and newer programming languages and versions of earlier programming languages
continually forthcoming. The new paradigm of object-oriented programming takes
us to a new conceptual design level in programming : it adds another level of
improvement in the appearance of the written programming code. However the

languages themselves do not enforce readable presentation and good programming style; they merely enable it. Taking advantage of the facilities for programming at a higher level, closer to natural language or mathematics, is achieved only through education and good training of the next generation of programmers. Some of what may be achieved in ultra-high level language programming is illustrated by an object-oriented graphics programming platform called CGE. This is basically a library that is to be linked into a user's application program at compilation time. But it contains declarations of object classes, methods and data that save the geometer from having to get involved in knowing the usual lower level details of programming. Additionally, coordinate values do not have to be entered by the programmer, and the positions, shapes and sizes of the geometric objects can be automatically selected by the platform (or else by the user with a pointing device). Euclidean geometry is coordinate-free and so is the CGE platform. CGE also incorporates constraint resolution by the Democracy Algorithm presented in [Rankin, 1991]. This means that the geometer is free to modify the graphics subject to the constraints that he has set up for it.

The Democracy Algorithm is an iterative process of information sharing amongst a society of intelligent agents (objects). The resulting resolution of the constraint equations generally cannot be precisely predicted, and the process shares many of the features of emergent phenomena [Huberman, 1991]. For the present application, the issue of obtaining a required position, orientation, or configuration of a constrained system is not important and so emergent phenomena aspects are not of concern here. In this paper the Democracy Algorithm, as given in [Rankin, 1991], is modified to work with a global list of key construction points. In this form, the agents no longer exchange their own data with each other, but with a universally accessible repository of data. This approach suits our problem and it means that the user must create all the construction points in advance and then use them for placing graphics elements (GEs).

The CGE library consists of object class definitions for the usual entities referred to in Euclidean geometry of straight line segments, circles, arcs of circles, squares, rectangles, ellipses and arcs of ellipses. It provides the methods for initializing, changing, displaying and erasing objects of each of these classes. Additionally there is a number of other utility functions provided that are not provided as object methods. For example, the procedure roughly_equal(P,Q) returns true if two points P and Q are visually coincident in the graphics output and false otherwise. The distance(P,Q) function returns the metric distance between the points P and Q and the angle(P,Q,R) function returns the radian angle subtended at point Q by the line segments QP and QR sweeping anticlockwise from QP to QR. A facility for dynamically displaying numeric values derived from a flexible construction is also provided in the new class type called observable. On initialization, objects of the class observable automatically select and lay exclusive rights to a section of the screen for display purposes. An object of this class continually displays its value in its own screen display area. Assigning a new value to such an object will cause the displayed value to be updated.

2 Geometrical Theorems as Constraint Systems

The theorems in traditional Euclidean plane geometry (see e.g. [Euclid, 1956], [Siddons and Snell, 1946]) apply to an indefinitely large set of cases. Each case where a theorem applies can also be displayed visually on a graphics screen in an obvious way. But more than one configuration of the graphics represents the same application case of the theorem since the theorems apply no matter what the position and orientation of the graphics image representing them is. But additionally, variation in the individual configurations of components in the image, such as points, line segments, arcs and circles may also be application cases of the theorem. Therefore, in displaying a geometrical theorem on a graphics screen, we wish to allow the viewer to be able to change the configurations of the components of the image, or the configuration of the whole image subject to the restrictions under which the theorem applies. As the viewer makes changes, he must receive visual feedback that indicates clearly to him that the theorem continues to hold true. This feedback may often be in the form of a numerical display of the values of one or more expressions involving angle or distance measurements on the case being displayed. This means that the graphics platform supporting the needs of geometers should be a constraint system [Rankin, 1991] [Leler, 1988] whereby geometrical elements can be constrained in ways naturally occurring in Euclidean geometry, and interactively displayed, as well as providing the interactive display of numerical quantities derived from the particular geometry.

The phraseology used in Euclidean geometry is still too high a level for direct implementation in software and we need to design a lower level language capable of expressing the same ideas. For example, all key defining points [Rankin, 1991], [Rankin and Burns, 1990] implicit in a theorem must be explicitly declared as is usual in current day programming languages. CGE provides a point class for this. Every point that the geometer will need in his constructions should then be declared at the start as an object of this class. The application code will also need to initialize each of these objects by a call to the class constructor method. This method requires no other parameter than the string name identifying the point concerned. As well as creating an object of the point class, the constructor method initializes its coordinate values by intelligent autoselection, and then displays the point as a labelled marker. (The visible graphics label is the string name given to the point in the constructor method parameter. The marker size, colour and style are set the same for all points.) The current implementation of intelligent autoselection is as follows. Random values for the x and y coordinates are first generated within the predefined acceptable screen ranges. All points that have been constructed are placed into a linked list structure by CGE. The tentative coordinates for a new point are tested against the coordinates of all points defined earlier which are in the linked list. If the new coordinates are within epsilon of the coordinates of any point in the linked list, then new random coordinates are generated and tested again and so forth. Once acceptable coordinates have been created the point is stored in the linked list and displayed. The non-visual coincidence of key points in a construction is a universal constraint that must be satisfied by all geometric constructions even under interactive modifications. From the linked list of key points, graphics entities are placed and displayed by selecting sets of key points as finite defining point sets as described in [Rankin, 1991].

As a simple example consider the first theorem from [Siddons and Snell, 1946]. If a straight line stands on another straight line, the sum of the two angles so formed is equal to two right angles.

To put this theorem into explicit form we would say the following: Create two distinct points called P and Q. Construct the line segment PQ. Create a new distinct point called R on the line segment PQ. Construct a fourth distinct point S. Compute the angles angle(S,R,P) and angle(S,R,Q) and display their sum. The displayed sum should remain constant (equal to p) no matter where the points P, Q, R and S are moved to subject to the constraints that they are all distinct and that R lies on PQ. To express this in a language based on object-oriented programming, the geometer must enter the following:

```
var
    P,Q,R,S,T : point_class;
    L1 : line_segment_class;
    sum : observable;
    finished : boolean;
begin
    begin_CGE;
    P.construct('P'); Q.construct('Q');
    R.construct('R'); S.construct('S');
    L1.construct(P,Q);
    L1.nearest_point(R,T); R.assign(T);
    sum.construct('angle SRP plus angle SRQ = ');
    sum.assign(angle(S,R,P) + angle(S,R,Q));
    finished := FALSE;
    move_a_point; if coincidence then restore_points;
    while not finished do begin
        resolve_constraints;
        if coincidence then restore_points;
        sum.assign(angle(P,R,S) + angle(S,R,Q));
        move_a_point;
    end;
    end_CGE;
end.
```

In this constraint system, the user can move any of the four points P, Q, R or S on the screen. If P is moved then the line segment PQ also moves and this leads to a new position for the point R which causes the line segment RS to move. However, there is no movement induced in the point S. The way an induced movement is computed for point R is to cause R to jump from its old position to the nearest point on the line segment PQ. (Other applications of the nearest point method have been described in [Rankin and Burns, 1990].) If this change in R results in a visual non-coincidence violation then the displacement of point P is rejected and the original point position of P is retained. Interactively selecting point Q and moving it results in similar constraint resolution as for the displacement of P. If the user displaces the point R, then the line segment PQ remains fixed and the point R jumps to the nearest point on the line segment PQ to the displaced position of R. Again if this position is too close to P or Q then the displacement is rejected and R is restored to its original position. Even if a movement in R is induced, the other points, P, Q and S do not move. Finally, if the user moves point S there is no effect on any of the other points, P, Q or R. If visual non-coincidence is violated by the displacement, then the displacement is rejected and S remains in its original position. Otherwise, S takes on the new position that the user sets and consequently the line segment RS will move.

As a second example, consider theorem 6 from [Siddons and Snell, 1946] which is dealt with in a similar way: The sum of the angles of a triangle is equal to two right angles.

To put this theorem into explicit form we would say the following. Create three distinct points called P, Q, and R. Compute the angles angle(Q,P,R), angle(R,Q,P) and angle(P,R,Q) and their sum and display the sum. Also display the edges PQ, QR and RP. Allow the user to move any of the points P, Q or R about and he will see that the sum always equals 2*p. To express this in a language based on object-oriented programming, the geometer must enter the following:

```
var
    P,Q,R : point_class;
    L1,L2,L3 : line_segment_class;
    a1,a2,a3,sum : observable;
    finished : boolean;
begin
    begin_CGE;
    P.construct('P'); Q.construct('Q');R.construct('R');
    L1.construct(P,Q); L2.construct(Q,R); L3.construct(R,P);
    a1.create(angle(Q,P,R));
    a2.create(angle(R,Q,P));
    a3.create(angle(P,R,Q));
    sum.create(a1.value + a2.value + a3.value);
    finished := FALSE;
    move_a_point; if coincidence then restore_points;
    while not finished do begin
        resolve_constraints;
        if coincidence then restore_points;
        a1.assign(angle(Q,P,R));
        a2.assign(angle(R,Q,P));
        a3.assign(angle(P,R,Q));
        sum.assign(a1.value + a2.value + a3.value);

        L1.show(WHITE); L2.show(WHITE); L3.show(WHITE);
        move_a_point;
    end;
    end_CGE;
end.
```

In this constraint system, the user can move any of the three points P, Q, or R on the screen. The three points can be placed anywhere on the screen without constraint except for the universal visual non-coincidence constraint. The program shows the triangle, the triangle angles and their sum.

More advanced theorems can better illustrate the implementation of dynamic constraint systems. Consider for instance, the theorem: The perpendiculars of a triangle are concurrent. For this constraint system, three points P, Q and R are digitized (or else selected by the computer). Then the line segments L1 = PQ, L2 = QR and L3 = RP are constructed. Next the perpendiculars are constructed: an infinite line I1 passes through P and perpendicular to L2, an infinite line I2 passes through Q and perpendicular to L3, and an infinite line I3 passes through R and perpendicular to L1. Then it will be seen that the point of intersection of I1 and I2 equals the point of intersection of I2 and I3. To allow the Democracy Algorithm to apply to this system we need to invent a new subclass called perpendicular. An object of this class is displayed as an infinite line and is initialized and assigned by three points say A, B and C. The infinite line then is that which passes through point A and is perpendicular to the line segment BC. (Infinite lines rather than rays or finite line segments were implemented as they are often necessary to reach the intersection point.) In an interesting variation of this theorem, perpendicular.init(A,B,C) was replaced with line_segment.init(A,D) where D is the nearest point to A on the line segment BC. The result was that the theorem continues to hold true but now the intersection point is always inside the triangle.

As an example of a theorem involving circular arcs: The angle of a circle segment is a constant. To construct this constraint system, select a point C, and two other points A and B. Construct a circle using points C and A : the circle is defined as having centre C and radius distance(C,A). Also construct an arc (a circle segment) with this centre C and the same radius. The arc starts from point A and turns anticlockwise to terminate on the infinite line through CB. Now select a fourth point P. From P compute the nearest point Q to it that is on the circle. Construct and display the line segments AQ and BQ. Take the angle angle(B,Q,A) as an observable. Allowing only the point P to be moved it will be seen that the angle displayed remains constant. If the other points A, B or C are moved then the angle value changes to a new value, but moving P (and hence Q) does not alter the new angle value displayed. This theorem only requires the class of circles to be provided in CGE. It uses the nearest point method which, as pointed out in [Rankin and Burns, 1990], is a very useful and even necessary method for all geometrical element classes of CGE.

3   Geometrical Object Hierarchy

There is a tendency to confuse subcases with the OOPs concept of subclasses. For example, fixed length line segments are a special case of line segments. If the geometric parameters of a line segment are x1, y1, r and theta, (where (x1, y1) are the coordinates of the first end-point, r is the length of the line segment and theta is its radian angle relative to the x-axis) then the geometric parameters of a fixed length line segment could be taken as x1, y1 and theta as the length r cannot be varied from the value it was initialized to (by the init method). So fixed length line segments are a subcase (the case when r is held fixed) of line segments. However when we make OOPs classes out of these, the class of line segments is properly a subclass of the class of fixed length line segments. This is because in OOP, subclasses have all the features or parameters of the superclass plus some new ones. Similarly, circles, with parameters xc, yc and r, are subcases of circular arcs, with parameters xc, yc, r, theta1, and theta2 (the case when the end angle equals the start angle), but the class of circular arcs is a subclass of the class of circles and so on with the many other instances of subcases that occur in geometrical constraint problems. Note that subcases of geometrical objects have fewer parameters than the more general case because the latter has had some restrictions placed on its parameters to define the subcase. In contrast, with the OOPs subclass concept, subclasses have all the inherited parameters of the parent plus some additional parameters. That is, geometric subcases actually correspond to OOP superclasses and vice versa. A problem with this for geometric applications is that, as we develop software or extend existing libraries (extensibility of compiled code being an important feature of OOP) we usually think of new classes to add that are subcases of existing ones for example the various strains of constrained line segment (fixed length, fixed angle, fixed length and angle). So in incremental development we wish to add on new subcases, but OOP makes it very convenient to be adding on new subclasses, not subcases.

However, it is possible to write the OOP code with the class of fixed length line segments as a subclass of the class of unrestrained line segments. For example we could set up the class of line segments with the parameters x1, y1, x2, y2 (the end- point coordinates). Now we make a subclass of this with the additional parameter r for the length of the line segment. When an object of this class of fixed length line segments is initialized, r has its value set. Any assignment to objects of class fixed length line segment must not use the inherited assign method of the superclass of line segments because this assign method allows the length of the line segment to change. Therefore the subclass of fixed length line segments has to implement a new assign method to override the inherited one. In fact, only the init, digitize and assign methods need to be rewritten for the subclass of fixed length line segments. Other methods like midpoint, move (which digitizes the new end-points and then invokes the assign method), enquire, nearest_point, show and hide can be directly inherited with no overriding methods. If we followed the normal intention of subclasses in OOP programming and made the class of line segments a subclass of the class of fixed length line segments then we could inherit all methods from the class of fixed length line segments except that we must override the digitize and assign methods. The important advantage of using inheritance in programming is that objects can be created incrementally with little additional programming effort for each added subclass, and this example, while going contrary to the usual OOP notion of what is a subclass and what is a superclass, shows that the advantages of inheritance programming are nevertheless applicable. The difference between programming subcases as subclasses rather than superclasses in this example was only the requirement that the init method must also be reimplemented (plus having to put up with having additional superfluous inherited parameters in the data structure area).

4   Improved Iterative Constraint Resolution

The Democracy Algorithm [Rankin, 1991] has been used for dynamically building and testing many different graphical constraint systems. All constraint systems in this context are created by selecting independent autonomous objects and linking them via message passing pathways according to the desired global design of the constraint system. All components of a constraint system are graphics elements

(GEs) which are OOPs objects defined by finite defining point sets (FDPSs) as in [Rankin, 1991]. Only point sets are transferred between the objects. Each object stores the input point FDPS values, then uses and modifies them to determine its own configuration according to its own inbuilt constraints, and then stores internally the modified FDPS values for other objects to receive if needed. For the Democracy algorithm, all GEs in the constraint system are maintained in a linked list in chronological order of creation and the pathways of point transfers are added to this as an extra data structure of pointers. The algorithm applies the current point positions to each GE in this list in turn receiving modifications of the point positions from each GE as it goes. The modifications to the input points are induced by the internal constraint equations encoded in each constrained GE class as described in [Rankin, 1991]. When there are no further changes in the input and output FDPS point set coordinates (to epsilon accuracy) for all GEs involved in the constraint system, then the iterations terminate with the new resolved solution to the constraints. It was noted that the stopping criterion of visual epsilon accuracy gave us very quick constraint resolution and usually in less than 10 iterations. It was also observed that this geometric constraint resolution technique applies to a wide variety of geometric constraint types [Rankin, 1991], and can be arranged into a hierarchy. By regarding a constraint system together with its Democracy Algorithm as a new constraint object that can be combined with other constraint system objects, a higher level of interacting objects arises and, in this higher level another Democracy Algorithm must operate to maintain the constraints set at this level. The constraints placed on a constraint system from its schematic diagram become the internal constraints for this constraint system regarded as a new object itself. These constraint system objects can be saved to disk as persistent objects, and reloaded whenever needed again in the future when they could be manipulated further, and combined together into new hyper-constraint systems. It remains to be seen what scope this approach will give to the study of constraint systems.

The design of the constraint system is coded in the GE list that is given to the Democracy Algorithm. This design is encoded as a large structure of additional pointers attached to the GE list as described in [Rankin, 1991]. In that reference, it was shown to be helpful to create the design from electronics-like schematic diagrams. The diagrams showed which points are joined (in common) amongst the GEs. They also indicated the flow of dependencies for point values between the GEs. It was noted in that paper that whilst for many constraint systems one-way dependencies were sufficient to computationally maintain the integrity (the valid appearance) of the constraint system, two-way dependencies ensured the maintenance of integrity in every case considered. However, this result only applies to pairwise joins. If, for example, three fixed-length line segments, L1, L2 and L3 are constrained to join at a particular choice of their end-points, say L1.P1, L2.P1 and L3.P1 then the structure of pointers needed to be changed. One approach considered was to make a ring where the L1.P1 input is derived from the L3.P1 output value, the L2.P1 input is derived from the L1.P1 output value and the L3.P1 input is derived from the L2.P1 output. This is symbolized by:

```
L1.P1 <-- L3.P1;
L2.P1 <-- L1.P1;
L3.P1 <-- L2.P1;
```

While this does generalize the two-way dependency of pair joins, tests have shown that again this does not maintain the integrity of the constraint system. However, by making a double-linked ring of pointers between all GEs involved at a multiple join, it has been found that the integrity of the constraint system does not become corrupted:

```
L1.P1 <-- L3.P1; L2.P1 <-- L1.P1; L3.P1 <-- L2.P1;
L3.P1 <-- L1.P1; L2.P1 <-- L3.P1; L1.P1 <-- L2.P1;
```

The extra code needed for this surprisingly reduced the execution time because convergence was more rapid.

In the Democracy Algorithm as described, points are not objects but the defining parameters of graphics objects, and graphics objects interact only with other graphics objects – all point data knowledge is kept locally in the graphics objects concerned. In the construction of the platform for Euclidean geometry it was decided to make all the key points of a construction global. In this approach, the user must create the key points of the geometric construction first and then select from them to place GEs. The Democracy Algorithm again goes through each GE in the GE list in turn, but each GE must now get its input points from the global list of key points of the construction. The algorithm updates the points it uses from this global list with the modified FDPS values that each GE produces. One can compare these two approaches in the familiar triangle example. In the first approach, the line segments L1, L2 and L3 have the double linked constraints:

```
L1.P1 <-- L3.P2; L2.P1 <-- L1.P2; L3.P1 <-- L2.P2;
L3.P2 <-- L1.P1; L2.P2 <-- L3.P1; L1.P2 <-- L2.P1;
```

(although the second links given in the second line are not really necessary in this case to preserve the integrity of the triangle [Rankin, 1991]). In the second approach, the constraints are expressed as:

```
L1.P1 <-- P; L1.P2 <-- Q;
L2.P1 <-- Q; L2.P2 <-- R;
L3.P1 <-- R; L3.P2 <-- P;
```

where P, Q and R are the global points. In the OOPs code the Democracy Algorithm for these reduces to:

```
repeat
    L3.enquire(E,F); L1.enquire(A,B); L1.assign(F,B);
    L1.enquire(A,B); L2.enquire(C,D); L2.assign(B,D);
    L2.enquire(C,D); L3.enquire(E,F); L3.assign(D,F);
until no further changes in L1, L2 and L3;
```

(where A, B, C, D, E and F are purely local point variables) for the first approach, and for the second approach:

```
repeat
    L1.assign(P,Q); L1.enquire(P,Q);
    L2.assign(Q,R); L2.enquire(Q,R);
    L3.assign(R,P); L3.enquire(R,P);
until no further visible changes in P, Q and R;
```

The first algorithm can be transformed to close similarity with the second through the identification of the local point variables F, B and D as the globals P, Q and R respectively. Then it can be seen that the first approach does effectively the same iteration steps as the second approach but lags a step in its updates on the first line segment parameter. The second approach always uses the latest values of the FDPS input points. However, tests show that the two approaches give about the same performance in the approach to convergence with the second approach being slightly faster on average. Of course there are major differences in the approachs with regard to the construction and manipulation of constraint systems. In the first approach the construction algorithm is:

```
repeat
    select a constrained GE type from the menu
    & then digitize its FDPS
    OR
    select join points from the menu,
    & then select a first GE on the screen and
      then a key point on it,
    & then select second GE on the screen and key point on it
    OR select displayed key point and move it to new position
until finished
```

In the second approach, the construction and manipulation algorithm is:

```
repeat
    create a key point
    OR select a constrained GE type from the menu
    & then select from the displayed key points for its FDPS
    OR select a displayed key point and move it
until finished.
```

The second approach has been adopted in this platform since an emphasis on key points is typical of problems in Euclidean geometry. It has also simplified the required data structuring for maintaining the design of a constraint system. A set of pointers in a double ring is not required to maintain the integrity of multiple joins in this approach.

5   Conclusion

The CGE library is an object-oriented graphics platform suitable for building application programs for geometers. The platform automatically builds constrained systems and incorporates a constraint resolver. This is a particularly useful tool for educationists who need to illustrate geometrical theorems in training students. The constraint resolver has the main features of the original Democracy Algorithm previously published. However, it is improved in a way that allows for multiple joins. Experimentation has shown that a singly-linked ring of merged end points is not sufficient to maintain the integrity of a multiple join but that a doubly-linked ring is sufficient in all known cases. However, in this application, a global list of OOPs point objects allows multiple joins without the need for ring structures. Also for this problem of providing a graphics platform for Euclidean geometry the universal constraint of non-visual coincidence amongst the key points of the construction has to be maintained. This is solved by rejecting interactive inputs that immediately give a violation of the constraint or yield a violation after the Democracy Algorithm has finished. When a modification is rejected the program sounds a warning and restores the previous configuration of key points.

6 Acknowledgements

The author is employed by La Trobe University, Bundoora, Victoria, Australia 3083 and this research was supported by a La Trobe University LMI School Grant.

References

Euclid (1956). *The Elements*. Dover Press.

Huberman, B. A. (1991). The performance of cooperative processes. In *Emergent Computation, Ed S Forrest*, pages 38–47. MIT Press.

Leler, W. (1988). *Constraint Programming Languages*. Addison-Wesley.

Rankin, J. R. (1991). A graphics object oriented constraint solver. In *Proceedings of the Second Eurographics Workshop*, in this volume.

Rankin, J. R. and Burns, J. (1990). New geometric intersection algorithm based on graphics object oriented programming. In Blake, E. and Wisskirchen, P., editors, *Advances in Object-Oriented Graphics I (Proceedings of the Eurographics Workshop on Object-Oriented Graphics, 1990)*, pages 89–107, Springer-Verlag, 1990.

Siddons, A. W. and Snell, K. S. (1946). *A New Geometry*. Cambridge Press.

Part VII

User Interfaces II

16

The Application Exposure: Bridging the User Interface and the Application

Tom Z.-Y. Zhou and William J. Kubitz

In a previous paper we described a new user interface model. This paper discusses further a crucial part of the model called the application exposure. Assuming that the application side is built in an object-oriented way, the application exposure allows application objects to be defined much more independently of the user interface support system than has been possible using traditional subclassing approaches, yet provides sufficient application information to the user interface side to support direct manipulation operations on application objects.

1 Introduction

Reusability is a crucial issue for object-oriented user interface (UI) support systems. "White-box" reuse [Johnson and Foote, 1988], or class reuse, of an object system (often known as a *framework*) is through subclassing of the existing class hierarchies. In contrast, "black-box" reuse, or component reuse, allows the programmer to choose components from a class library, customize them with parameters, and assemble them into a functional module. In general, component reuse is much easier than class reuse. In our view, a UI support system should be primarily component-reusable, relying on class reuse only when the system must be extended.

We feel that many existing systems [Krasner and Pope, 1988, Sibert et al., 1986, Barth, 1986, Vlissides and Linton, 1989, Myers et al., 1990] do not put enough emphasis on component reuse. Although there are good examples of component reuse in these systems, such as the "pluggable views" in Smalltalk and the "Interactors" in Garnet [Myers et al., 1990], as a rule new applications are almost always built by subclassing the existing class hierarchies. That is, the framework provides a collection of "generic" objects that possess interactivity, while an application subclasses these objects to add application specifics. As such, reusing these frameworks is often not as easy as one would wish.

Another problem with the subclassing approach is that many applications, especially 3D ones, are quite complex and have many application-specific considerations as to how their objects should be represented. In solid modeling applications (see [Mäntylä, 1988]), for example, many different variations of a so-called "winged-edge" data structure may be used for the same kind of boundary representation (or BR) object to suit different sets of application algorithms. Forcing the application objects to follow a certain format imposed by a framework can be too restrictive.

Our goal is to build a more component-reusable UI framework to support 3D applications. Since subclassing inherently constitutes a tight coupling between the UI support system and the application, we decided that our system must allow the application to be built as a separate class tree. In so doing, we required a mechanism with which to couple the application to the UI functionality "horizontally". This coupling must be adequate for purposes of user interaction, yet loose enough that it does not impose restrictions on the way the application is built and does not require the application programmer to learn low level details of the support system in order to implement this linkage. We formulated a layered model of the user interface [Zhou and Kubitz, 1992] in which the *application exposure* (AE) layer was exactly designed to achieve this coupling. Our conviction is that an object-oriented approach offers new ground on which we can avoid traditional problems, such as inadequate semantic feedback, that have hindered horizontal coupling in traditional systems [Pfaff, 1985]. With object-orientation, each application object constitutes a localized context making it much easier for the UI to acquire application semantics from the individual objects involved in the interaction.

The AE layer is divided into two portions: one that exposes application operations and one that exposes application representations. Application representations may take many forms but are specified completely by the (real or contrived) geometric (or structural) description and material properties of the application objects. The real issue is, then, how to expose the application object properties necessary for producing a suitable representation along with the operations on the object that are relevant to the current needs of the user. These operations may be local to the user interface or may be application operations which must be presented to the user through the user interface.

2 Exposing Application Representations

The exposure of representations applies not only to application objects having intrinsic geometric properties, but to all application objects having any form of visualization. That is, it applies generally to all objects having a visual representation of any kind. 3D solid models, spatial grids, particle systems, surfaces, and curves, for example, are all ways of defining geometric representational properties. In each of their defining classes, the application programmer must add an *exposure method* which is able to traverse any instances of the class and express their geometric representations in a format imposed by the UI. In other words, the method will generate objects in a standard format containing the application data, and return them to the UI. In a similar way, the material properties of the object must be made available to the user interface in order to properly represent surface properties. In this way, the user interface can manage the graphical representation of the application object that is presented to the user. This graphical representation may in fact be specified by the application and it can be generated for the user interface in the same manner as it would be by the application itself, that is, by using a modern graphical modeling support system such as Egbert's GRAMS [Egbert and Kubitz, 1992], suitably augmented.

2.1 Graphic Objects

Interface Graphic Objects [IGOs] are of two kinds, those whose defining properties (geometry and material) originate in the application and are "passed through" the user interface so that the UI has control of the representation presented to the user (which can be chosen by the application or the UI, as needed) and those UI "assistance objects" whose defining properties and representations are both entirely determined by the UI itself. Passing application object definitions through the UI prior to chosing the representation (unless dictated by the application) has the advantage that the UI may choose a representation best suited to a given operation, which may not have originated with the application, but rather with the user interface. Thus, as the context switches between the UI and the application, the representation may be changed to the one best suited to the task at hand. This is also extremely useful when the UI is serving as the common interface to multiple applications used to operate on the same underlying application data. This scheme is possible because of the decoupling of the application modeling from the graphics modeling, and because the application and the user interface share the same geometric and material specification scheme and the same graphics modeling system.

The standard format is defined by a graphics class hierarchy, such as that provided by GRAMS, depicted in Figure 1. Objects defined in this hierarchy are simply graphic representational objects provided by a large graphics modeling library. As stated above, while all the representations come from the same modeling hierarchy the defining information comes from the application or the user interface. The user interface manages the screen presentation in both cases. In this case of the UI itself, this includes assistance objects used to help the user perform certain alignments and those used to provide visual representations for both mediators and activators [Zhou and Kubitz, 1992]. Thus, the term IGO is used to mean a graphics object managed by the user interface.

Objects in this class tree are not orthogonal. In general, objects defined in the `PrimitiveGO` subtree can be used to adequately convey geometric descriptions for all covered applications, assuming that those applications do not use higher order geometric constructs than quadrics. But since applications often work at more elevated structural levels, more complex GO classes are added to simulate the common geometric object structures that are well-established among applications. Thus, the class `BRLikeGO` defines GOs that best represent a specific kind of application object, namely solid models defined by their boundaries. The objects defined by `UniformGO` are convenient for shadowing application objects with uniform finer details, such as particle systems and spatial grids. The class `CompositeGO` is for representing application objects composed of other application objects. In particular, `CSGLikeGO` is for shadowing solid objects built with so-called normalized boolean operators $+*$, $-*$, and $\cap*$, while `AggregateGO` is suitable for compositions of heterogeneous objects.

Providing these higher-level GOs in addition to the primitive GOs substantially narrows the possible structure and semantic gaps between application objects and the objects created to represent them in the UI, making the task of exposing application representations easier and more efficient. From the standpoint of the UI, these higher-level objects are also more convenient to manipulate.

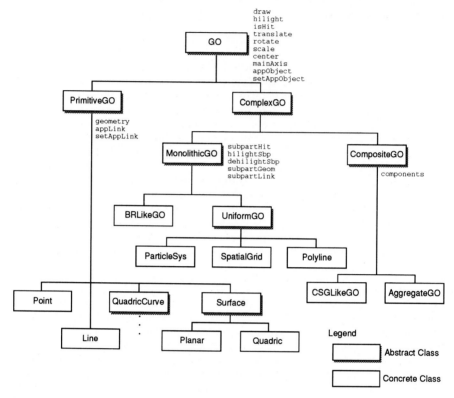

Figure 1: Class hierarchy of generic objects

2.2 Properties of GOs

IGOs are the graphical representations of application objects (or UI objects) whose definitions have been exposed to the UI by the application. Once chosen, the representations are managed exclusively by the UI even though operations on the underlying application objects may cause the representation to change form (but not the chosen visualization type). This situation prescribes the following properties for IGOs.

- IGOs only need to reflect the properties of application objects that are user interaction-relevant (to the current user interface and/or the application context).

In 3D applications such as solid modeling, such properties include primarily the geometric representations of application objects. The UI needs this information to produce appropriate visual representations (visualizations) of the application objects, to handle high level processing of hit-detections, to compute possible on-screen constraint conditions, etc. Properties of application objects that are not relevant to the context of the current operations need not be accurately depicted by the IGOs. In fact, one of the most important features of an IGO is to clearly and accurately depict, even emphasize, the properties of the underlying application object that are relevant to the current context.

The class BRLikeGO is a good example. The boundary representation in solid modeling defines solid models in terms of their boundaries. Typically, a BR contains not only the geometric description of the boundary elements but also the topology of them, expressed in an elaborated form known as "winged-edge" data structure. For solid modeling applications, this topological information is very important because it allows algorithms that modify solid models via Eular operations, as well as those that evaluate solid models, to work efficiently, or to work at all. However, the UI does not itself perform similar operations on the IGO visualizations of such BR objects, even though the visualizations presented on the screen may be used to allow the underlying applications to do so. Therefore, there is no need to include the full topology in the definition used to produce the visualization of the class BRLikeGO. The proper visualization form for an application object is dependent on the use. Systems like GRAMS offer a number of different visualizations to the application. In addition, as mentioned, the UI can intervene in the choice of the visualization used. When an operation is invoked through the user interface that modifies the underlying application data (as many application operations would), then clearly the defining information of the representation is changed. This may or may not cause the visualization to change, depending on whether or not the defining data from the application object used by the visualization is affected by the changes. In most cases, of course, the application would choose to use a visualization that *does* show the changes as that is the essence of interactive systems. In spite of this, there might be uses where a simplified visualization (which is apt to be less computationally demanding) is used to invoke an operation and then the visualization is switched to a more sophisticated one (which is likely more computationally demanding) to view the result of the operation.

Thus, IGOs may not always need to depict application objects at a high level of accuracy on a continuous basis. Typically, a solid modeling application manipulates BR models by applying so-called "local modifications" to them, such as rounding ("blending") a sharp edge, lifting an interior point of a face, or even splitting a model into parts. These operations cause faces, vertices, and edges to be added to or removed from a solid model, or may even, as in the case of splitting, create new BR models. Obviously, the application must handle all these situations. The BR objects in the application must be able to update themselves when undergoing such operations. However, in many cases there is no need for the UI to continuously follow suit by displaying the detailed visualization of these BR objects. This would be true, for example, if the only purpose of the UI representation was to help in identifying the lifting point on a face or placing a cutting plane for splitting a face. In this case, a simplified representation would be sufficient until after the operations had been performed by the application, after which the application representation for the updated BR objects would need to be redrawn (probably using a higher quality representation) so that the user could see the precise results. In other words, IGOs need not continuously update themselves during all operations since it may be sufficient for them to be updated at the completion of an operation. This will save substantial computation time.

By ignoring the application specifics that are irrelevant to the UI (though perhaps important to the application), IGOs can be more general, and in many cases simpler, than the application objects they represent. It is not unusual for a single GO class to be used to represent several different types of application objects.

- IGO operations (as opposed to application operations) are used exclusively by the UI and can be hidden from the application.

All IGOs must accommodate general UI operations. First of all, as representations of application objects they must be able to display and highlight themselves to supply visualizations of application objects like any graphic objects. They must also support hit detection (with the support of the graphics system) so as to let the user select screen image objects and thus UI and application objects. Finally they must accommodate dragging (translation), rotation, and scaling operations, like all graphic objects, so as to allow dynamic visual feedback when the visualized objects are so operated upon at any level (user, UI system, application, etc.) The methods defined on the abstract top class of the GO hierarchy in Figure 1 represent the operations that all GOs support.

Since composite GOs reflect a kind of object that is hierarchically constructed, they must provide ways for reaching lower-level objects. Thus, the method `components` is defined on the abstract class `CompositeGO`. This method is invoked by the UI when making context shifts [Zhou and Kubitz, 1992].

Many application objects contain finer detail that do not qualify as sub-objects. For example, vertices, edges, and faces in a BR object, or meshes in a grid object, do not contribute to the BR object or the grid object in the same way sub-objects do to their composite. In general, applications do not define objects at a level lower than the smallest semantically useful one, although the raw data at the lowest level must be accessible via a method that understands the data structure. Thus, there is no need for hit detection below the object level if an application is properly designed. Methods must exist in the UI to support subpart selection [Zhou and Kubitz, 1992] from the application data base (assumed to be object-oriented), but this does not necessarily imply selection through object hit detection by the user.

The UI always has access to the geometric and material information of application objects and thus has the information needed to handle UI constraint conditions between representations. This information is available through the application exposure for the particular application or UI object. The methods `geomDesc`, defined for all primitive GOs, and `center` and `mainAxis`, defined for all complex GOs, provide this information.

Since the above GO operations concern the UI and/or the graphics support system, they can be hidden from the application side, thereby greatly simplifying the application programmer's view of the user interface.

- GOs exhibit different views to the UI and to the application.

The user interface shares the GO view held by the graphics modeling system rather than the high level, AGO view of the application. This facilitates many of the low-level (and graphics) operations that must be performed by the UI but are unknown to the application. For UI support, just as for generic graphics support, the GO class tree follows a strict type hierarchy. This provides the benefit of polymorphism in the manipulation of IGOs by the UI. On the other hand, operations are not the only determining factor for the organization of this class hierarchy. For example, the classes `Planar` and `Quadric` share the same abstract super class and the same set of operations, but they represent different geometric objects. The fact that both of these IGOs can be operated upon in exactly the same way by the UI is largely irrelevant to the application. More important is the fact that a quadric surface must be represented with a quadric IGO, not a planar IGO. Thus, in the eyes of the application programmer, the IGO tree is only a class library in which each class defines a type of object of a certain geometric nature and provides one or more *constructor*(s) that can be called upon to create instances of that class.

2.3 Multiple Representations for GOs

In a modern graphics modeling system such as GRAMS, multiple visualizations (different graphics representations) of a given defining object are possible. Thus, multiple visualizations of IGOs are possible. The visualizations adopted for IGOs may affect the efficiency of commonly used IGO operations, such as rendering (including viewing transformations), hit detection, and geometry conversion. Often a single visualization will not be adequate for supporting all UI operations on a given object. For example, the geometry of a sphere might be normally stored as the coordinates of its center and the radius. This form might be quite convenient for hit detection, but be less useful for explicit geometric and perspective transformations or scanline and wireframe algorithms, which are likely to be used by the IGO methods to produce different visualizations. Other examples are the form in which the geometry of planes and CSG objects are stored. Fortunately, a system like GRAMS provides automatic conversion of high level graphic objects to lower level primitives, thus removing this burden from the user interface.

Thus, the application programmer is not burdened with converting application object definitions into forms ideal for IGOs. It would be a violation of the encapsulation offered by the graphics support system to do so because it amounts to opening the internal details of GOs to the application side. The application is allowed to use the most appropriate AGO as its representation unless the UI overides this choice because of the specific needs of the user interface itself. The user interface can cache the result of an internal geometry conversion performed by the graphics support system if the UI requires access to the converted form of the data, or as a means of increasing the efficiency and/or improving system response time.

Caching IGO Geometry, Transformation Matrix, and Material Property

An IGO cache is provided for each IGO for storing the final form of the geometry as derived by the graphics support system the entity's original mathematical description supplied by the application. For example, it might store {center coordinates, radius} for a sphere or {vector, distance} for a plane. The geometry cache for an IGO is filled with either application supplied or computed data, depending on the needs of the chosen visualization. For example, if the application object is a plane, then the normal and the distance to origin are used to fill the IGO's cache directly. If, on the other hand, the object is a planar polygon then the values computed by the graphics support system are used to fill the cache. Similar considerations apply to storing the current transformation matrix and the final form of the material properties for the IGO. The material properties may also have been derived from the original specification supplied by the application. Complex objects, such as BR-like and CSG-like GOs, use geometry caches to hold their centers and axes. Since these data are unlikely to be supplied directly by the application objects, but are also needed by the graphics system, they too can be obtained directly from it. The geometry cache is used to answer geometry inquiries at the UI level and to eliminate the (usually) time consuming conversion process that takes place in the graphics system if only the high level geometric description is available. By supplying the geometric description required by the chosen visualization, the rendering speed is improved considerably and interactivity is enhanced. Hit detection is performed by the graphic system. The UI uses the result of the hit detection supplied by the graphics system.

Efficiency of IGO Generation and Regeneration

The creation of an IGO cache, as discussed above, is sometimes expensive since no conversion is involved and the specification from the application can be used directly. However, there is no way to know in advance what visualization may be chosen, so providing a cache for all possibly active IGOs is the only logical choice. In general, each time an application object is changed in such a way that the appearance of its current visualization changes, or a new visualization is chosen, the IGO representation changes and the IGO cache must be reloaded with the newly derived values. So a legitimate question is: To what extent will the visualization regeneration process impede the response time of the UI? The answer is very little. Dragging, rotation, and scaling, for example, are among the most demanding operations in terms of response time. But since the application object in these cases is only undergoing an affine transformation which does not really change the application object's representation, there is no need for regeneration at each step. Regeneration is necessary primarily when an existing object is modified, a new visualization is chosen, new application objects are introduced, or as the result of a splitting or combining operation. In these cases, fortunately, response time is not quite so critical since users are usually willing to tolerate a larger response time when an operation produces a result considered to be more significant by the user.

2.4 IGO Visualization

We now give a few examples of IGO visualization invocation, with the minimum use of pseudo C++ code. In the first example, the application objects are defined in a normal BR format. Suppose that the application accepts both planar and quadric surfaces for its solid models. Since the intersection of two quadric surfaces can be quite bizarre (think of the intersection of two cylinders), also assume that the application uses polylines to approximate such intersection curves. Thus a BR object may have quadric faces, but its edges are always polylines.

Every application object in the BR format contains three lists that hold the geometric descriptions for the object's vertices, edges, and faces. The application object also contains a sophisticated piece of data representing the topology of its elements: the winged-edge structure. Fortunately, this structure can be ignored by the IGO visualization.

There is a `BRLikeGO` constructor that can use all three lists:

```
BRLikeGO::BRLikeGO(Point* vertList, Line* edgeList,
                   Surface* faceList);
```

This constructor will generate a BR-like GO and return a pointer to it. Note that the three arguments are also pointers to GO types, namely `Point`, `Line`, and `Surface`. The exposure method defined on the application object will traverse its three lists and invoke constructors of the classes `Point`, `Line`, and `Surface`, respectively, to prepare the three arguments. Once this is done, it calls the `BRLikeGO` constructor to generate its shadow GO.

Now suppose that the application objects are loosely defined BRs. Such an object contains a list of vertices and a list of faces, each face being a sequence of indices into the vertex list. There is a simpler `BRLikeGO` constructor designed for this case that takes only one argument:

```
BRLikeGO::BRLikeGO(Planar* faceList);
```

`Planar` is also a GO class. One of its constructors may take a plane description and another a planar polygon. In this case the latter constructor is obviously more convenient and will be used by the exposure method when it traverses the face list.

As in the last example, consider the so-called "generalized primitives", such as a block given as a triplet {width, height, length}. If the programmer sees such a block as the intersection of six planar half-spaces, he may choose to visualize the object with a `CSGLikeGO` constructor, which takes a boolean operator (expressed as a text string) and a variable number of GOs (in this case, six `Planar`s) as the arguments. The `Planar` constructor that takes a plane description as the argument will now be used. The final call will look like this (constructors are called with "new"):

```
new CSGLikeGO("Intersect",
              new Planar(1, 0, 0, 0), // normal, distance
              new Planar(-1, 0, 0, width),
              //...
              );
```

Depending on data available in the application, it is also entirely possible that the programmer will choose to shadow the object with a `BRLikeGO` constructor.

3 Exposing Application Operations

The exposure of application representations discussed so far is mainly used in direct manipulation operations. For both direct manipulation and the command mechanism [Zhou and Kubitz, 1992], application objects must also expose their operations. A classical example of this kind of exposure is the "pluggable views" of Smalltalk [Krasner and Pope, 1988]. The pluggability works as follows: if a *model* (an application object in Smalltalk terminology) decides that some of its methods should be invokable by the user, it can define a menu method which, when called, will return an association list containing the user-invokable methods and the associated text strings that can be used to display these messages in a menu. The list must be in a standard format accepted by the system. A *pluggable view* is paired with a *menu controller* and can be "plugged" into any model with the standard menu message defined. When the user presses a mouse button at the view, the view will send the menu message to the model to get the list and pass it to the controller. The controller will then display a menu filled with the text strings and accept the user's choice. Finally the message associated with the item chosen by the user is sent to the model. This scheme can also be implemented with other object-oriented languages.

3.1 Application Operations with Arguments

The Smalltalk pluggability is very restrictive in that it only allows the user to invoke application operations without arguments. As a generalization of this simple pluggability, the AE layer of our system must be able to expose application operations that do take arguments. Now the situation is much more complicated. First of all, the number of arguments and the argument types, or collectively, the *signature*, for each exposed function must be conveyed to the UI. Without this information the UI will not be able to furnish the proper arguments to invoke the application operation. Furthermore, since the functions defined on an application object probably have different signatures, using an association list to expose and invoke them is no longer a viable solution. But this second question is more implementation oriented and we shall focus on the first question in our discussion here. Again, brief pseudo C++ code will be used when necessary.

Suppose the following functions are defined on an application object of class X and are intended to be callable by the user:

```
class X {
public:
    void* func1(int, String, Y*);
    void* func2(Z*, float);
    void* func3(Coord*);
    //...
};
```

Also suppose that an exposure method exposeOps is defined on X. This function will supply the UI with each user-callable function's name and signature. Thus, for func1, func2, and func3, exposeOps will return:

```
"Function 1", 3, "int", "String", "Y*"
"Function 2", 2, "Z*", "float"
"Function 3", 1, "Coord*"
```

The issue here is: How would the UI interpret the information? There are actually three categories of arguments, each requiring a different treatment.

One category includes types provided by the implementation language understood by both sides. In the case of C++, these are int, float, char*, etc. The only trick here is that, if the application has renamed a type, say char*, as String, it must expose the original type name instead of the "proprietary" type name. Interaction techniques for preparing such arguments are fairly standard. If the application operation expects an argument of type char*, for example, the UI will use a dialog box to let the user input the string.

Another category includes application-defined objects with which the user interacts — in other words, to which the UI has access. Suppose the application operation expects an argument of type Y, where Y is a class of the application. Since the user interacts with objects of class Y, the argument object must be either in a UI-maintained buffer as a result of a previous operation or selectable by the user from the selection context. The only thing the UI must do is check if the candidate is of type Y. This explicit type inquiry can be answered with another exposure method, say exposeType. Note that it is not enough for exposeType of class Y to simply answer "Y". If Y is strictly a specialization of class Z, then an instance of Y can always be used in place of an instance of Z in any operation. Therefore, exposeType must also answer an object's super classes as long as they form an "Is-a" relationship down the chain. If a candidate of type Y answers "Y, Z", then the UI knows it qualifies as a type Y as well as type Z argument.

Objects in the third category need more consideration. An argument may be an application-defined structure. This structure is internal to the application, yet the application expects the user to fill in its fields. In general, the UI has no knowledge at all about any application-specific structures. Therefore even if the UI is given the name of such a type, it will not be able to do anything with it. The solution is for the application to provide each internal structure with a constructor which takes a flat list of arguments to fill the structure. For example, Coord is a nested structure defined in the application,

```
struct Aux {char* ss; char* tt;};
struct Coord {int x; int y; int z; Aux aux;};
```

then a constructor

```
Coord::Coord(int, int, int, char*, char*)
```

should be added to the structure Coord. Now, exposeOps should list func3's signature as

```
5, "int", "int", "int", "char*", "char*"
```

instead of

```
1, "Coord*".
```

Grouping information can be included along with the signature so that the UI will know to use a single dialog box to get all these values. After the UI has gathered all the values, they can be repacked into type Coord using the constructor. This repacking will be done on the application side by a "hook" function responsible for actually invoking the exposed operations.

3.2 Automatic Generation

Writing the exposure methods manually would be tedious and error-prone. However, a quick examination reveals that these methods are highly mechanical and repetitive and, therefore, can be produced largely by a text scanner after the programmer provides, to the scanner, the application functions to be exposed. Assistance from the application programmer is needed for more sophisticated cases. The conversion from a single argument of type `Coord*` into five arguments of basic types discussed in the Section 3.1 is probably a place where programmer intervention is needed. Tracing operations defined on the super classes and joining them with those defined on the current class may also need programmer intervention.

3.3 Static Application Objects

So far the term "application objects" has been used to refer to those objects that are the primary subjects of the operations and are created, modified, and deleted dynamically during an interaction session. Besides these ordinary objects, the UI must also deal with other application entities. For example:

- Classes that define ordinary application objects. Creation of an application object must deal with the defining class. In Smalltalk, an instance creation message is sent to the defining class. In C++, one of the class's constructors is invoked. In both cases, classes are the subjects of the operations. The operations are usually invoked by the user.

- "Processing engines". In C++, for example, a collection of *static* functions can be grouped into a class. These operations are not meant to be invoked on the instances of the class. Rather, they are used to process the objects passed to them as the arguments. Such a class actually serves as a processing engine, and some processing engines may need to be controlled by the user.

Entities like these are application objects in a more general sense. They differ from ordinary application objects in that

- They are static. They come into existence whenever the program starts and are never deleted.

- They do not contain geometric representations that mandate how they should be visualized in the UI.

- Their operations, collectively, can be partitioned into fixed, disjoint subsets. For example, the instance creation operations of all classes can be gathered into a creation group, and each processing engine can form an operation group. This is in contrast to the ordinary application objects where, given an object, the available operations depend on its position in the class tree.

Although the principles discussed in the previous sections still apply, static objects deserve a slightly different treatment than ordinary objects. In fact, the operation exposure for such objects is somehow simpler and can be done more efficiently. Since it is not necessary for static objects to answer inquiries at runtime, the programmer can prepare "exposure inserts" for them that can be planted into the UI components.

3.4   Related Work

The operation exposure portion of the AE layer is not completely novel. Besides the Smalltalk pluggability mentioned earlier, the callback mechanism widely used in recent UI toolkits accomplishes a similar result. The underlying principles, however, are different. Rather than requiring the application to expose its operations to the UI, callbacks rely on the programmer to "hardwire" actual application function calls into the UI components.

Hardwiring callbacks can be difficult, and callbacks are often associated with "spaghetti" code. The problem is not necessarily caused by the callback mechanism per se, but rather by the environment where it is applied. Current UI toolkits were originally designed to rely on application-provided callback functions to wire widgets together, while actually this job can be done more independently of the application. In addition, callbacks emerged at a time when applications were built overwhelmingly in a procedural rather than object-oriented way. Without the object abstraction and other benefits offered by object-oriented programming, it is very difficult to organize application functions in a orderly and logical way so as to expose them and to let the UI understand the exposure. This left the callback as the only practical solution prior to object-oriented methodology.

By contrast, the operation exposure takes an object-oriented view of the application. The UI is now interacting with application objects rather than functions and procedures. Selecting an object for manipulation establishes a specific operation context associated with the object, and that context can be made known to the UI at runtime. The localized, per-class exposure is well-organized and much more manageable than traditional callbacks. Note that the operation exposure does not completely exclude callbacks. The "exposure inserts" for static objects (Section 3.3) are in fact similar to callbacks. For dynamic objects, however, callbacks are indeed of little use.

The operation exposure also bears similarities to the Nephew UIMS/Application interface [Szekely, 1989] and MIKE [Olsen, 1986]. Like the callback mechanism, these two earlier systems also view the application side as consisting of functions and procedures and attempt to formulate a well-defined interface to those procedural entities. In a procedural world, however, this means that the UI must be given extensive information on the entire set of available application operations and on how to validate operands for these operations. This can be very difficult for a complex system.

4   Concluding Remarks

We are currently prototyping with the model described in [Zhou and Kubitz, 1992]. Although there are still technical details to be fully worked out, the general idea of the AE layer discussed in this paper appears to be quite promising. Figure 2 is a sample screen dump showing our prototype in operation. The user is working on several application objects (a car body and several wheels) through their exposure in the UI. The objects seen on the screen are actually IGOs generated by these application objects.

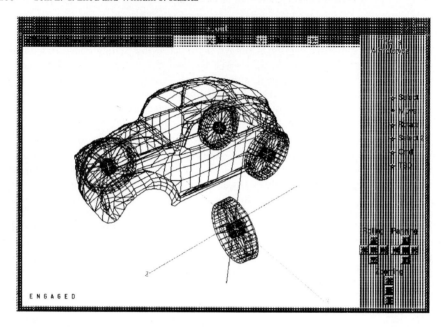

Figure 2: The assembly of a Beetle

The application exposure is not effortless to build, but it is certainly more manageable than building an application on the basis of a given framework. For example, to expose application representations, the programmer must learn about the relevant properties of GOs, which consists primarily of the nature of these GOs (e.g. what GOs can be used to represent what kinds of application and user interface objects) and the use of their constructors. Since the application programmer must know this information already in order to use the graphics system, very little additional effort is required. On the other hand, if one were *building* application classes based on the GO class tree, one would need to learn how GO classes are defined and how they interact with other elements of the framework, such as those responsible for windowing, event dispatching, viewing transformation, and so on. In addition, the graphics system would be embedded in the application as has been traditionally, and reusability would be defeated. This is much more difficult than learning the "external properties" of GOs.

References

Barth, P.S., An Object-Oriented Approach to Graphical Interfaces. *ACM Trans. Graphics*, 5(2):142–172, April 1986.

Egbert, P.K., and Kubitz, W.J., Application Graphics Modeling Support Through Object-Orientation. *IEEE Computer*, pages 84–91, September 1992.

Johnson, R., and Foote, B., Designing Reusable Classes. *JOOP*, 1(2), June/July 1988.

Krasner, G.E., and Pope, S.T., *A Cookbook for Using the Model-View-Controller User Inter-*

face Paradigm in Smalltalk-80. ParcPlace Systems, January 1988.

Mäntylä, M., *An Introduction to Solid Modeling.* Computer Science Press, 1988.

Myers, B.A., Giuse, D.A., Dannenberg, R.B., Zanden, B.V., Kosbie, D.S., Pervin, E., Mickish, A., and Marchal, P., Garnet: Comprehensive Support for Graphical, Highly Interactive User Interfaces. *IEEE Computer*, pages 71–85, November 1990.

Myers, B.A., A New Model for Handling Input. *ACM Trans. Information Systems*, 8(3):289–320, July 1990.

Olsen Jr., D.A., MIKE: The Menu Interaction Kontrol Environment. *ACM Trans. Graphics*, 5(4):318–344, October 1986.

Pfaff, G.E., editor. *User Interface Management Systems.* Springer-Verlag, Berlin, 1985. (Roundup of Seeheim workshop).

Sibert, J.L., Hurley, W.D., and Bleser, T.W., An Object-Oriented User Interface Management System. In *Proc. SIGGRAPH '86*, pages 259–268, August 1986.

Szekely, P., Standardizing the Interface Between Applications and UIMS. In *Proc. UIST '89*, pages 34–42, November 1989.

Vlissides, J.M., and Linton, M.A., Unidraw: A Framework for Building Domain-Specific Graphical Editors. In *Proc. UIST '89*, pages 158–167, November 1989.

Zhou, T.Z.-Y., and Kubitz, W.J., An Object-Oriented View of the User Interface. *Computer Graphics Forum*, 11(3), September 1992. (Proc. Eurographics '92).

Part VIII

Experiences

17

An Interactive 3D Graphics Class Library in EIFFEL

Russell Turner, Enrico Gobbetti, Francis Balaguer, and Angelo Mangili

An object-oriented design is presented for building interactive 3D graphics applications. The design takes the form of a library of classes written in Eiffel, an object-oriented language with multiple inheritance, static typing, dynamic binding, garbage collection, and assertion checking. The classes form a set of reusable components from which a variety of other interactive 3D graphics applications could easily be constructed. A discussion of the overall design goals and philosophy is given. This is followed by a summary description of the purpose and implementation of each of the component class clusters. Finally, the issues are discussed of applying object-oriented techniques to interactive 3D graphics, including encapsulation of existing software and the implementation on a Silicon Graphics Iris workstation.

1   Introduction

A new three-dimensional style of interacting with computers is emerging. This style relies on fast, high-quality graphics displays coupled with expressive, multi-degree-of-freedom input devices to achieve real-time animation and direct-manipulation interaction metaphors. 3D interactive techniques are already being used in systems that require the creation and manipulation of complex three-dimensional models in such application domains as engineering, scientific visualization or commercial animation. Other possibilities include the newest virtual environment research which strives for a more intuitive way of working with computers by including the user in a synthetic environment.

The design and implementation of an interactive 3D application are extremely complex tasks. The application program has to manage a model of the virtual world depicted on the screen, and to simulate its evolution in response to events from the user. These events can occur in an order which is determined only at run time. In particular, an interactive, event -driven application must be able to handle the multi-threaded style of man-machine dialogue associated with direct manipulation interfaces, and it must be able to make extensive use of the various asynchronous input devices at the disposal of the user. These can vary from the keyboard and mouse to more sophisticated devices such as the spaceball or DataGlove.

Seen from a software engineering viewpoint, the design of interactive 3D applications can benefit from object-oriented techniques in several ways. For example, data abstraction can be used to support different internal data representations, multiple graphics drivers can be encapsulated in specific objects, a variety of subclasses can offer the same interface for the manipulation of graphical objects, and the distribution of information can be used to manage the parallelism inherent in direct manipulation programs. From the point of view of a user, the direct manipulation metaphor allows the intuitive behavior and relationships of the objects on the screen to mirror the class and instance hierarchies of the data objects. Object-oriented construction is therefore a natural approach for the design and implementation of an interactive 3D graphics system.

We had already gained some experience building object-oriented software with the development of a research user-interface toolkit for the Silicon Graphics Iris workstations [Turner et al., 1990] using a custom-made object-oriented extension to C based on the concepts of Objective C [Cox, 1986]. This experience showed us the limitations of using a hybrid language for the implementation of an object-oriented design. Because the language was an extension of a traditional language, it was difficult to completely enforce the object-oriented paradigm, often resulting in a mixture of procedural and object-oriented styles. In addition, the language provided no multiple inheritance, and no static typing, which limited its expressiveness and sometimes influencing design decisions. For example, code duplication was often necessary in cases where multiple inheritance should have been used instead. Another big problem with our system was its lack of garbage collection, which required us to spend too much time chasing memory bugs and devising complex algorithms to destroy object structures.

As a result, we became convinced of the importance of using a pure object-oriented language for our work, and Eiffel was chosen for the 3D library because of its characteristics which corresponded closely to our needs. In particular, Eiffel supports multiple inheritance, static typing, dynamic binding, garbage collection, assertion checking and the ability to call other languages easily. We were interested to find out if these powerful object-oriented features would help in the process of 3D design and we also wanted to test if it was possible to use a pure object-oriented language like Eiffel for an area with such large constraints on performance as interactive 3D graphics.

In this chapter we will present the design and implementation of a set of classes in Eiffel which can be assembled to create these types of applications. Section 2 discusses our design goals and methods, section 3 presents a detailed description of the various clusters of classes making up the library, section 4 describes how these classes are assembled into applications and section 5 discusses some of the issues we have encountered.

2 System Design

2.1 Identification of Principal Class Clusters

We initially spent most of our time in group discussions about the design of the system. The software development tools for Eiffel encourage the grouping of related classes into what are called *clusters*. We therefore decided to split the problem into several principal clusters to be developed in parallel by different people, with each cluster carried through the design process to implementation. The identification of these clusters was based on an analysis of the 3D graphics application domain and on our previous experience designing other graphical systems. This process is typical of the bottom-up approach that object-oriented design tends to promote. The clusters we identified were:

- a modeling cluster, to represent the various components of graphical scenes;

- a rendering cluster, to provide several rendering facilities;

- a dynamic cluster, to provide ways to encode interactive and animated behavior;

- a user-interface cluster, to provide standard interaction widgets and devices.

We also developed some lower-level clusters for providing data structure and mathematical functionality. One of these, the mathematics cluster, provides standard mathematical objects such as VECTOR and MATRIX, as well as classes more specific to computer graphics such as TRANSFORM_3D and QUATERNION.

For the purposes of describing the class structure of the clusters, we made use of object-relation diagrams, as in [Rumbaugh et al., 1991], and pictured in Figure 1. The definition of the static structure of the design is usually the first step in the design process, and these diagrams allowed us to give a schematic presentation of this structure which combines both instance relations and inheritance relations. These diagrams became a standard way for us to exchange ideas during the design meetings.

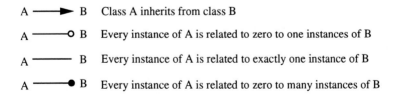

Figure 1: Object-Relation Diagrams

These diagrams are the only formal notation we used during the design process. No other types of diagrams or special notations were used. These diagrams are useful but we tend to resist more formalized schemes (data flow diagrams, for example). These other techniques could be of some use, particularly if used together with some CASE tools for maintaining diagrams up-to-date with respect to the code, and we may consider them in the future. Fortunately, Eiffel's assertions and invariants offer a way to represent the programming contracts between different components of the system. We therefore sometimes use fragments of Eiffel code early in the design instead of pseudo-code or data-flow diagrams.

2.2 Conventions

To encourage more regular interfaces, and to improve the reusability of our classes, we adopted some conventions for naming Eiffel features. Some of these conventions are:

- features that return an alternate representation of an object always begin with *as*. For example, *as_quaternion:* QUATERNION, which can be applied to instances of MATRIX_4D;

- features that modify the value of *Current* as a result of some computations based on the parameters always begin with *to*. For example, *to_sub(left, right: like Current),* which can be applied to instances of NUMERIC_OBJ;

- features that store the results of their computations in one of their parameters always contain the suffix *_in*. For example, *row_in(i: INTEGER; v: VECTOR),* which can be applied to instances of MATRIX.

One result of these conventions is that features tend to follow the style of modifying Current or one of the parameters instead of creating a new object. Therefore, it is the client's responsibility to allocate all the necessary objects, and this can reduce the overhead due to allocation and collection of unnecessary temporary objects.

We put some effort into defining preconditions, postconditions and invariants for all the routines and classes because, by specifying the programming interface contract, they are a key element for promoting reusability. Assertions formally define the behavior of the classes and therefore we use them early on in the design phase. They also provide a certain form of documentation and help during debugging. Assertions also help to produce efficient software. By clearly defining the responsibilities of each component, defensive programming techniques can be avoided.

2.3 Encapsulation

One of the important features of Eiffel, in our opinion, is the ability to encapsulate routines written in other languages. Because this can be done cleanly, it helps to promote pure object-oriented design. It is also essential if we are to acheive one of the main goals in object-oriented programming which is reusability. Decades of programming effort have been spent in developing and testing large software libraries in various languages. Some of these libraries, for example the FORTRAN BLAS and LAPACK libraries, provide a functionality that could not be particularly improved upon by reimplementing them in an object-oriented language. Hybrid languages such as C++ [Stroustrup, 1986] and Objective-C [Cox, 1986] try to encourage this reuse by allowing the programmer to continue developing their software using object-oriented extensions. Unfortunately, this approach does not enforce a clean separation between the object-oriented and non-object-oriented portions of the software. By putting an object-oriented gloss on traditional languages, the software engineering problems of the traditional languages are perpetuated into the object-oriented languages.

On the contrary, the Eiffel approach is to define a clean and localized interface with the non-Eiffel language components. This does not compromise the object-oriented paradigm upon which the language is based. Our VECTOR and MATRIX classes are implemented on top of the BLAS and LAPACK standard FORTRAN libraries, and for us the ability to reuse this functionality was an important aspect of the development. A great deal of functionality at a high performance was added in a small amount of time, without sacrificing the object-oriented design.

3 Overview of Principal Clusters

3.1 The Graphical Model

Interactive 3D graphics applications must be able to respond to asynchronous input events as they happen, so designers must build their programs to behave properly no matter when and in what order the events will occur. This is usually done by maintaining a global data model which represents the current state of the application program at any moment during its execution. In an object-oriented system this global data model, called the graphical model, consists of a hierarchy or directed acyclic graph of instances representing the virtual objects to be manipulated. Many different aspects have to be considered when designing the graphics model, such as rendering, interactive behavior, inheritance of attributes and maintaining internal consistency. Several class structures have been proposed in the literature for representing three-dimensional hierarchical scenes. Examples are found in the modeling and rendering library Dore [Pacific, 1992], [Fleischer and Witkin, 1988], which describes an object-oriented modeling testbed, [Grant et al., 1986], which presents a hierarchy of classes for rendering three-dimensional scenes, [Hedelman, 1984] which proposes an object-oriented design for procedural modeling, and the object-oriented 3D interaction toolkit UGA [Conner et al., 1992].

Interactive 3D graphics systems are typically concerned with manipulating models arranged in a hierarchical fashion. This hierarchy can be represented as a tree of homogeneous transformations which define the position, orientation, and scaling of the reference frames in which graphical primitives are defined.(see [Boulic and Renault, 1991]).

The classes from which the graphical model is built are contained in the modeling cluster, which is presented in Figure 2.

The WORLD_3D class represents a three-dimensional scene and contains the top level of the graphical modeling hierarchy and all the other global information that the application manipulates such as the environmental illumination parameters (packaged in instances of AMBIENT).

The transformation hierarchy is represented by instances of NODE_3D which maintain a transformation object and also may contain child nodes so as to form a tree. It is used to specify the position, orientation, and scaling of the reference frames to which the models are attached. In addition, the NODE_3D contains pointers to other objects which maintain information about the node such as MATERIAL and

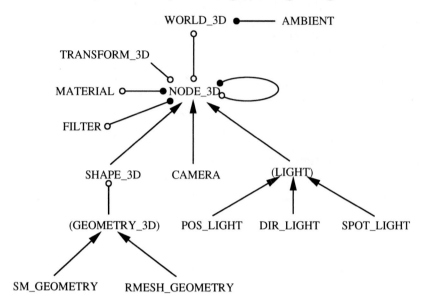

Figure 2: Basic modeling classes

FILTER. These objects may be multiply referenced and their attributes inherited through the instance hierarchy by delegation. The NODE_3D itself can be subclassed into three varieties: lights, cameras, and shapes, which represent the three basic types of objects in the hierarchy.

Instances of MATERIAL are used to define the reflectance properties of physical surfaces. They contain information such as the color and intensity of the emission, diffuse, and specular components as well as shininess and transparency factors for the specular reflection. Instances of FILTER represent a two-dimensional image which can be projected onto the contents of the node in various ways to achieve texture mapping.

Instance of LIGHT represent a light source and maintain information about its color and intensity. Subclasses of LIGHT, such as DIR_LIGHT, POS_LIGHT, and SPOT_LIGHT define various types of light sources and maintain more specific information such as direction, location in space and angle of projection.

An instance of CAMERA represents a virtual camera positioned in the scene, and maintains information about its viewing frustum and its perspective projection. It is through virtual cameras that the 3D world is rendered on a 2D screen.

The SHAPE_3D class represents the concept of a physical object having a geometric shape in Cartesian space. Geometries are defined in a separate class, to make them more general and reusable. By implementing SHAPE_3D so as to reference an instance of a GEOMETRY_3D, it is possible, for example, to define operations on abstract geometry, independant of the other shape characteristics. Also, since the geometries can be multiply referenced, a single geometry may be used in multiple locations in the hierarchy, with different node characteristics. In this way, the hierarchical structure of the scene can be designed independently of the geometries.

Initially, simple geometries can be used which then are easily replaced by more elaborate ones as work progresses. Complex hierarchical structures like skeletons can be designed and reused several times with different geometries attached to them to change their appearance.

The GEOMETRY_3D class can be subclassed to provide various types of geometries. Examples are: SM_GEOMETRY, which defines a geometric object by specifying its surface as a mesh of triangular facets, and RMESH_GEOMETRY, which represents objects as rectangular meshes of three-dimensional points.

3.2 Multiple Inheritance

One notable aspect of Eiffel is its support for multiple inheritance. In fact, the language and the standard clusters that come with it tend to support a very fine-grained approach to multiple inheritance, which we have adopted in our design philosophy. The result is a large number of relatively small classes, many of them deferred, which encapsulate a single concept or piece of functionality. Figure 3 illustrates this type of inheritance for the NODE_3D class, although we usually do not show it in so much detail in our other object-relation diagrams.

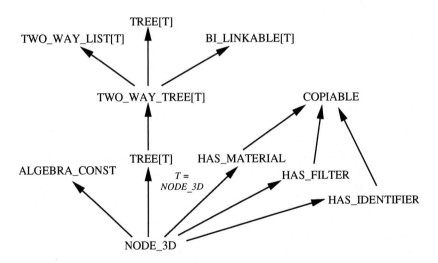

Figure 3: Multiple Ancestors of the NODE_3D Class

In this way, multiple inheritance allows us to compose the NODE_3D's behavior as a collection of partial views, each one defining a particular programming contract and functionality.

3.3 Rendering

For 3D interactive graphics, two of the most important types of operations are rendering the visual appearance and implementing the dynamic behavior of the different graphical objects. An important design question that arises is: where should the graphical appearance and dynamic behavior be encoded? Two possible solutions are: to encode them directly in the model (e.g. by adding a specific *render* feature to the various graphical objects), or to design a new set of classes that are able to perform these operations.

When designing simple two-dimensional class libraries, such as user-interface toolkits, these kinds of operations are usually encoded directly in the model. For more sophisticated applications, however, this kind of approach is usually not feasible because there may be no simple way for a graphical object to perform these operations based on its own internal data.

Taking as an example the operation of rendering a three-dimensional scene, several arguments suggest the creation of auxiliary classes:

- there are potentially many different algorithms for drawing graphical scenes which can coexist in the same system. For example: ray-tracing, radiosity, or z-buffering techniques. The details of these techniques should not have to be known by every graphical object.

- rendering may occur on several different types of output devices such as the frame buffer, a texture map, or an output file, and it is not necessary for all this knowledge to be spread out among all the graphical objects.

- several rendering representations, such as wire-frame or solid, may be selectible on a per graphical object basis. The same object may be viewed by several different windows at the same time, each view using a different representation.

- some rendering algorithms may require access to global modeling data simultaneously. For example, a hidden surface algorithm may need to depth sort a polygon display list.

Obviously, the rendering operation needs much more information than just the type of object to be rendered. Also, a single graphical instance can be rendered in several different ways depending on the type of renderer and the type of representation. We therefore decided to design and implement a new set of classes to maintain this additional information and to implement the various rendering algorithms.

The rendering cluster is composed of a set of classes that are used to render a three-dimensional scene. Figure 4 illustrates the basic design of this cluster:

Five basic sorts of classes can be identified:

- renderers (subclasses of RENDERER). These represent particular techniques for rendering entire scenes. The actual rendering algorithm is implemented in these classes. An important subclass of RENDERER is LIGHTED_RENDERER, which describes renderers that use illumination parameters to compute a visual representation of the scene.

- cameras (subclasses of CAMERA). These are objects able to return geometric viewing information such as perspective and viewpoint.

- worlds (subclasses of WORLD). These are objects which contain a modeling hierarchy and other information such as global illumination parameters.

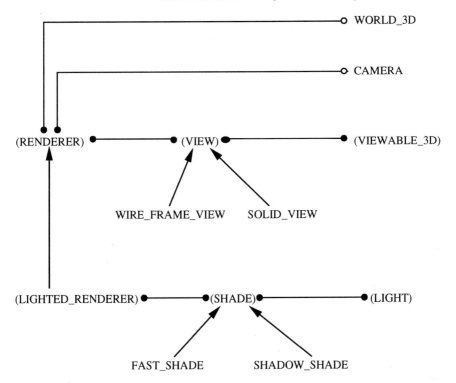

Figure 4: Basic rendering classes

- viewable models (subclasses of VIEWABLE_3D such as SHAPE_3D in the modeling cluster). These represent visible objects which have position, orientation and scale in Cartesian space, as well as a geometry, and a material.

- views (subclasses of VIEW). These are objects which define how a viewable object should be represented.

In this architecture, the view objects act as intermediaries between the models and the renderer, telling the renderer what technique (e.g. wireframe, solid, highlighted) should be used to display each graphical object. This provides a clean separation between a model and how it is viewed. Since multiple views may reference the same model, an application can have, for example, more than one window onto a world, each representing the objects in different ways.

When a renderer displays a particular graphical object, it first consults its views and their attached viewable objects to determine the necessary drawing algorithm. This type of rendering operation, the binding of which depends on more than one target, can be described as polymorphic on more than one type.

Object-oriented languages with dynamic binding like Eiffel, which dispatch on the basis of the target type at the moment of feature application, offer a way to select between different implementations of the same operation without using conditional statements. This ability to have the data determine the algorithm is one of the major advantages of object-oriented programming and can be used even when the dispatching has to be done on more than one type. We have done this for the rendering operation, which is implemented by applying a feature to each polymorphic variable we want to discriminate and letting the dynamic binding make all the choices [Ingalls, 1986].

To illustrate how this method works, we will look at the various classes that form the rendering cluster. To render a scene, a *render* feature is applied to a renderer instance, which has the task of displaying all the objects that are attached to its views. To do this the renderer, after some initializations, sets up the camera and applies a *render* feature to all its views with itself as a parameter.

Each time the *render* feature is applied to a view, it communicates back to the renderer information about what kind of geometries are attached to it through its viewable objects. This is done by storing the current renderer and applying a *view* feature to all the viewable objects known by the view. The viewable objects perform a similar kind of operation by applying the *portray* feature to the model's geometry and respond to the *view* feature call with a more specific viewing feature depending on the type of view object. For example, a *view_rmesh* feature will be applied by objects conformant to RMESH, a *view_sm* feature by objects conformant to SM_GEOMETRY, and so on. So, every subclass of VIEW must implement a new *view_...* feature for each of the types of geometries that need to be distinguished. The specific view features themselves are implemented in VIEW subclasses by calling back to the current renderer with the specific render feature (e.g. *render_wf_rmesh*) to display the object in the desired representation. It is only at this point that the graphical object is actually displayed on the screen. Figure 5 shows a typical example of the sequence of feature invocations resulting from the *render* feature being applied to a renderer.

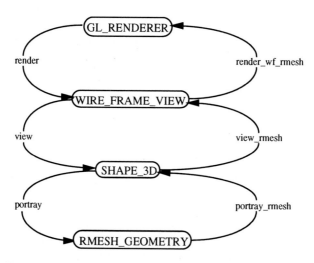

Figure 5: Multiple Dispatching for a Render Feature Call

As Figure 5 shows, rendering a single object sets off a chain of feature calls which pass through the view, the viewable model and its geometry and back again ultimately resolving to the appropriate rendering feature. In this way, the composition of the instance data structure alone automatically determines which specific rendering algorithm is invoked.

3.4 Dynamics and Input

Implementing interactive and animated behavior is among the most problematic aspects of computer graphics design. These can actually be thought of together as the problem of dynamic graphics. How does the application change its graphical output in response to asynchronous input? Viewed in this way, input from the user results in interactive behavior, while input from other data sources or real-time clocks results in animated behavior.

The first problem a sequential application (a single process with one thread of control) must solve is multiplexing between different asynchronous input sources and handling the various input data in a consistent time order. The standard way to do this in object-oriented toolkits is to have a central input-gathering algorithm responsible for selecting between the various input queues (e.g. the windowing system, various devices, and inter-process communication channels) and extracting each input event in the proper time order, resulting in a single time-ordered queue of input events which can be handled sequentially. For an application which assumes this purely input-event-driven model, the basic dynamic behavior algorithm then takes the form of a loop as follows:

```
Initialize the application and select input channels
from start until over loop
     Go into wait state;
     Wake up when input arrives; Respond to input;
end
```

In this event loop structure, the dynamic behavior of the application is implemented in the section *Respond to input*. A natural object-oriented way to model a workstation with multiple input devices is for each input device (e.g. mouse, spaceball, keyboard) to be represented by a separate instance of a particular input device class. To implement such a model, the first action taken in response to an input event is to update the input device object representing the source of this data. For example, when the application receives an input event indicating that the user moved the mouse, the state of the mouse object has to be updated.

Once an input device object has been updated, the state of the application has changed and some action must be performed to respond to this input event and implement the dynamic behavior of the program. For example, if we want the virtual camera viewing the scene to move when the user moves his spaceball, a mechanism must be devised to implement this. An obvious way to do this is to implement a feature in the CAMERA class that is called every time the state of the spaceball changes. However, for similar reasons that led to the separate rendering and modeling classes described in the previous section, it is often better to move the code implementing the dynamic behavior into a separate object, which we call a *controller*. In the case of the virtual camera, we would implement a camera controller object which can be attached to it. The controller knows how to update the camera parameters in response to spaceball events. We call these controller objects dynamic objects because they change their state in response to external input.

The encapsulation of an object's graphical appearance allows more complex graphical assemblies to be constructed from graphical components. We would like to be able to build more complex dynamic behavior in a similar way by assembling dynamic objects together. To do this effectively, a mechanism must be developed to represent the changes of state of dynamic objects in response to input and to maintain the dependencies between dynamic objects so they can be updated. We call these changes of state *events,* and implement the updating of dependent objects through the proper distribution of events.

To model the dynamic behavior of an application, as described in the previous section, we have created two clusters of classes: an input cluster for maintaining and multiplexing between multiple input channels and a dynamic cluster for representing and distributing events.

Figure 6: The Input Cluster

The design of the input cluster is represented in Figure 6. It is adapted from the set of inter-process communication classes developed by Matt Hillman [Hillman, 1990] and partially reuses most of its components.

The NET_NODE class represents objects that can form and accept socket connections with other processes, and merge input from all of these sources into a single event stream. It is through these connections, which are represented by instances of NET_CONNECTION objects, that asynchronous input from the various input devices, from the window system, and from remote processes arrives to the application. The input data is represented by objects of type NET_MESSAGE which are able to both read from and write to a network connection. On top of these basic classes, we have implemented several extensions by means of specialized connection objects and features. One of these is the user interface toolkit presented in the next section.

Figure 7: The Dynamic Cluster

The distribution of events are modeled in the dynamic cluster whose principal components are shown in Figure 7. Three types of objects are used in modeling the dynamic behavior of our applications: *events, handlers,* and *dynamic objects.* A dynamic object maintains a list of the different types of events it can send out to other objects, that is, a list of instances of a specific subclass of EVENT for each type of event it can transmit. A dynamic object transmits an event every time it has to communicate a change of state, the type of event indicating what kind of state change occurred in the dynamic object. Each event instance maintains a list of handler objects, called *subscribers,* which are objects that need to be informed whenever the event is transmitted. These subscriber objects then handle the event to implement their dynamic behavior.

A dynamic object generates an event by applying to its event instances a feature called *transmit.* This feature is implemented in the EVENT class by applying a specific handling feature to all of its subscribers. This handler feature, which is implemented separately by each subclass of EVENT, has the source of the event (i.e. the dynamic object which transmitted the event) as its only parameter. For example, an event of class BUTTON_DOWN transmits the button down event by application of the feature *handle_button_down,* and an event of class BUTTON_UP transmits by applying *handle_button_up.* As in the rendering cluster, this distinction is made completely through the dispatching mechanism inherent to the dynamic binding and not through conditional statements.

This particular representation of dynamic object behavior follows the concept of an event being a signal between two connected objects, a source and a target. The only information transmitted by the event itself, however, is its type, which is indicated by the name of the feature called. Any other data must be explicitly queried from the source by the handler of the event. The handler can then update its internal state and perform actions according to the changes of state in the source objects and its own internal behavior. In a similar manner, secondary events can be transmitted by handlers that are themselves dynamic objects. In this way, the overall behavior of an application can be encoded to a large degree in the graph of connections traversed by the events.

The ability to handle events is represented by the HANDLER class, which implements the details of event dispatching. Several deferred subclasses of HANDLER exist, each one defining a general dynamic object that can handle certain types of events. Handler classes can be implemented by inheriting from these general handlers and redefining the handler features to respond to specific events. In this way, the dynamic behavior of an individual object is encoded entirely within its event handler features.

Dynamic objects are a very important concept in our system design: graphics applications written inside our framework can in fact be thought of as big networks of dynamic objects that transmit events and handle them in real time.

3.5 User Interface

The user interface cluster provides the sorts of interactive capabilities associated with modern graphics workstations, in particular, a mouse, a windowing system, and standard types of 2D interaction widgets, like text input, sliders, and buttons. It also encapsulates, in an object-oriented way, some of the newer 3D input devices such as the Spaceball or the DataGlove.

This functionality was already available to us from an earlier development effort by our group to create a user-interface toolkit, called the Fifth Dimension Toolkit, for use in our laboratory. When that project started, we had no access to an object-oriented language, so we developed a technique for doing object-oriented programming in C based on [Cox, 1986]. In designing this toolkit, which was inspired to a large extent by the NextStep AppKit [Thompson, 1989], we consciously tried to make as purely object-oriented a design as possible.

A particularly useful feature of the 5D toolkit is an interface builder tool, modeled after the NextStep's interface builder, which allows panels of widgets to be arranged and their attributes edited interactively. The resulting user-interface widget panels can then be stored in a human-readable (and editable) ASCII file and loaded in by an application program at run-time.

Given this functionality and the fact that numerous other application programs had already been developed using the 5D Toolkit, we decided not to start over from scratch in Eiffel but rather to encapsulate the 5D toolkit in an Eiffel class. This presented some problems, however, because encapsulating an object-oriented software library is considerably more difficult that a non-object-oriented one. Unlike traditional subroutine libraries, which usually do not maintain their own data structures or state, an object-oriented software library allocates memory and sets up a network of interrelated data structures. Any encapsulating Eiffel code, therefore, must either duplicate all of the underlying object's internal data structures itself, raising problems of consistency, or it must separately encapsulate each of the objects maintained by the encapsulated object. For us, this problem was further complicated by the fact that the toolkit event distribution mechanism, in which any dynamic object can send an event to any other object, would require events to be sent in both directions across the language boundary. Since we wanted our Eiffel objects to receive events from the 5D Toolkit objects, an event translating mechanism had to be build.

Our solution was to associate a parallel Eiffel instance of single class, UI, for every instance of a 5D toolkit object. Since the toolkit objects are dynamically typed, the single UI class encapsulating all the toolkit functionality is reasonable. Most of the 5D toolkit objects are lower level and do not need to be directly accessed by Eiffel, so a mechanism was devised so that the parallel Eiffel UI object for each toolkit object is created only on demand when it is needed in the Eiffel application. When the instance is no longer referenced on the Eiffel side, it is garbage-collected by Eiffel even though the 5D toolkit object still remains. An interface was also built to translate 5D toolkit events into Eiffel event types as they occur. Because the Eiffel types of events were largely inspired by the toolkit, this was not too difficult, but the problem of mapping one system of user-interface event types onto another is in general not trivial.

4 Building Appplications

Figure 8 gives a typical example of how various classes from the modeling, rendering and dynamic clusters are combined to form an application structure. In this case, a flight controller object is attached to a particular node in the modeling hierarchy. This controller subscribes to *new_transform* events from the trackball object. When the trackball receives a *mouse_moved* event, it responds by transmitting a *new_transform* event. When this is received by the flight controller, it responds by updating the new position of the node.

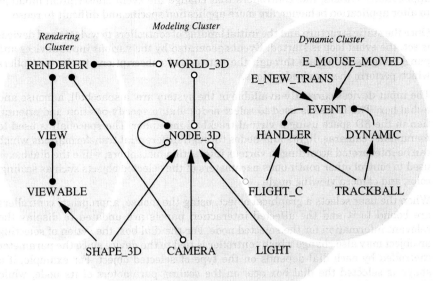

Figure 8: Example of Application Program Structure

Using the Eiffel 3D class library, an interactive 3D application program can be implemented by constructing a top-level class. When the program is started, it invokes the *Create* feature of this class, which instantiates the various objects, assembles them, and starts the event handling loop. The first part of the *Create* algorithm initializes the data structures, and loads in all the panels of user interface objects from files created by the user-interface builder. It then creates windows to contain these panels and to display the three-dimensional scenes. The visibility state of the different windows are set to reflect the initial state of the program. The event handling loop is then started up and managed by a top-level handler class which, in response to user input, implements the various application program commands.

The application appears to the user as a collection of windows displaying either three-dimensional views of the world, or widget control panels. Combinations of windows may be made visible at any given time as desired. After the interface objects have been instantiated, controllers are then bound to the different widgets and devices using the subscription mechanism presented earlier. Specific instances of user-interface widgets can be identified by their names, created using the interface builder.

The interactive behavior of the application is determined by both the internal behavior of the controllers, as implemented in their event handler features, and by their connections to input devices, interaction widgets and other controllers. Some of the controllers that were written are general purpose and reusable in other

286 Russell Turner, Enrico Gobbetti, Francis Balaguer, and Angelo Mangili

applications. Others, like controllers that change the event subscription bindings to alter application behavior, are more application specific and difficult to reuse.

Once the static structure and the initial binding of controllers to widgets and devices is set, the event loop is started. Events generated by the various input devices and panel widgets propagate through the network of subscriptions to the controllers which perform the required actions.

The input devices currently available in the system are: a spaceball, a mouse and a dial box. The mouse is used to select nodes and to specify position and orientation in the 3D space using a virtual trackball metaphor. The spaceball is used to manipulate cameras, lights and nodes through differential transformations which can be interpreted according to various interaction metaphors, while the dial box is used to control other continuous parameters of the selected objects such as scaling, color, and camera viewing angle.

When the user selects a graphical object, using the mouse, appropriate controllers are bound to it and the affected interaction panels are updated to display the relevant information for the selected node. For the dial box, the action of selecting an object may also change which controller is tied to the device since the parameter controlled by each dial depends on the type of selected object. For example, if a shape is selected the dial box acts on the scaling parameters of its node, while if a camera is selected the dials control the field of view and the clipping planes. Usually, the spaceball is set up to control the camera, while the mouse, through its trackball controller object, controls the currently selected node. Using a menu, the user can modify these default bindings and change the control metaphor for the selected node or the current camera.

5 Discussion

5.1 Building Reusable Components

The bottom-up approach, which object-oriented design tends to promote for building applications, leads to the creation of software systems that are large assemblies of reusable basic components. We have to admit, however, that components are not usually reusable from the beginning, and some effort is usually required to make them general enough for exploitation in different applications.

The first step for making a component reusable is to make it usable in the first place. To ensure that this is true, client applications need to be written and the resulting feedback used to improve the design. For this reason, we believe that building test applications to obtain a first draft of class libraries is necessary, and for most non-trivial class libraries preferable to directly building components from first principles. One such test application that we have built is a key-frame animation system, which allows objects to be animated by interactively placing them in key positions and then interpolating a spline curve to obtain a smooth motion [Gobbetti et al., 1993].

Object-oriented techniques make it possible to exploit the similarity of structure of all applications in a particular domain by creating frameworks that define and implement the object-oriented design of an entire system such that its major components are modeled by abstract classes. High level classes of these frameworks define the general protocol and handle the default behavior, which is usually appropriate for most of the cases. Only application-specific differences have to be implemented by the designer through the use of subclassing and redefinition to customize the application. The reuse of abstract design which is offered by this solution is even more important than simply the reuse of code.

Several well known application frameworks exist, particularly in the area of user interfaces. Examples are: Smalltalk's MVC [Krasner and Pope, 1988], Apple Computer's MacApp [Schmucker, 1986], and the University of Zurich's ET++ [Weinand et al., 1989].

We believe that our dynamic, modeling, and rendering clusters are a first step towards developing a framework for our interactive three-dimensional graphics applications. However, much work still remains to be done to make this framework general enough for the creation of future applications.

5.2 Performance

Performance is an important concern when building interactive 3D graphics programs. Poor performance is often used as a criticism of using pure object-oriented techniques for the development of such applications, and as an argument in favor of using languages that freely mix the procedural and the object-oriented paradigm such as C++ or Objective-C.

The development of the key-frame animation system showed us that high performance applications can be obtained using a pure object-oriented language such as Eiffel without compromising the design. This particular application, built using the Eiffel class library, is able to render fully shaded scenes containing several thousands of polygons at interactive speed (more than ten refreshes per second) on a Silicon Graphics Iris, allowing the user to edit and animate three-dimensional shapes using a direct manipulation metaphor.

Several factors permitted this kind of high performance. The fact that Eiffel is purely object-oriented and statically typed allows the compiler to perform important optimizations (such as inlining, unneeded code removal, and simplification of routine calls), resulting in high-performance code without compromising the purity of the design. Optimization of several important aspects of our software system was often obtained by creating specialized subclasses that handle special cases. The ability to encapsulate highly-optimized FORTRAN numerical routines also contributed.

The availability of garbage collection in Eiffel often allowed us to simplify algorithms and data structures, resulting in more compact and efficient code. Since the garbage collector is incremental, it is possible to use it in interactive programs only at those times when it does not disturb the user. By carefully designing the components to minimize creation of temporary objects, we have been able to limit the CPU cost of object allocation and deallocation to under 10 percent. Previous experience developing a user interface toolkit using an object-oriented extension of C showed us the importance of these memory issues. In this system a great deal of design effort was spent in defining and maintaining appropriate data structures and storage schemes in order to properly destroy unreferenced objects.

6 Conclusions

Interactive 3D graphics is still in its infancy as a user interface paradigm. The challenge of building applications that realize the full potential of modern 3D computer graphics hardware remains immense. However, the development of object-oriented design techniques represents a significant advance toward the goal of creating reusable and extensible software components and assemblies for interactive 3D graphics software construction.

Our experience using a pure object-oriented design strategy and implementation language for building a general-purpose interactive 3D software library was very positive and showed us that these techniques are well suited for creating high-performance applications made of assemblies of reusable components in the field of interactive 3D graphics. In practice, it is almost impossible to build up a complete software system from scratch, and therefore even a pure object-oriented design needs some way to interface with existing software in traditional languages. We feel that the best way to do this is to have a well-defined separation between the object-oriented and traditional components of the software, in which the object-oriented components can be thought of as a higher-level language layer on top of the traditional language layer. This paradigm could be extended to a multi-layered approach with a declarative layer, based on constraint or logic programming, built on top of the object-oriented layer.

Most of the components that were created during this project are still being used and extended for our current work, making it possible for us to concentrate our efforts in solving the specific problems of new application domains. We are therefore continuing to use Eiffel and object-oriented techniques for our current research work, which focuses on the fields of neural networks, cooperative work for animation, and physically-based simulation of deformable models.

References

Boulic, R. and Renault, O., 3D Hierarchies for Animation. In *New Trends in Animation and Visualization*. John Wiley, 1991.

Conner, D. B., Snibbe, S. S., Herndon, K. P., Robbins, D. C., Zeleznik, R. C., and Dam, A. V., Three-Dimensional Widgets. In *SIGGRAPH Symposium on Interactive Graphics*, pages 183–188, 1992.

Cox, B. J., *Object Oriented Programming: An Evolutionary Approach*. Addison-Wesley, Reading, Massachusetts, 1986.

Fleischer, K. and Witkin, A., A Modeling Testbed. In *Proc. Graphics Interface '88*, pages 127–137, 1988.

Gobbetti, E., Balaguer, J. F., Mangili, A., and Turner, R., Building an Interactive 3D Animation System. In Meyer B, N. J., editor, *Object-Oriented Applications*. Prentice-Hall, 1993.

Grant, E., Amburn, P., and Whitted, T., Exploiting Classes in Modeling and Display Software. *IEEE Computer Graphics and Applications*, 11(6), 1986.

Hedelman, H., A Data Flow Approach to Procedural Modeling. *IEEE Computer Graphics and Applications*, 1(4), 1984.

Hillman, M. F., A Network Programming Package in Eiffel. In *Proc. TOOLS 2*, pages 541–551, Paris, 1990.

Ingalls, D., A Simple Technique for Handling Multiple Polymorphism. In *Proc. ACM Object Oriented Programming Systems and Applications*, 1986.

Krasner, G. and Pope, S., A Cookbook for Using the Model-View-Controller User Interface Paradigm in Smalltalk-80. *Journal of Object-Oriented Programming*, 3(1):26–49, 1988.

Pacific, K., *Dore Programmer's Manual*. Kubota Pacific, Inc, 1992.

Rumbaugh, J., Blaha, M., Premerlani, W., Eddy, F., and Lorensen, W., *Object-Oriented Modeling and Design*. Prentice Hall, Englewood Cliffs, New Jersey, 1991.

Schmucker, K., *Object-Oriented Programming for the Macintosh*. Hayden, 1986.

Stroustrup, B., An Overview of C++. *SIGPLAN Notices*, 21(10):7–18, 1986.

Thompson, T., The Next Step. *Byte*, 14(3):365–369, 1989.

Turner, R., Gobbetti, E., Balaguer, F., Mangili, A., Thalmann, D., and Magnenat-Thalmann, N., An Object Oriented Methodology using Dynamic Variables for Animation and Scientific Visualization. In *Proceedings Computer Graphics International 90*, pages 317–328. Springer-Verlag, 1990.

Weinand, A., Gamma, E., and Marty, R., Design and Implementation of ET++: a Seamless Object-Oriented Application Framework. *Structured Programming*, 10(2):63–87, 1989.

Authors' Addresses

Shenchang Eric Chen
Kenneth Turkowski
Douglass Turner
Apple Computer, Inc.
20705 Valley Green Drive
M/S 60-W
Cupertino, CA 95014
USA

D. Brookshire Conner
Andries van Dam
Dept. of Computer Science
Brown University
Providence, RI 02912
UNITED STATES

Eric Cournarie
Michel Beaudouin-Lafon
LRI
Université de Paris-Sud
BAT. 490
F-91405 Orsay Cedex
FRANCE

Rui Gomes
Rui Pedro Casteleiro
Fernando Vasconcelos
INESC/IST
Rua Alves Redol 9-2D
P-1000 Lisboa
PORTUGAL

Richard Helm
Tien Huynh
Kim Marriott
John Vlissides
IBM T. J. Watson Research Center
P.O. Box 218
Yorktown Heights, NY 10598
UNITED STATES

Heinrich Jasper
Universität Oldenburg
FB Informatik
Postfach 2503
D-26111 Oldenburg
GERMANY

William Leler
Ithaca Software
1001 Marina Village Parkway
Alameda, CA 94501
USA

Angelo Mangili
Scientific Computation Center
Swiss Federal Institute of Technology
CH-6900 Manno, Switzerland

John R. Rankin
Department of Computer Science and
Computer Engineering
La Trobe University
Kingsbury Drive
Bundoora, Victoria 3083
AUSTRALIA

Zsofia Ruttkay
Vrije Universiteit
Department of Mathematics and
Computer Science
Postbus 7161
1007 MC Amsterdam
THE NETHERLANDS

Adelino F. Da Silva
Grupo de Eng. Sistemica
Universidade Nova de Lisboa
P-2825 Monte da Caparica
PORTUGAL

Russell Turner
Enrico Gobbetti
Francis Balaguer
Computer Graphics Laboratory
Swiss Federal Institute of Technology
CH-1015 Lausanne
SWITZERLAND

Remco Veltkamp
CWI, IS
Kruislaan 413
1098 SJ Amsterdam
THE NETHERLANDS

Johan Versendaal
Willem Beekman
Marco Kruit
Charles van der Mast
Delft University of Technology
Department Information Systems
Julianalaan 132
2628 BL Delft
THE NETHERLANDS

Peter Wisskirchen
GMD
Schloss Birlinghoven
D-53757, St. Augustin
GERMANY

Tom Z.-Y. Zhou
William J. Kubitz
Dept. of Computer Science
University of Illinois at
Urbana-Champaign
1304 W. Springfield Ave.
Urbana, IL 61801
UNITED STATES

Focus on Computer Graphics

(Formerly EurographicSeminars)

Advances in Computer Graphics Hardware III. Edited by A. A. M. Kuijk.
VIII, 214 pages, 88 figs., 1991

Advances in Object-Oriented Graphics I. Edited by E. H. Blake, P. Wisskirchen.
X, 218 pages, 74 figs., 1991

Advances in Computer Graphics Hardware IV. Edited by R. L. Grimsdale,
W. Straßer. VIII, 276 pages, 124 figs., 1991

Advances in Computer Graphics VI. Images: Synthesis, Analysis, and
Interaction. Edited by G. Garcia, I. Herman. IX, 449 pages, 186 figs., 1991

Intelligent CAD Systems III. Practical Experience and Evaluation. Edited by
P. J. W. ten Hagen, P. J. Veerkamp. X, 270 pages, 116 figs., 1991

Graphics and Communications. Edited by D. B. Arnold,
R. A. Day, D. A. Duce, C. Fuhrhop, J. R. Gallop, R. Maybury, D. C. Sutcliffe.
VIII, 274 pages, 84 figs., 1991

Photorealism in Computer Graphics. Edited by K. Bouatouch, C. Bouville.
XVI, 230 pages, 118 figs., 1992

Advances in Computer Graphics Hardware V. Rendering, Ray Tracing and
Visualization Systems. Edited by R. L. Grimsdale, A. Kaufman.
VIII, 174 pages, 97 figs., 1992

Multimedia. Systems, Interaction and Applications. Edited by L. Kjelldahl.
VIII, 355 pages, 129 figs., 1992. Out of print

Advances in Scientific Visualization. Edited by F. H. Post, A. J. S. Hin.
X, 212 pages, 141 figs., 1992

Computer Graphics and Mathematics. Edited by B. Falcidieno, I. Herman,
C. Pienovi. VII, 318 pages, 159 figs., 1992

Rendering, Visualization and Rasterization Hardware. Edited by A. Kaufman.
VIII, 196 pages, 100 figs., 1993

Visualization in Scientific Computing. Edited by M. Grave, Y. Le Lous,
W. T. Hewitt. XI, 215 pages, 121 figs., 57 in color, 1994

Photorealistic Rendering in Computer Graphics. Edited by P. Brunet,
F. W. Jansen. X, 286 pages, 175 figs., 1994

From Object Modelling to Advanced Visual Communication. Edited by
S. Coquillart, W. Straßer, P. Stucki. VII, 306 pages, 128 figs., 1994

Object-Oriented Programming for Graphics. Edited by C. Laffra, E. H. Blake,
V. de Mey, X. Pintado. VIII, 304 pages, 102 figs., 1995

Photorealistic Rendering Techniques. Edited by G. Sakas, P. Shirley, S. Müller.
approx. X, 446 pages, approx. 140 figs., 17 in color, 1995

Springer-Verlag
and the Environment

We at Springer-Verlag firmly believe that an international science publisher has a special obligation to the environment, and our corporate policies consistently reflect this conviction.

We also expect our business partners – paper mills, printers, packaging manufacturers, etc. – to commit themselves to using environmentally friendly materials and production processes.

The paper in this book is made from low- or no-chlorine pulp and is acid free, in conformance with international standards for paper permanency.